About the Author

Roger D. Sorrell received a Master of Letters degree in Modern History from Corpus Christi College, Oxford, which he attended on a Rhodes Scholarship. He received his Ph.D. from Cornell University.

ST. FRANCIS OF ASSISI AND NATURE

ST. FRANCIS OF ASSISI AND NATURE

Tradition and Innovation in Western Christian Attitudes toward the Environment

Roger D. Sorrell

New York Oxford
OXFORD UNIVERSITY PRESS
1988

Oxford University Press

Oxford New York Toronto
Delhi Bombay Calcutta Madras Karachi
Petaling Jayab Singapore Hong Kong Tokyo
Nairobi Dar es Salaam Cape Town
Melbourne Auckland

and associated companies in
Berlin Ibadan

Published by Oxford University Press, Inc.,
200 Madison Avenue, New York, New York 10016

Library of Congress Cataloging-in-Publication Data
Sorrell, Roger D. (Roger Darrell), 1954–
St. Francis of Assisi and nature.
1. Nature—Religious aspects—Christianity—History
of doctrines—Middle Ages, 600-1500. 2. Francis, of
Assisi, Saint, 1182-1226—Views on nature. I. Title.
II. Title: Saint Francis of Assisi and nature.
BT695.5.S68 1988 231.7 85-10135
ISBN 0-19-505322-2

Acknowledgments for permission to quote extended passages
will be found on pp. vii and viii.

2 4 6 8 9 7 5 3 1

Printed in the United States of America
on acid-free paper

To Francis of Assisi,
that most gentle and creative man,
whose legacy all humanity lovingly
passes down through the ages.

Acknowledgments

Special tribute must go to Dr. Brian Tierney, of Cornell University, without whose constant support and reasoned criticism this work would never have gone to print. Also, I must acknowledge a debt of gratitude to two earlier scholars whose works stimulated me greatly. Edward A. Armstrong's book, *St. Francis: Nature Mystic. The Derivation and Significance of the Nature Stories in the Franciscan Legend*, was invaluable as a complete collection and initial analysis of many anecdotes investigated here. Lawrence Cunningham's work, especially in his *Saint Francis of Assisi,* provided excellent foundation for a careful approach to the difficult issues in the area of Francis' dependence on Christian tradition.

To those dear friends Kevin Schuda, William Berleman, and Moya Duplica, who helped by their generous moral support and reading of drafts, I also owe special gratitude.

The Scripture quotations contained herein are from the Revised Standard Version Bible, ©1946, 1952, 1971 by the Division of Christian Education of the National Council of the Churches of Christ in the U.S.A., and are used by permission. Excerpts from *Lyrics of the Troubadours and Trouvères*, translated by Frederick Goldin, © 1976 by Frederick Goldin, are reprinted by permission of Doubleday, a division of Bantam, Doubleday, Dell Publishing Group, Inc. I also gratefully acknowledge permission from the respective publishers to quote passages from the following: L. Cunningham's *Brother Francis: An Anthology of Writings by and about Saint Francis of Assisi*, © 1972, Harper & Row; Augustine's *Confessions* (edited and translated by R.S. Pine-Coffin), © 1961, and Augustine's *Concerning the City of God against the pagans* (translated by H. Bettenson), © 1972, Penguin Books; Plotinus' *The Enneads* (translated by S.

MacKenna, 4th ed.), © 1969, Faber & Faber; E.A. Armstrong's *Saint Francis: Nature Mystic. The Derivation and Significance of the Nature Stories in the Franciscan Legend*, © 1973, University of California Press; O. Englebert's *Saint Francis of Assisi: A Biography* (translated by E. Cooper, 2nd ed.), © 1972, and *Saint Francis of Assisi, Writings and Early Biographies: English Omnibus of the Sources for the Life of Saint Francis* (edited by M. Habig, 3rd ed., rev.), © 1973, Franciscan Herald Press; L. Bieler's *Ireland, Harbinger of the Middle Ages*, © 1963, *Mysticism and Philosophical Analysis* (edited by S. Katz), © 1978, and *Mysticism and Religious Traditions* (edited by S. Katz), © 1983, Oxford University Press.

Seattle R. D. S.
June, 1988

Contents

Abbreviations, xi

Introduction: The Myth of the Medieval View of Nature, 3

1 The Ascetic Tradition and the Early Franciscan Outlook, 9

2 Traditional Elements in Francis' Interpretation of Creation, 39

3 Francis' Transcendence of Tradition and Its First Major Impact on His Attitude Toward Creation: The Sermon to the Birds, 55

4 Francis' Special Regard for Creation, 69

5 Tradition and Its Impact on the *Canticle,* 98

6 The Controversy over the *Canticle*'s Meaning, 115

7 The *Canticle*: Francis' Ideal Vision of Creation, 125

8 Francis: Reality and Legacy, 138

Appendix I: Francis and Catharism, 147

Appendix II: Analysis of the Early Franciscan Sources, 149

Appendix III: The Sermon to the Birds in the Early Sources, 152

Notes, 159

Bibliography, 185

Index, 195

Abbreviations

SELECTED WRITINGS BY FRANCIS

EX	*Exhortation to Praise God (Exhortatio ad Laudem Dei)*
LH	*Praises before the Office (Laudes Horarum)*
RB	*Rule of 1223 (Regula Bullata)*
RNB	*Rule of 1221 (Regula non Bullata)*
SV	*Praises of the Virtues (Salutatio Virtutum)*

EARLY LIVES AND LEGENDS

F	*The Little Flowers of St. Francis (I Fioretti di San Francesco)*
P	*The Legend of Perugia (Legenda Perugina)*
ML	Bonaventure, *Major Life of Francis (Legenda Maior)*
MNL	Bonaventure, *Minor Life of Francis (Legenda Minor)*
MP	*The Mirror of Perfection (Speculum Perfectionis)*
3 Comp.	*The Legend of the Three Companions (Legenda Trium Sociorum)*
TM	Thomas of Celano, *Treatise on the Miracles of Blessed Francis (Tractatus de Miraculis Beati Francisci)*
VP	Thomas of Celano, *First Life of Francis (Vita Prima)*
VS	Thomas of Celano, *Second Life of Francis (Vita Secunda)*

ST. FRANCIS OF ASSISI AND NATURE

INTRODUCTION

The Myth of the Medieval View of Nature

The topics we will explore include some of those areas of medieval thought which are the most misunderstood and misrepresented in the modern era. Medieval reactions to the natural environment, and, in particular, St. Francis' reactions to nature, are issues that have been subjected to a very great deal of partisan distortion and mythologizing, and the legacy of this treatment is very much with us. One would have hoped that academic history would correct popular misconceptions in these areas, but in fact academic history itself has, until recently, often created and furthered the popular stereotypes. For when one reads the works of those noted historians who helped form present-day opinion on the subject of medieval beliefs about nature, one finds a curious paradox. The very historians who most flaunted their rationalism and enlightenment in studying the Middle Ages exhibit nothing less than undisguised disdain when they come to discuss the medieval Church's view of the natural environment. Their clear eyes become clouded. They make vast and emotion-laden generalizations. Their reaction stems from superstition: a superstitious horror of a specific form of Christian piety—asceticism—which at times influenced medieval attitudes toward the physical universe. In this area, great rationalists have held great prejudices.

Gibbon, the titan of medieval historians, devoted a whole chapter of his *Decline and Fall of the Roman Empire* to a bitter attack upon the early medieval Christian ascetic movement.[1] The historian's contempt, expressed in his calculated and ironic style, launched one of the greatest literary blitzkriegs in history. He has been quoted as saying:

> There is perhaps no phase in the moral history of mankind of a deeper or more painful interest than this ascetic epidemic. A hideous, distorted, and emaciated maniac, without knowledge, without patriotism, without natural affection, spending his life in a long routine of useless and atrocious self-torture, and quailing before the ghastly phantoms of his delirious brain, had become the ideal of nations which had known the writings of Plato and Cicero and the lives of Socrates and Cato.[2]

One has no difficulty imagining the devastating effect such bitter prejudice would have upon those attempting to evaluate the beliefs and actions of the hermits and monks—precursors of Francis—who actually had a remarkable ecological outlook and impact.

> An ascetic ideal was the original stimulus in evolving a philosophy of man as a creator of new environments. The early saints purposefully retired from the world, and they fancied that by their clearings they were re-creating the earthly paradise, re-asserting the complete dominion over all life that existed before the Fall. The attractive force of these retirements, both to other monks and to the laity, and organized efforts at conversion, led to Christian activism, in which taming the wild was a part of the religious experience.[3]

Only in very recent times could such an unprejudiced and insightful analysis have been made.[4] For Gibbon's fiery condemnation of the "ascetic epidemic" itself infected historians who followed him, leading to gross overgeneralizations and to the creation of the myth that there was basically only one medieval view of nature—that of fanatical monks (usually nameless), who were pathetically unable to appreciate their natural surroundings due to their pathological suspicion of demonic temptation through the sensory world. Even in twentieth-century writers one may still encounter pot shots taken at "the" medieval view of nature, aimed with all the accuracy of an arquebus. Coulton,[5] whose history of the Church in the Middle Ages was intended to explode old myths about that period, concluded instead by perpetuating almost as many as he extinguished. He dismissed medieval views of the physical environment with typical bombast.

> The Church suspected nature: seldom does a monastic writer describe the beauties of the field or forest or water; and even then, perhaps, only to mark how short a step from those delights to the pains of hell. The flight of rooks which St. Edmund Rich saw between Oxford and Abingdon was a flight of devils; St. Dominic saw the devil in a sparrow that hindered his reading; therefore he plucked it alive; the charming nature-touches in Francis and

> Anselm and Hugh of Lincoln are not typical, but highly exceptional. Nature was cursed since the Fall.[6]

More recent writers such as Arnold Toynbee and Lynn White, Jr., who are concerned about ecological issues, have attempted to portray the ascetic tradition as part of the supposed "monotheistic disregard for nature"[7] that became prevalent when Christianity displaced pagan concepts of the *genius loci*—the spirit inhabiting and protecting places.[8] Francis is the hero who somehow freed himself from these callous and irresponsible attitudes of the Dark Ages.[9] But the documents do not support such a narrow and harsh view of Christian thought and action during the period.

Because of misconceptions like those above, we must begin our study with a thorough re-examination of early medieval views of nature. A survey of the range and diversity of medieval outlooks will revise or refute many of the misleading and distorting conclusions that have been made about this period. We will investigate the various transformations of ascetic and monastic views of creation through the period, so as to set the stage properly for a discussion of Francis' attitudes toward the natural environment.

Francis' opinions have been the source of tremendous controversy and an equally great amount of misinterpretation and distortion. He has been seen as a pantheist,[10] a Protestant,[11] a devout Catholic,[12] a Catholic liberationist,[13] and a heretic who miraculously escaped the stake.[14] The biographer who called Francis' life "a life for all seasons"[15] made a statement more true than he realized.

Today, Francis has proven *too* relevant—some of his ideas and attitudes seem to relate to current thought so well that they almost demand to be plucked out of context and taken up into contemporary modes of thinking that distort their original sense and place them at the mercy of modern values and expectations. His actions gain new motivations; his beliefs new bases; his untranslatable medievalisms (when discovered) seem quaint and out of place—even repulsive.[16] The temptation is too great, and Francis is remade to fit a modern image. One recent researcher criticizes this tendency.

> To identify Francis as a medieval prototype of the "now" generation is to simplify the image of a man who is infinitely more complex. It is also to cloud over other facets of the personality and significance of a man who has a far wider right to the attention of our own age. . . . The tendency to view Francis as a sort of charming, medieval "nature freak" is a case in point. . . . But the plain fact of the matter is that Francis was a medieval

man. If his example and teachings transcend the period in which he lived, he nonetheless did live in that period.[17]

One of the most extreme of these modern reinterpretations portrays Francis as a heretical animistic revolutionary, who "tried to depose man from his monarchy over creation and set up a democracy of all God's creatures"[18]—an interpretation easily refuted by studying the early documents. In addition, to take this one so-called democratic element out of Francis' conceptions and equate it with a modern word having many anachronistic associations is to invite distortion and confusion. Other researchers seem to have been irritated that Francis did not wholly conform to their modern preconceptions or expectations. Consider some remarks of Morris Bishop, whose biography of Francis tends to view the saint from the background of the late 1960s. "Curiously, this lover of all life did not take the next logical, almost inevitable, step and refuse to eat meat."[19] And at another point, "He felt, indeed, a pathological need for public confession and abasement. In a sermon he boasted that during the Advent fast he ate vegetables fried in bacon fat."[20] Francis hardly boasted, nor was his constant confession "pathological." Both issues here are easily explained as results of Francis' new apostolic ideals and the medieval respect for austerity.[21] In all the above cases the medieval context has been lost, and either different motives are imputed or Francis is seen as hypocritical or even mentally disordered.

For a satisfactory historical understanding of Francis' thought, the unoriginal or even typically medieval elements in his conceptions and actions must not be ignored or suppressed to emphasize the "progressive." That will merely result in distortion and frustrating incomprehension. Seen in their own context, Francis' expressions represent neither an incoherent mélange nor a systematic harmonization, but an organic, living synthesis, a complex and at times difficult balance of the traditional and the original, which is appropriate for Francis' deepest values, his own experiences, and his own time. This living synthesis was Francis' greatest achievement, and was founded on Francis' superb intuitive grasp of Christian doctrine and its potential—a grasp that was acknowledged with awe by scholars of the time.[22] It is this superb intuitive balance and faithfulness to Christian ideas that make Francis a reformer and innovator within a tradition instead of a revolutionary and a heretic.

The Early Sources

The sources this book is based on may not be those most familiar to many readers. The most famous texts relating the unforgettable stories about

Francis are *The Little Flowers of St. Francis*, and the *Major Life* of St. Francis, composed by St. Bonaventure. Neither of these famous works, however, possesses the greatest degree of trustworthiness for our present subject area, as both were composed many years after Francis' death.[23] Bonaventure's *Major Life (Legenda Maior)* contains little or no original material not found in earlier sources and presents Francis as seen through the eyes of a university-educated scholastic who had never met him. The *Little Flowers (Fioretti)* is an Italian translation of an early fourteenth century Latin account, the *Actus Beati Francisci et Sociorum Eius*, which arose from an oral tradition that is given to elaboration of miraculous elements, and sometimes confuses the chronology of events it relates.[24]

For stories and viewpoints most closely associated with Francis, we must turn to other works remaining to us. First there are the extant letters, poems, and other works by Francis himself.[25] Two years after Francis died, Thomas of Celano wrote the *First Life of Francis (Vita Prima).*[26] As Celano was a sophisticated and well-trained Franciscan who had met Francis personally, his *Vita Prima* is the earliest and most respected source for many of the stories about Francis. In 1244, almost twenty years after Francis' death, his Order issued a call for a collection of new material from those who still remembered him.[27] Some of this material was compiled in a document composed by a few of Francis' most intimate and trusted disciples, among whom was the famous Brother Leo, an especially intimate and articulate companion of Francis. This material quite possibly survives, in part at least, in a document called the *Legend of Perugia (Legenda Perugina).*[28] It thus arguably reflects the views of Francis and his inner circle of followers. Celano's *Second Life of Francis (Vita Secunda)* uses this and earlier material, and was written in 1246. We will draw our evidence primarily from these earliest sources, and employ the later ones only with caution.

Francis, Nature, and Ecology

Though this book is about Francis and nature, Francis himself never used the term *natura*, and this lack is revealing in a saint who often is portrayed as a "lover of nature." Francis instead talks of the "heavens," "earth," and "the world," and "all creatures which are under the heavens."[29] The terms—and indeed, his whole outlook—arise not from a modern concept of nature as the intricate array of scientific laws governing the universe, or the personification of these laws, but from the terms and conceptions he found in the Vulgate Bible, especially in the Psalms and Canticles of the liturgical offices he recited daily.[30] The Biblical literature Francis draws on is rich in specific terms for things in creation, but rarely indulges in abstract conceptualization—instead it depends on a certain poetic suggestiveness for descriptive power. It also asserts the belief in a divine creation, organized according to a plan that is hierarchical and unchanging, with all parts having their established positions and dependent on divine will and action.[31] This was the most fundamental basis for Francis' conception of the natural world.

The terms used in this study will aim to mirror Francis' basic conceptions to a certain degree so as not to obscure the assumptions he made. Instead of using the term "nature," this book will speak of "creation," or will discuss various "creatures" more specifically. The word nature will appear only as a qualifier (for example, "nature mysticism," the "natural world," or the "natural environment") to be used in the sense of the nonhuman, nonartificial constituents of the material universe.

For similar reasons, the terms "ecology" and "ecological" will be used sparingly here, as they hold various connotations foreign to Francis' time. Yet it is fair to say, at least on a basic level, that the beliefs of Francis do pertain to what we would call "ecology" in a popular sense, for they very much involve a concern with the relationship between humankind and other creatures. Indeed, perhaps that is the simplest and most apt way of describing the focus of this book: the study of Francis' place in the medieval Christian tradition of thought about humankind's relationship to the rest of creation.

1

The Ascetic Tradition and the Early Franciscan Outlook

EARLY CHRISTIAN ATTITUDES TOWARD CREATION

Certainly there is no lack of evidence to show that Christianity molded the attitudes of many medieval people toward creation in striking (and some would say negative) ways. Consider these lines by St. Columba:

> Day of the king most righteous,
> The day is nigh at hand,
> The day of wrath and vengeance,
> And darkness on the land.
>
> Day of thick clouds and voices,
> Of mighty thundering,
> A day of narrow anguish
> And bitter sorrowing.
>
> The love of women's over,
> And ended is desire,
> Men's strife with men is quiet,
> And the world lusts no more.[1]

Or these, by an early scholar at Malmesbury:

> Storm and destruction shattering
> Strike fear upon the world,
> The winds are out, and through high heaven
> Their bacchanals are hurled.
> Their league is broken, burst the girth,
> And launched their fury on the earth.

Torrent on torrent falls the rain,
Dark are the lovely Pleiades,
Their seven lamps are out, and dark
The houses where abode the stars.
And Sirius shines no more at all,
And heaven is hung with blackest pall. . . .[2]

Yet even amid the horrifying and apocalyptic images of the last work, one can point out traces of another view of creation—the classical. There were in fact several attitudes distinctly different from the ascetic attitude toward creation that existed together simultaneously in the Christian Middle Ages. The most important of these might be characterized as follows: the classical or classically influenced poetic interpretation; the view stemming from the scientific or philosophic tradition; and the folk or barbaric outlook. Each of these has so many representations in the literature left to us that an attempt to discuss them in detail would necessitate a book in itself. This study will thus present here only a tiny sampling of the vast spectrum of possibilities in each area.

The Poetic Tradition

Raby[3] has traced the history of the Latin lyric through the Middle Ages. This secular lyric tradition, which had produced such works as Vergil's *Eclogues* and *Georgics*, held an honored position for descriptions of natural settings. Ausonius (died c. 395), a late antique poet, left such lines as the following, which are rather typical products of their tradition.

Spring, and the sharpness of the golden dawn.
Before the sun was up a cooler breeze
Had blown, in promise of a day of heat,
And I was walking in my formal garden,
To freshen me, before the day grew old.

I saw the hoar frost stiff on the bent grasses,
Sitting on fat globes on the cabbage leaves,
And all my Paestum roses laughing at me,
Dew-drenched, and in the East the morning star,
And here and there a dewdrop glistening white,
That soon must perish in the early sun. . . .[4]

His tribute to the Moselle is one of the haunting masterpieces of late antique poetry.

What color are they now, thy quiet waters?
The evening star has brought the evening light,
And filled the river with the green hillside;
The hill tops waver in the rippling water.
Trembles the absent vine and swells the grape
In thy clear crystal. . . .[5]

Go now, and with Phrygian marble slabs
Lay out smooth floors spreading an expanse of marble through
thy dark halls!
But I, scorning what wealth and riches have bestowed,
Will marvel at Nature's handiwork, and not at that where
ruin wantons,
Recklessly prodigal and delighting in her waste.
Here firm sands spread the moist shores
And the foot resting on them leaves no recording print behind.[6]

Ausonius' friend, Paulinus, produced a Christianized variant of the "Spring" poem.

Spring wakens the birds' voices, but for me
My Saint's day is my spring, and in its light
For all his happy folk the winter flowers.
Keen frost without, midwinter, and the year
Rigid with cold and all the country white,
But gone the harder winter of the soul. . . .[7]

Fortunatus showed the potential to combine lyric emotion and a dramatic natural setting in another way.

Wild is the wind, but still thy name is spoken;
Rough is the sea; it sweeps not o'er thy face.
Still runs my love for shelter to its dwelling,
Hither, O heart, to thine abiding place.

Swift as the waves beneath an east wind breaking
Dark as beneath a winter sky the sea,
So to my heart crowd memories awaking,
So dark, O love, my spirit without thee.[8]

Poems celebrating spring or linking human feelings to the environment are known throughout the Dark Ages, as Raby shows. In some cases, the same Carolingian monasteries associated with ascetic reforms may have produced the extant poems, which make use of natural observation and delight in classically imitative natural images[9]—either from mere love of classical models[10] or from actual appreciation for creation.[11] The tradition continued up to the troubadour era.

The Scientific Tradition

If one interprets "scientific" in a broad sense, one may establish three levels of such writings in the Middle Ages: the popular, the encyclopedic, and the original philosophic. The popular level included such Latin texts as bestiaries, which reflect the common tendency of the Middle Ages to link creation with the Creator through symbolism, mixing observation derived from antiquity with Christian interpretation.

> The Panther is an animal with small spots daubed all over it so that it can be distinguished by the circular dots upon the tawny and also by its black and white variegation. . . .
>
> Pliny says that animals with sharp claws cannot bear babies frequently, since they get damaged inside when the pups move about. . . .
>
> The true Panther, Our Lord Jesus Christ, snatches us from the power of the dragon-devil on descending from the heavens. . . .[12]

A line of Christian encyclopedists—Isidore, Bede, and Rauban Maur, to name the best known—also passed on much classical science, ranging from astronomical observations and calendrical data to abstract speculation. Isidore's *De natura rerum*, for example, transmitted the idea of the World Soul,[13] as did pagan compendia such as Macrobius' *Commentary on the Dream of Scipio*.[14]

On an original level, such philosophers as Augustine and John Scotus Eriugena drew on Latin and Greek sources to produce intellectual syntheses bearing the marks of some classical views of creation. Augustine, in spite of an ambivalence toward the sensory world, could enthusiastically appreciate its beauty.

> Then there is the beauty and utility of the natural creation, which the divine generosity has bestowed on man, for him to behold and to take into use, even though mankind has been condemned and cast out from paradise into the hardships and miseries of this life. How could any description do justice to all these blessings? The manifold diversity of beauty in sky and earth and sea; the abundance of light, and its miraculous loveliness, in sun and moon and stars; the dark shades of woods, the colour and fragrance of flowers; the

> multitudinous varieties of birds, with their songs and their bright plumage; the countless different species of living creatures of all shapes and sizes, amongst whom it is the smallest in bulk that moves our greatest wonder—for we are more astonished at the activities of the tiny ants and bees than at the immense bulk of whales. Then there is the mighty spectacle of the sea itself, putting on its changing colours like different garments, now green, with all the many various shades, now purple, now blue. . . .[15]

John Scotus Eriugena, in the ninth century, created an original synthesis of Christian doctrine with classical philosophy.[16] He envisioned a universe which, despite the fall from its first purity, was permeated with divine goodness and progressing toward restoration. In addition to being absorbed within a Cosmic Soul,[17] the universe gained its whole orientation and direction from Christ as Logos: "Everything comes from Him and goes toward Him, for He is Beginning and End."[18] God, conceived of in a Christianized Neoplatonic manner, diffused order and form into the universe.

> So a grant of the Divine Goodness is the establishment of the universe and the distribution of all creatures according to general and special reasons, a distribution which the Superessential Goodness, God, lavishes universally upon all from the highest down, i.e., from the intellectual nature, the highest of all creatures, to corporeal, which holds the last and lowest place in the universe.[19]

Sources similar to those Scotus drew on—Augustine, Boethius, Origen, Pseudo-Dionysius—inspired the writers of the twelfth century School of Chartres, whose works, such as Bernard Silvester's *De mundi universitate*, William of Conches' *De philosophia Mundi*, and Alan of Lille's *Anticlaudianus*, contain a positive, Neoplatonically derived view of the natural world.[20] Again, this is such a vast subject area that we can do no more than provide an example of its positive and philosophically sophisticated attitude toward creation. Here is a passage from *Anticlaudianus*.

> Nature, which decrees every single thing with profound wisdom, has its own ordinances for these abodes (bodies), and with far-seeing eye shapes the laws which it promulgates through the wild world. She examines the cause of things and the seeds of the universe. . . . That mind has a wisdom beyond man; it is flavored with the relish of divine intellect, from whose deep fount a river flows that gives your minds discernment. Nature's mind, then modelled on so great an exemplar, does not lie inactive.[21]

Passages such as these may be seen as intellectual support and background for Francis' untutored expressions a few years later.

THE FOLK-BARBARIAN TRADITION

There was another level on which attitudes toward the natural world were expressed in the Middle Ages—one we find preserved in vernacular literature of all types, from lyric poems, to epics, to the later troubadour songs.[22] Later chapters will investigate the effect of some of this literature on Christian thought. For now, an Anglo-Saxon charm for unfruitful ground will furnish an example of the attitudes toward creation that might arise in a vernacular tradition:

> Erce, Erce, Erce, Mother of Earth,
> May the All-Wielder, Lord Eternal,
> Give flourishing acres of sprouting shoots,
> Acres bountiful bringing to harvest
> Tall stalks and shining growth. . . .
> Be healed, O Earth, O Mother of men,
> Be hale and growing by grace of God:
> Be filled with food for the use of men.[23]

Similar simple and popular sentiments may have had their impact upon Francis—for example, consider the lines of his *Canticle of Brother Sun*: "Be praised, my Lord, for Our Sister, Mother Earth,/ Who nourishes and governs us,/ And produces various fruits with many-colored flowers and herbs." Undoubtedly some Italian folk songs of shepherds and peasants did exist in Francis' time.[24]

Above all, Francis was a religious man—a hermit, and a wandering evangelist. We must now examine the religious tradition which provided the background for his ideals and expressions.

THE ASCETIC-MONASTIC VIEW OF CREATION

In the 1860s, the Count de Montalembert published a massive history of Western monasticism which attempted to counter the charges of Gibbon and others.[25] The first volume contained a chapter entitled "Services Rendered to Christendom by the Monks." It proclaimed, among other things, that Western monks were

> profoundly impressed by the beauty of nature and the external world. They admired it as a temple of the goodness and light of God, as a reflection of

> His beauty. They have left us a proof of this, first in their choice of situation for the greater number of their monasteries, which are so remarkable for the singular suitableness and loveliness of their site; and also in the descriptions they have left of these favorite spots.[26]

A few other studies, such as that of Biese,[27] tentatively asserted that some sporadic appreciation for the environment existed in the Middle Ages, with the exception of some of the "darkest" periods.[28] Historians of these supposedly benighted eras then retaliated with new evidence demonstrating that their period or cultural area was not devoid of the refined human sentiments and values at issue.[29]

Workman, an early twentieth-century monastic historian, also noted many instances in which ascetics manifested "larger sympathies with beasts and birds" and appreciated other things in creation.[30] Later, however, even one Franciscan historian spoke of those many (but curiously nameless) medieval ascetics who "considered the marvels of nature causes of temptation and moral perversity: the devil was hidden in the smile and glance of a woman, in the perfume of a flower, in the smell of a fruit, the clucking of a hen, the slight rustling of leaves. . . ."[31] Ascetic suspicion and avoidance of women may be understood, but to extend the generalization to the other areas is to oversimplify and basically misrepresent vitally important ascetic attitudes on the subject of creation.

With the publication of Glacken's monumental study of attitudes toward the environment from classical times to early modern Europe,[32] careful and unemotional analysis of the Dark Age eremetic tradition became a reality based on a secure foundation. As Glacken began to discover, when the expressions arising from the ascetic tradition are examined on their own terms as a coherent unity, and not taken out of context and generalized in the assumption that the "negative" elements represent all the important conceptions at issue, the researcher is confronted with attitudes much more profound and interesting than the stereotypes would seem to indicate. One discovers a tradition actually possessing a great potential for appreciation of the natural environment, a tradition which often expresses sentiments of a universal relevance, and at times even resembles certain modern American associations with the natural environment, as Williams demonstrates.[33] Furthermore, and most important, it is now very easy to demonstrate that, contrary to old stereotypes, idealistic and fervent ascetic movements were most dependable sources of revitalized interaction with creatures of the natural world and appreciation for the environment. There was a definite and comprehensible link between asceticism and a particular complex type of appreciation for creation from the earliest

Egyptian hermits to the Franciscans. In fact, as this view was inherited and developed, almost every major ascetic movement or revival in the Middle Ages led to renewed interest in the natural world, and to similar expressions of emotion or appreciation for it. All these ascetic expressions shared basic tenets in their views of creation, however much they also differed from one another in other respects. Thus when seen from this perspective, Francis' expressions, though sometimes innovative, become to a substantial extent another sign of a common tendency, and are some of the grandest and most explicit manifestations and elaborations of common presuppositions.

A brief look at some early ascetic movements will reveal both their similarities and their differences. The early Egyptian ascetics[34] retreated from a troubled, competitive society and harsh taxation[35] to caves, abandoned tombs, and crude huts within the desert. These they learned to appreciate in a very complex manner, linking together associations that produced an extremely typical tension and dialectic.

Athanasius, biographer of the first great hermit, Antony (died c. A.D. 350), relates that when Antony was divinely led to his inner mountain retreat he, "moved by God, loved the place."[36] When a philosopher asked him how he lived without books, he reportedly answered, "My book is the nature of created things. In it when I choose I can read the words of God."[37] Chitty notes how the early holy men "had a positive love for the stark beauty of their wildernesses."[38] Their positive reaction was startlingly original and unclassical. Even more interesting were the values under the surface of this reaction. The early hermits, in their stern heroism, denied their old allegiances to cities, farms, and kin (and later, feudal ties)—sources of communal safety as well as tension. They threw themselves, without any social protection, into a hostile new environment that demanded the hardiness of the greatest frontiersman. Fully expecting a struggle with themselves and with forces in the environment, they nevertheless depended in a new and purer way upon the merciful promises of their God to hear them in their times of need and aid them in their battle against their evil impulses and the evil in an unrestored natural environment inhabited by fierce beasts and demons.[39]

> Antony, the prototype of all hermits, went into the desert to fight the demons of the caves, and of the sands, the dragon and lilith. In the spiritualization of geography and in the evolution of Christian anthropological types, the desert of the ascetic with its wild beasts was at once the sublimation of the arena of the pre-Constantinian martyr and the intimation of the paradise of Adam before the Fall.[40]

The natural environment that the ascetic inhabited was thus "the wilderness of temptation and the wilderness which is a provisional paradise with saints and beasts in harmony, obedient to Christ."[41] "The desert, for the ascetics as for the Biblical Israelites, was, in effect, at once the haunt of demons and the realm of bliss and of harmony with the creaturely world."[42] New Testament passages such as Romans 1:20 ("Ever since the creation of the world his invisible nature, namely, his eternal power and deity, has been clearly perceived in the things that have been made. . . .") and 1 Timothy 4:4–5 ("For everything created by God is good, and nothing is to be rejected if it is received with thanksgiving, for then it is consecrated by the word of God and prayer.") provided a clear ontological justification for the belief that creation's goodness and harmony were to be restored for the true Christian. An excellent recent study by William Short further elaborates upon these beliefs, and documents their wide currency in late Roman and medieval Christian society.[43]

The encounters with various creatures that arose out of this complex dialectic included instances of conflict with demon-possessed animals and environments, thaumaturgical control of creatures and elements, sentiments of love and mercy expressed toward animals, and appreciation of the ascetic's natural surroundings. This particular type of appreciation of the environment derived from very closely linked ascetic ideals. The modern perspective, which would dismiss the elements of conflict and miracle-working as primitive superstition and praise the others as enlightened, is simply irrelevant to the historical situation, and discourages rather than encourages sympathetic understanding of the true ethos of the ascetic life and the real potential for appreciation of the environment arising from it.

The miraculous element in many of the anecdotes about the early ascetics (and about Francis himself) requires comment. While modern rationality justly regards claims of the miraculous with suspicion, medieval readers would have believed the stories, or at least many of them. Celano and other earlier hagiographers sometimes quote the sources they had interviewed in person, or give more indirect information intended to authenticate their accounts.[44] They recognized in at least an elementary way the problems of credibility, but definitely expected the reader to accept their information at face value. While a hagiographer may occasionally embroider or invent (especially if his subject lived long before his time), modern critics should resist overgeneralizing their skepticism and consider accounts on a case-by-case basis. Furthermore, simply because early observers see an incident as containing something miraculous does not mean the incident could not have occurred in a way explicable without attributing to it supernatural causation. The people of the period projected a powerful ideology (as we shall see) upon incidents that were perhaps unusual, but often not inexplicable.

The popular and mythic character of many early hagiographic sources should not blind the modern reader to the only-too-human elements in the predicaments of the early ascetic heroes. They renounced their social commitments, their cities or farms, with troubled and tempted minds. They faced their new and lonesome environment with faith and determination, but also with fear and ineptitude. One Egyptian hermit almost died from eating poisoned plants until he learned from animals which plants were safely edible.[45] Wild sounds in the natural environment terrified early hermits,[46] and they linked them with the demonic temptation they faced in the first trying period of adjustment to life alone in the wilderness. Often the reaction of the environment to the saint mirrored his inner state—and not only in the mythologized sense understood by the early hagiographers. The hermit's first doubts, fears, and temptations would have come at the very time of his difficult adjustment to life away from a protected social environment, and they would be linked to his fears of wild beasts and the unexpected and harsh conditions he now faced with feelings of inadequacy. The hermit's quick resolve to work and support himself was not only a fulfilling of the Biblical injunctions, but also a reflection of the psychological need to gain a sense of security and control over his new environment. This resolve would be transferred later, with widening implications, to monastic orders.

To the naive, fearful, and lonely former city dweller or renegade peasant, the slowly developing ability to take care of himself by finding or growing secure sources of food would have evolved alongside increasing spiritual growth and stability. Thus it is no wonder the two were intertwined and that the struggle of adaptation to a new and wild environment became a part of the spiritual struggle around which the whole ascetic's life was centered. On an ideological level, the finding of a demonic presence in the ascetic's natural surroundings represented Christian recognition of the pagan belief in the *genius loci*, insofar as the early ascetics interpreted these guardian spirits as evil spirits in still unrestored creation. They were to be fought and exorcized. And who now can imagine the joy and new sense of security the frightened and lonely ascetic would have felt at the approach of curious and perhaps even friendly wild animals (as they sometimes are when never previously confronted by humans)? No wonder his ability to tame these and overcome the demonic forces which occasionally used them or hid in his environment was considered proof of his spiritual progress and his command over his newly productive and pacified environment. His regaining of "paradise" was all too perceptible in the physical environment. Well-known ascetics who followed this progression of taming and regaining their retreats included Antony, Cuthbert, and, to some extent, even Francis.[47]

THE RANGE OF EXPRESSIONS IN THE EAST AND EARLY WEST

That the ascetic ideal and ethos were remarkably powerful stimuli to appreciation of the environment in different ways to various individuals within the tradition may be seen from the letters of early educated Christian ascetics such as Basil (died 379), who describes the environment surrounding his ascetic retreat as a classical idyll inspiring his own Christian tranquillity.

> It is a lofty mountain overshadowed with a deep wood, irrigated on the north by cold and transparent streams. At its foot is spread a low plain, enriched perpetually with the streams from the mountains. The wood, a virgin forest of trees of various kinds and foliage which grows around it, almost serves as a rampart; so that even the Isle of Calypso, which Homer evidently admired as a paragon of loveliness, is nothing in comparison with this. . . . My hut is built on another point, which uplifts a lofty pinnacle on the summit, so that the plain is outspread before the gaze, and from the height I can catch a glimpse of the river flowing around, which to my fancy affords no less delight than the view of the Strymone as you look from Amphipolis. . . . The Iris, on the other hand, flowing with a swifter course than any river I know, for a short space billows along the adjacent rock, and then, plunging over it, rolls into a deep whirlpool, affording a most delightful view to me and to every spectator, and abundantly supplying the needs of the inhabitants, for it nurtures an incredible number of fishes in its eddies. Why need I tell you the sweet exhalations from the earth or the breezes of the river? Other persons might admire the multitude of the flowers, or the lyric birds, but I have no time to attend to them. But my highest eulogy of the spot is, that, prolific as it is of all kinds of fruits from its happy situation, it bears for me the sweetest of all fruits, tranquillity.[48]

Even allowing for Basil's enthusiasm, it is hard to concur with Gibbon's description of the saint's retreat as the "savage solitude of Pontus."[49]

Basil's thought reveals many different levels of appreciation for his surroundings, ranging from the perspective of ascetic necessity, in that the location fulfills his requirements for the inducement of undistracted contemplation; to its utilitarian aspects, in that it provides well for settlers around it; to the (classically influenced) paradisal associations it brings forth from him. It is a more complex and intellectualized statement, but it arises from the same ethos and traditional eremetic ideal, and probably expresses feelings similar to those of many other ascetics who never could have articulated them so well. When Basil says, "for the contemplation of Nature abates the fever of the soul, and banishes all insincerity and presumption,"[50] he speaks for thousands who retreated to natural solitude. When Jerome writes back to the West, "to me the town is a prison, and solitude is a paradise,"[51] he expresses what many others would implicitly have believed. Basil and Jerome expressed their feelings in words; the others voted with their feet.

Sulpicius Severus, writing in the late 300s, demonstrates how the Eastern ideals were transferred to the Western ascetic movement.[52] His dialogue *Postumianus* may have functioned as a sort of newsletter from the Orient, reporting on the famed Egyptian hermits and asserting that now there was someone in the West who was comparable to them: Severus' hero Martin of Tours.[53] This Martin is famous for cutting down a pine tree venerated by pagans, in an incident showing divine power.[54] Severus' intent in the *Postumianus* was to show that whatever the Egyptians could do, Martin could do several times better. This turned out to be problematic in cases of the reports concerning the Egyptian ascetics' relationship with their environment and creatures within it. Severus reports five impressive incidents which prove there was a strong ideal of harmony with creation in Egyptian asceticism.[55] Most are touching stories about usually wild animals becoming loyal pets, and have the same associations about them as Glacken attributes to later comparable relationships: They are "explained by the primitive innocence which these heroes of penitence and purity had won back, and which placed them once more on a level with Adam and Eve in the terrestrial Paradise."[56] In one incident a hermit addresses a penitent wolf,[57] not attributing to it rationality in a pantheistic sense, but attributing the wolf's consciousness to the special intervention of God as a sign to humans to recognize divine power and to "show how animals were submissive to Adam before he transgressed God's commandment and was driven from the paradise of delights," as another early source puts it.[58]

Severus is hard put to equal these beautiful stories, but he replies by boasting that "it was a very ordinary thing for Martin to vanquish the fury of beasts or the venom of serpents."[59] He sees nothing amiss in comparing this sort of miraculous incident to the ones above. And indeed, both incidents can be taken to demonstrate the same concept—the purity of the holy man restoring the harmony and goodness of original creation.

So Severus narrates his incidences of the saint's thaumaturgy without a blush.[60] But at other times Martin in kindness saves a hare from hunting dogs, and draws moral allegorical truths from things of creation.[61] The important factor here is that Severus wholeheartedly accepts the Eastern ideals and associations and considers them an integral part of the new Western movement.

This powerful complex of ideas was passed on and found expression in the many newly begun or very vital Western ascetic movements, for which the *Life of Antony* and Severus' works were staple reading all through the Middle Ages. In the early Italian eremetic and Benedictine tradition, the *Dialogues* of Gregory the Great (c. 594) present stories of conflict, thaumaturgical control, and harmony in a manner typical of that seen before. One incident is a classic example of how ascetics might associate the natural environment with temptation. According to Gregory, Benedict of Nursia had a difficult struggle conquering his sensual desires.

> One day when the saint was alone, the Tempter came in the form of a little blackbird, which began to flutter in front of his face. It kept so close that he could easily have caught it with his hand. Instead, he made the sign of the cross and the bird flew away. The moment it left, he was seized with an unusually violent temptation. The evil spirit recalled to his mind a woman he had once seen, and before he realized it his emotions were carrying him away. . . . He then noticed a thick patch of nettles and briars next to him. Throwing his garment aside he flung himself into the sharp thorns and stinging nettles.[62]

As in Martin's life, animals were seen as forms of the demonic presence.[63] Yet in other anecdotes, Gregory tells how the monk Florentius, feeling lonely, asks God for a companion, since his earlier monastic brother had left him. Somewhat surprisingly, he receives a bear, which in his extreme simplicity he accepts as his new fellow monk.[64] At another time, Benedict's sister, Scholastica, weeps in trying to persuade him to spend more time with her, and, in a remarkably poetic correspondence between environment and emotion, a rainshower arises during her tears, thus forcing Benedict to stay.[65]

With the introduction of Christianity to Ireland and England, the traditional ideas were adapted to the special circumstances of the insular setting. Armstrong notes that early Celtic literature abounds with an attitude of "pleasurable interest in nature," and discusses some of the early Christian stories reflecting this.[66] In England, Bede's *Life of Cuthbert*, perhaps influenced by both Irish and continental traditions, furnishes more examples than usual of the typical sorts of encounters.[67] Felix's *Life of Guthlac*, written in the early 700s, breaks new ground. The fact that the hagiographer's subject and patron were both members of an Anglo-Saxon royal house[68] seems to have stimulated the writer to produce an "epic life" appropriate for the circumstances. He drew upon two noble epic traditions of literature—classical Vergilian and Anglo-Saxon. The continental ascetic ideal is broadened and fertilized by connection with the contemporary Anglo-Saxon epic tradition.

Vivid evocations of the natural word's beauty and power provide haunting symbolic settings for Guthlac's spiritual stages of growth and physical journeys. They are a Christianized expression faithful to the psychologically resonant natural descriptions in the Anglo-Saxon poetic tradition. Although they are set in the normal context of the ascetic's struggle with himself and his new harsh environment, they contribute a heretofore unprecedented sense of the awesome presence of the natural world symbolically and physically important to Guthlac. For instance, during a gloomy night of spiritual struggle, Guthlac decides to renounce his empty ambition for kingship and riches. He awakes to a resplendent morning.

> So when the mists of the dark night had been dispersed and the sun had risen in fire over helpless mortals, while the winged tribe chirped their morning songs from the beaks that birds possess, then he dressed and raised his limbs from his rustic bed and, signing himself with the sign of salvation on his breast, bade his companions choose another leader for their expedition. . . .[69]

The description struggles for a sort of fateful grandeur, aided by echoes of Vergilian gravity (*cum sol* mortalibus egris *igneum demoverat ortum*).[70] The environment gains a portentious glory through its own imposing presence, not through divine action or saintly power. Later, Guthlac (Aeneas) leaves the safety of the monastery, and, guided by the fisherman Tatwine (Charon) on a skiff (the infernal barge), explores his new home, the marshland (the Styx).

> It is a very long tract, now consisting of marshes, now of bogs, sometimes of black waters overhung by fog, sometimes studded with wooded islands and traversed by the windings of torturous streams. . . . No settler had been able to dwell alone in this place before Guthlac the servant of Christ, on account of the spectres of demons which haunted it. Here Guthlac, the man of God, despising the enemy, began by divine aid to dwell alone among the shady groves of this solitude.[71]

This dire and haunting setting, complete with Vergilian resonances and clearly expressing through its descriptive language the fears and doubts of the adventuring hero—a psychological projection often found in Anglo-Saxon poetry[72]—again relies on evoking the imposing grandeur of the environment's presence for its effect.

Guthlac is in fact portrayed as an epic Antony. Like the Egyptian saint, he inhabited tombs and huts. He "deeply loved" the "desert" and went there specifically "despising the enemy"[73]—the demons it held as land at the time unrestored by Christian presence. But significantly, through synthesis with the secular traditions to which the ascetic values were open, Guthlac's spiritual conflicts acquire overtones of epic combat, and his appreciation for his environment is related in a manner which endows that environment with a new importance, a new power and glory. The different cultural context will be a crucial factor in comprehending Francis' original modifications of the tradition he inherits. The new elements in Guthlac's attitude toward the environment, arising from his redefinition of the ascetic life as a life of noble adventure, illustrate a principle often true in the Middle Ages: A radical redefinition of ascetic life in general also leads to a redefinition of the ascetic's relationship with creation, since the latter grows out of the former in an integrated complex of thought.[74]

The Irish also had redefined the ideal of the ascetic life. Edward Armstrong has amply discussed the characteristics of the early Irish ascetic tradition, in which the particularly Celtic conception of the ascetic life as one of wandering pilgrimage (*peregrinatio*) stimulated adventurous exploration and a heightened awareness of the natural environment.[75] By the ninth century, this Irish outlook had produced its most distinctive and fascinating expression, the *Voyage of St. Brendan*,[76] the famous legend of Irish monks exploring the natural world. In the centuries between its compilation and Francis' time, it became immensely popular on the European continent. One reworking of it

> was well-known in the courts and chateaux by the trouvères, in the form of a poem in the twelfth century. . . . Its success was tremendous. It was the epoch of the Breton cycle, and it made the tour of Europe, adapted, in prose or as a poem, in all the languages of Europe.[77]

Armstrong believes that Irish influence had a direct impact on Francis.[78] Although his conjecture is provocative, the evidence (or rather, the lack of it) currently supports instead the view of Tommasini,[79] who argues against direct influence by the Irish on Francis. Tommasini accounts fully for the similarities in Irish and Franciscan expressions by noting their similar ascetic experiences and parallel independent interpretations of Biblical passages. Francis himself never referred to any Irish hagiography, nor does he manifest special devotion to Irish saints. His early biographers, who were very alert to the sources that influenced Francis, never mention any Irish connections. Still, it remains possible that Francis may have heard the *Voyage* legend through troubadours or jongleurs, as Peter Waldo heard the legend of St. Alexis.[80] If Francis did, the *Voyage* stories were told to him in the context of the other new troubadour expressions of joy in and appreciation for the natural world—an influence we will discuss later. In a general sense, it is still possible to agree with Armstrong's suggestion that "Irish penetration of the Continent contributed and prepared an ambience favourable to the emergence and success of Franciscanism,"[81] whether or not Francis knew any particular Irish legends.

In the *Voyage of St. Brendan*, the saint and his companions journey over land and sea at the edges of the then-known world; they constantly cross from the recognizeable everyday physical world into the unknown and strange, from the level of literal significance in the world to the spiritual or mythic "reality" hidden in it. The drama of the actual sea voyages seems to be reflected fittingly in the heightened sense of spiritual conflict or harmony experienced in various encounters within this strange territory, where the natural merges with the supernatural until the two are indistinguishable.

Brendan and his crew wish to sail to an island called the "Paradise of Birds."[82] On their way to it they stop on another island to purify themselves in expectation. When Brendan steps onto the island, he sings the Hymn of the Three Young Men:[83]

> Bless the Lord, all works of the Lord,
> sing praise to him and highly exalt him forever. . . .
> Bless the Lord, all things that grow on the earth,
> sing praise to him and highly exalt him forever. . . .
> Bless the Lord, all birds of the air,
> sing praise to him and highly exalt him forever. . . .[84]

Immediately upon completing this canticum, Brendan warns his monks sternly not to fall into temptation, reminding them of divine power over creation. The monks were to keep firmly in mind God's power over His own creation and call on Him in danger. For Brendan, the greatness of creation was clearly matched by its temptations. Yet in his chanting of the Hymn of the Three Children, Brendan gives voice, for the first time in recorded ascetic tradition, to that vital Biblical passage which fervently and at such great length looks on creation as the good work of a good God and urges it to unite with humankind in praising its Maker. Here the ascetic ideal of the harmony of humanity with creation reaches a new height.

When the seafarers reach their "Paradise of Birds," the birds chant praise to God and give Brendan his instructions for the rest of his pilgrimage.[85] This story is in fact the closest parallel in the Irish tradition to Francis' addresses to creation, such as his Sermon to the Birds. Yet there are important distinctions which Armstrong does not take into account in his discussion of the Irish tradition.[86] First, Brendan does not chant the canticum to anything specific in creation, nor does he actually speak to these birds. Further, Brendan's experiences take place in such a half-supernatural, half-physical world that the birds probably should be interpreted as angelic souls or spirits, as they are interpreted elsewhere in the story and in many other medieval stories.[87] But in Francis' case there is never any suggestion that the creatures addressed are anything other than the actual birds, insects, or other living creatures concerned.

Irish continental influence may be traced in the lives of St. Columban and St. Gall. Both of these saints were renowned for their domestication of wild animals.[88] The story of how Columban came to choose Bobbio as the site of his new monastery in Italy proves again how the fervent ascetic ideal could lead to an appreciation on many levels of natural surroundings.

> At that time a man named Jocundus appeared before the king [Agilulf, king of the Lombards] and announced that he knew of a church of the holy Apostle Peter, in a lonely spot in the Apennines; the place had many advantages, it was unusually fertile, the water was full of fishes, it had long been called Bobium from the brook that flowed by it. There was another river in the neighborhood, by which Hannibal had once passed a winter and suffered the loss of a very great number of men, horses, and elephants. Thither Columban now went, and with all diligence restored to its old beauty the church which was already half in ruins.[89]

The place seems to be appreciated not only for its fertility and quiet solitude, but also for its historical significance. Columban's restoration of the ruined and forgotten church cannot but remind the student of Francis of that saint's own similar efforts (see, e.g., *VP* 18).

Many authors, including medieval ones, have charted the fervent rise and languid decline of the early ascetic movements.[90] Reform attempts usually followed, however, accompanied again by new expressions of appreciation for the natural environment. The following poem, almost Chinese in its delicacy and lyricism, was a product of the ninth-century Irish ascetic revival.[91]

> I have a bothy in the wood—
> none knows it save the Lord, my God;
> one wall an ash, the other hazel,
> and a great fern makes the door. . . .
> This little secret humble place
> holds tenure of the teeming woods;
> maybe you will come to see?—
> but alone I live quite happy.
>
> Smooth the tresses of yew-green yew-trees,
> glorious portent;
> place delicious with great green oakwoods
> increasing blessing.
>
> Tree of apples, huge and magic,
> great its graces;
> crop in fistfulls from clustered hazel,
> green and branching. . . .
>
> Resting there are herded swine,
> goats and piglings;
> wild swine, too deer and doe,
> speckled badgers.
>
> Great woodland bands troop like fairies
> to my bothy;
> and great delight when timid foxes
> show their faces. . . .
>
> I hear the soughing of the pine-trees
> and pay no money;
> I am richer far through Christ, my Lord,
> than ever you were.[92]

Again we see the common theme illustrated. Revived or reinterpreted ascetic ideals, arising out of the inherited tradition of beliefs and preconceptions, take on innovative forms. In this case, the ascetic's response to creation is one of fascination and delight, a bit similar to some of Francis' expressions. These verses also witness to the strange curiosity or friendliness of animals in the wild.

Carolingian expressions of appreciation for the natural environment have long been studied.[93] A poem of Alcuin's seems to reveal sentiments similar to the Irish poem above.

> Beloved cell, retirement's sweet abode!
> Farewell, a last farewell, thy poet bids thee!
> Beloved cell, by smiling woods embraced,
> Whose branches, shaken by the genial breeze
> To meditation oft my mind disposed.
> Around thee too, their health-reviving herbs
> In verdure gay the fertile meadows spread;
> And murmuring near, by flowery banks confined,
> Through fragrant meads the crystal streamlets glide,
> Wherein his nets the joyful fisher casts,
> And fragrant with the apple bending bough,
> With rose and lily joined, the garden's smile;
> While jubilant, along thy verdant glades
> At dawn his melody each songster pours,
> And to his God attunes the notes of praise.[94]

Carolingian reform also began to bring monks back closer to their environment. Benedict of Aniane, the Benedictine reformer, is reported to have "guided the plow with the plowman, used the ax with the woodsman, reaped with the reapers."[95]

Stockmayer[96] records many instances of appreciation for the natural environment springing from the extension of Christianity and, more particularly, monasticism, spreading into eastern Germany during late Carolingian and early Ottonian times. Groups of monks looked for a contemplative paradise where a "beautiful forest would give secret solitude."[97] The extensions of cultivated land produced by the founding of new monasteries brought about radical alterations in the environment, and began a trend of increasing cultivation that has continued up to the present, as Glacken maintains.[98]

In other examples, a certain Bishop Altmann was so intrigued by local stories he heard in his new diocese that he climbed and explored the nearby mountains—thus anticipating by a few centuries Petrarch's famous ascent of a mountain. Altmann established an oratory in the mountains and was buried in his most beloved spot there.[99] Ansfried, a young squire of Otto I, climbed into the mountains in the dead of winter to feed the birds he loved[100]—bringing to mind Francis' similar concern for his beloved larks in the winter season (*LP* 110). Finally, in a confrontation very similar to that of Martin and the pagans over the pine tree, Bishop Otto, the apostle of Pomerania, threatened to fell a magnificent oak tree worshipped by the local rustics. But he accepted promises that henceforth the tree would not be venerated, and agreed with the people of the vicinity that the tree should be spared "due to the usefulness of its fruits and the pleasantness of its shade."[101]

THE CISTERCIANS

Spiritual leaders of the twelfth century, like those of the third and fourth centuries, manifested a revived and intense concern that Christianity return to the literal practice of what they conceived to be the true original Christian way of life. As Grundmann's fundamental study illustrates,[102] the twelfth century was a time of transition, in which the ideal of the "apostolic life" (a term which in the earlier Middle Ages was applied to the life of ascetics and regular canons),[103] underwent major redefinition; various Christian reformers, stimulated by monastic reforming zeal and the broadening appeal of the papal reform efforts,[104] attempted to return to the "true sources" of the apostolic life and model their beliefs, practices, and mode of living on what they saw there in a more literalistic manner.[105] Both the Cistercian and Franciscan reform movements (as well as various heretical movements such as the Cathars)[106] arose in this context. The Cistercians betray this origin most in their fervent insistence on following the Benedictine Rule literally, and by zealously paring away customs and observances considered unnecessary accretions.[107] The Franciscans most obviously reflect the new pressures and broadening reform ideals of their era in several ways: their redefined observance of apostolic poverty, their origins in and appeal to the pious laity,[108] and their rejection of regular orders for the ideal of apostolic wanderlust in evangelism (and even martyrdom).

In spite of obvious differences, the two orders resembled each other in many ways.[109] Both conceived themselves to be the *pauperes Christi*—the poor people of Christ—and this ideal reinforced devotion to asceticism, manual labor, and certain preferences for austere living conditions.[110] Both orders thought of their members as jongleurs or minstrels of God—though the conception of what this meant differed greatly.[111] In both orders the attitude toward the things of creation derived directly from the basic guiding conception of the type of apostolic life accepted by and imposed on the members. And while each order exhibited innovations in its outlook, both also expressed earlier ascetic attitudes to a substantial degree.

THE CISTERCIAN REFORM AND CISTERCIAN ATTITUDE TOWARD CREATION

The Cistercian attitude toward the environment was an integral part of and natural development from the whole Cistercian reforming ideal. The same urge that led the early Cistercians to revise liturgical observance of the Benedictine Rule led them to accept with fervor (at least at first)[112] Benedict's command that true monks should perform manual as well as spiritual labor. One comment of Benedict's on the subject is particularly striking considering later Cistercian beliefs.

> But if the circumstances of the place or their poverty require them to gather the harvest themselves, let them not be discontented; for then are they truly monks when they live by the labour of their hands, like our fathers and the apostles.[113]

Benedict's honorable concession to poor monasteries was evidently interpreted to mean that to work in the fields and harvest was to live the true life of the desert fathers and apostles. St. Bernard himself directed the harvest at Clairvaux—it was considered "one of the most meritorious works."[114]

Bernard's letters reveal he saw great spiritual benefit to be gained from contact with the natural world through the manual labor of the early Cistercians. He writes Henry Murdach, "Believe me who have experience, you will find more laboring in the woods than you ever will among books. Woods and stones will teach you what you can never hear from any master."[115] Another time he writes to Aelred of Rievaulx, encouraging him to compose a treatise on charity in spite of Aelred's protests of literary unskillfulness. He urges Aelred to show not what he has learned from grammarians but what he has been taught by the Holy Spirit, and then says:

> But I do not quail before the steepness of mountains, or the roughness of stones, or the deep hollows of valleys, since in those days [to come] the mountains will flow with sweetness, the hills with milk and honey, and valleys will abound with grain, the honey will rise up from the rock, and olive oil from the hardest stones. Christ's sheep will feed themselves amid the rocks and mountains. And so I maintain that you have broken out with your hammer something from those stones by your great wisdom, something you have not taken from the matters of the schools. For you have sensed some things in the noonday heat, under the shade of trees, that you have never learned in schools.[116]

This inevitably brings to mind Basil's comment about how the contemplation of creation inspires humility and banishes pride, which of course Bernard would associate with stylistic embellishments learned in schools. But Leclercq says of these passages:

> When St. Bernard speaks of the "book of Nature" and of all that can be learned "under the shade of trees," he is not thinking of the beauty of the surroundings but of the labor that the preparation of a field necessitates, and of the prayer, reflection, and the mortification that is furthered by work in the field.[117]

His interpretation is too narrow. The passage shows clearly that Bernard associated work in the fields with both spiritual growth and a paradisal vision of creation restored in the coming apocalypse. These same paradisal associations appear in early Cistercian descriptions of Rievaulx (where Aelred was abbot).

> The name of their little settlement and of the place where it lies was derived from the name of the stream and the valley, Rievaulx. High hills surround the valley, encircling it like a crown. These are clothed by trees of various sorts, and maintain in pleasant retreats the privacy of the vale, providing for the monks a kind of second paradise of wooded delight. From the loftiest rocks the waters wind and tumble down to the valley below. . . . And when the branches of lovely trees rustle and sing together and the leaves flutter gently to the earth, the happy listener is filled increasingly with a glad jubilee of harmonious sound. . . .[118]

These Cistercian comments clarify one another and fully justify Gilson's opinion that the early Cistercians presuppose their life "is in permanent contact with nature, and that the sites habitually chosen for Cistercian monasteries, in one of those lonely valleys dear to St. Bernard, had become integrated by him to the mystical life itself."[119] Bernard's remarks to Aelred in fact reveal an interpretation of the spiritual significance of creation that can be linked with other Cistercians, and his belief that important values must be "sensed"[120] while in the shade of trees greatly resembles the much more elaborated sentiments found in the later Cistercian *Description of Clairvaux* discussed below.

Daniel's description of the area around Rievaulx should put to rest the old view that the early Cistercians preferred to locate their monasteries in blasted heaths and dreary vales.[121] The evidence suggests rather that on the whole they selected sites that were manageable and potentially very productive.[122] The paradisal imagery shows how ideas in the ascetic tradition have been taken up with new fervor by the Cistercians, who believed that their new reformed apostolic life was fittingly established in the "restored paradise" surrounding their new cloister sites. There is a profound harmony between the perfect natural beauty of the site and the renewed perfection of the monastic life set within it.[123]

Early Cistercians, who chanted the Psalms with much feeling while they worked,[124] had discovered the important literal significance of the the message of Psalms and the Canticle of the Three Young Men, which exhort creation to praise God, as Francis would do later. Idung of Prüfening, in the midst of a free-wheeling debate with a (fictitious) Cluniac opponent over authenticity of customs,[125] proclaims:

> You are a simple-minded theologian if you do not know that inanimate creatures, devoid of sense and life, speak to God and praise God. What else is the meaning for us of the Hymn of the Three Children and the very last praises in the Psalms where all creatures are invited to praise God?[126]

CISTERCIAN ADVANCES BEYOND THE TRADITIONAL ASCETIC VIEW

Two later Cistercian sources, Caesarius of Heisterbach's *Dialogue on Miracles*[127] and an anonymous Cistercian's *Description of Clairvaux*,[128] demonstrate how the Cistercians drew on the potential in the old ascetic interpretation of creation and altered it in profound new ways. As these two sources are contemporary with Francis, or nearly so, they will provide excellent comparisons with the early Franciscan attitude toward creation.

Caesarius, writing between 1220 and 1235,[129] relates an incident which occurred as monks were laboring in the fields one day. He remarks that while it is against divine will to keep birds for amusement, storks are permitted to nest at Cîteaux and other places "because by them not only the monastery but all the places round are cleared of foul worms."[130] One fall day they made ready to migrate.

> . . . [W]hen they had marshalled their ranks for traveling abroad, that they might not be thought ungrateful for the hospitality granted them, they sought out the brotherhood which at that moment was working in the fields, and flew round them with many hoarse cries and made them all wonder, not knowing what they wanted. And the prior said to them: "I suppose they are asking permission to go"; and raising his hand blessed them. At once, wonderful to say, with great cheerfulness they flew off together, making the monks feel ashamed, who think little of receiving or waiting for the blessing, when they set out for a journey.[131]

The whole ethos of this incident is nearly indistinguishable from that of Franciscan examples probably contemporary to it. The prior did not preach to the birds or blend his praise of God with their songs, as did Francis,[132] yet the same general feeling of affinity with the rest of creation pervades this incident, as it would with many early Franciscan stories. Perhaps this similar ideal led the Cistercians to take the interest they did in Franciscan legends during the thirteenth century—an interest which resulted in the preservation of invaluable copies of early Franciscan documents ordered destroyed by the Franciscan chapter of 1266.[133]

Caesarius, showing a debt to the moralistic ascetic tradition the Cistercians inherited, pointedly compares the pious actions of the birds to the laxity of humans: The birds asked for the proper blessing before leaving, while monks neglect this. The actions of animals are seen as models for human actions, as they would be also with the Franciscans (*ML* 8:7; *LP* 110; *VS* 47). At other times in these *Dialogues*, other traditional incidents occur, such as human conflict with demon-possessed creation[134] and thaumaturgical alteration of natural objects.[135] These, as we will see later, could fit comfortably within the range of Franciscan expressions.

THE HIGHEST EXPRESSION OF THE CISTERCIAN IDEAL: THE *DESCRIPTION OF CLAIRVAUX*

The *Description of Clairvaux*,[136] written by an anonymous early Cistercian, is one of the most beautiful documents of the Middle Ages, and represents at its height the Cistercian ideal of harmony with creation. It is little known, and though Glacken comments on it, he wrongly attributes it to Bernard.[137] The *Description* demonstrates the tremendous power of the ideas in the ascetic tradition, reinforced by the particular new Cistercian ideal of work amid glorious creation. The work is suffused with the guiding ideal of humankind's noble, divinely given duty to shepherd and perfect creation, and restored creation's reciprocal love for humanity's gentle and rational rule. As Leclercq says:

> The cloister is a "true paradise," and the surrounding countryside shares in its dignity. Nature "in the raw," unembellished by work or art, inspires the learned man with a sort of horror: the abysses and peaks which we like to gaze at, are to him an occasion of fear. A wild spot, not hallowed by prayer and asceticism and which is not the scene of any spiritual life is, as it were, in a state of original sin. But once it has become fertile and purposeful, it takes on the utmost significance.[138]

In the *Description*, monks labor with great dedication and joy to reclaim the wild land around Clairvaux.

> The top of the mountain is the scene of numerous labors of the monks; works as pleasant as they are peaceable—to collect dry branches, and gather them in bundles to burn them; to grub up the brushwood which disfigures the ground, and to prepare it for the fire, for which alone it is fit; to uproot the brambles and destroy them. . . .[139]

This restoration of the environment to humanity's proper sway will allow the best and most beautiful trees to prosper, "so that there may be no impediment to the sturdy oak which salutes the heavens with its lofty top, to the graceful lime-tree which spreads its arms, to the ash tree whose wood is so elastic and easily split, or to the leafy beech. . . ."[140] Many other expressions in the *Description* reveal this Cistercian "English country garden" ideal (recently compared to the Franciscan view),[141] which maintains that when humankind exercises proper dominion over reclaimed creation, two goals are thus harmonized: Creation's beauty is perfected and humanity is properly served by now-willing servants. Consider the harmony between tended natural beauty and human needs served by creation in the following passage.

> Where the orchard ceases begins the garden, through which run little channels of water, or rather little streams separate and divide it into squares. . . . Here, too, is a pleasing sight afforded to the eyes of the sick brethren when they go to sit on the verdant bank of a pool filled with pure and running water, where they can catch the sports of the little fish in water clear as crystal, which swim to and fro in shoals like marching armies. The water of these pools serves at the same time for nourishing the fish and for watering the vegetables in the garden. . . . This stream passes and repasses the many workshops of the abbey, and everywhere leaves a blessing behind it for its faithful service.[142]

The channels of water provide sport and food for fish, diversion for people, nourishment for garden vegetables, and cleansing for the monastery's workshops. Utilitarianism is harmonized with aesthetic delight; creation serves humanity willingly and even sports with joy in the presence of humans. The writer of the *Description* believed, as did Francis, that it was a human obligation to praise the things of creation and be grateful for willing service.

> . . . I am accused of ingratitude by that sweet fountain of whose waters I have so often drunk, which has merited so well of me, and which I have repaid so

ill. It reminds me in a tone of reproach that it has often quenched my thirst, that it has given me water to wash my hands and even my feet, that it has rendered to me many such offices of kindness and benevolence. . . .[143]

In other ways God's goodness works through creation to aid people physically and spiritually.

The sick are wont to sit upon the green turf, and when the excessive heats of the dog-days burn the earth and dry up the rivers they sit sheltered under the trees, and defended from the heat by their shadow. Under their leafy screen the sun's rays are softened, and their sufferings are soothed as they breathe the air fragrant with the scent of hay. The pleasant green of the trees and of the turf rests their eyes, and the fruit which hangs before them promises them delight when ripened. . . . Their ears are agreeably occupied by the sweet and harmonious concerts of birds of varied plumage. See how, in order to cure one sickness, the goodness of God multiplies remedies (in creation). . . .[144]

This hints at Bernard's link between the monastic life and its harmony with the natural setting. Another more fervent passage seems to proclaim Bernard's thoughts with beautiful elaboration.

That spot has much charm, it greatly soothes weary minds, relieves anxieties and cares, helps souls who seek the Lord greatly to devotion, and recalls to them the thought of the heavenly sweetness towards which they aspire. The smiling countenance of the earth is painted with varying colors, the blooming verdure of spring satisfies the eyes, and its sweet odor salutes the nostrils. But while I view the flowers, while I breathe their sweet scent, the meadows recall to me the histories of ancient times; for while I drink in the sweetness of the flowers, the thought occurs to my mind of the fragrance of the clothing of the Patriarch Jacob, which the Scripture compares to the odor which mounts from a fruitful field. When I delight my eyes with the bright colors of the flowers, I am reminded that this beauty is far above that of the purple robe of Solomon, who in all his glory, could not equal the beauty of lilies of the field. . . . In this way, while I am charmed without by the sweet influence of the beauty of the country, I have not less delight within reflecting on the mysteries which are hidden beneath it.[145]

Humankind and creation need each other. Humanity governs and thus perfects creation; creation ministers to people physically and spiritually. Its beauties are painted by the hand of divine wisdom.[146] They remind the observer (as they would Francis) of that higher spiritual beauty and scriptural passages which elevate and glorify the particular things seen.

The passage may clarify what Bernard meant when he distinguished between that knowledge "sensed" under the shade of trees and that learned in schools. Through the great sensual delight creation has to offer—the happy face of the earth, the fragrance and color of spring flowers—human minds are led away from the cares of worldly toil. They are calmed and aided to meditate more easily on the mysteries of divine goodness. The beauty in creation itself moves people to ascend from the sensual to the spiritual; it thus furthers spiritual training and refreshment.

Specific Relationships between Cistercian and Franciscan Thought

The many passages given above demonstrate that there are extensive similarities between Cistercian and early Franciscan attitudes toward creation. Some of these similarities derive from shared basic Christian ideals—for example, the belief that the things of creation have a duty to serve humankind. Francis himself said, "Every creature says and proclaims, 'God made me for thee, O man!' " (*LP* 51). It is then humankind's reciprocal duty to be grateful for creation's services and appreciate the beauty and benefits the material world gives to them. According to Francis,

> These creatures minister to our needs every day: without them we could not live; and through them the human race greatly offends the Creator. Every day we fail to appreciate so great a blessing by not praising as we should the Creator and Dispenser of all these gifts. (*LP* 43)

Both the Cistercians and Francis (*VP* 58; *F*II:1–2) expressed great enjoyment in being amid the natural environment, especially when they linked the elements of creation to spiritual matters. They took delight in associating something observed in creation with pleasant and appropriate Biblical passages relating to it. These associations often are unusually literal, in contrast to bestiary allegorization of Biblical passages. For instance, the *Description of Clairvaux* quotes the Song of Songs and applies it literally: "I have sat under the shade of the tree which I desired, and its fruit was sweet to my taste."[147] Francis and the *Description*'s author quote from Jesus' well-known comparisons of natural to human beauty.[148] Today we might quote Shelley or Wordsworth when impressed by the environment's beauty.

The *Description*'s lyricism and meditative appreciation of creation's beauty stop short of the rapturous joy and mystical absorption which so clearly characterize Francis' nature mysticism: "We who lived with him saw him find great cause for interior and external joy in all creatures; he caressed and contemplated them with delight, so much so that his spirit seemed to live in heaven and not on earth" (*LP* 51). Francis' love of being out amid the natural environment was not limited to enjoying the surroundings of a monastery or fields,[149] as it often was with the Cistercians. But both considered that things of creation were more partial to them than to those who were not friars or monks, respectively.[150] At times this perceived partiality and friendship led to refreshingly humorous encounters or expressions, as when the *Description*'s author apologized to a beloved fountain for mentioning it last.[151] Francis once held a waterfowl and then released it, whereupon it flew away, "showing its joy by a certain movement of its body" (*VS* 167; *ML* 8:7).

The differences between the Cistercian and early Franciscan ideals must not be overlooked. The conceptions in the *Description* reveal a singularly dynamic vision of human involvement with creation. There is a distinct emphasis upon the practical and technical domination of creation, in a systematic manner, for its use by humankind.

> The river climbs to this height by works laboriously constructed, and passes nowhere without rendering some service, or leaving some of its water behind. It divides the valley into two by a sinuous bed, which the labour of the brethren, and not Nature, has made. . . .[152]

This element might at first seem to be a horrifying confirmation of Toynbee's alleged "monotheistic disrespect for nature,"[153] and to imply a license to exploit the environment, with just pride, for humanity's own ends. However, this would be an unfair extrapolation and distortion. The Cistercian view emphasized consistently the close bonds and harmony between humankind and the rest of creation. Humanity and the rest of creation in fact achieve perfection together because of human efforts at tending and organizing the environment, and creation's willing response to humanity's rational guidance. Creation repays human care by aiding people physically and spiritually. They are partners in a common effort.

> But the river does not hesitate nor refuse any who require its aid; and you may see it causing to rise and fall alternately the heave pestles (of the fullers) . . . and so relieves them of the heaviest part of their labour. . . . How many horses would this labour tire! Of how many men would it weary the arms! And the kindly stream relieves us from it altogether, although without it we should have neither food to eat, nor raiment prepared to put on. *It shares with us our fatigues*, and for all the labour which it undertakes the whole

> day long it expects no other recompense than that when it has completed diligently all its tasks it may be permitted to go free upon its way [emphasis added].[154]

This sophisticated Cistercian synthesis, an attempt to reconcile a deep reverence for creation with a need for technical domination of the environment for protection, security, and support, was the product of a settled, permanent monastic community. As such, it was intensive, systematic, and yet circumscribed in outlook. It is an adaptation and elaboration of assumptions present in earlier medieval tradition, which had not lacked examples of dedicated and organized monastic efforts prefiguring the Cistercian.[155] But these developments, derived from monastic life and monastic ascetic tradition emphasizing technical ingenuity and systematic modification of the physical environment, contrast with elements of Francis' thought which harken back to earlier, simpler, eremetic life and ideals. The Franciscan approach arose from a more primitively organized social grouping very much attached to a life of wandering and individual meditative retreat. It was impractical for large and complex social units because of its resistance to formal organization, permanent habitation, and extensive alteration of the environment.

Francis would indeed have used simple tools in his renovation of the tiny churches he worked on early in his religious career. Moreover, as the Order grew, he would allow his brothers to inhabit friaries and build their own churches. But this was different from promotion of large-scale engineering feats or large construction projects for the benefit of the Order. As Francis' comments show, projects of this sort clashed with his ideals that his followers should exist in absolute poverty and non-attachment to places or property in their lives of wandering evangelism (see especially *LP* 8–16). Francis had learned a different sort of respect for creation through his experiences with the eremetic life. Also, because of his eremetic ideal he was totally determined (in spite of his delicate constitution)[156] to endure harsh environments with complete austerity, refusing to rely on monastic organization or extensive human imposition upon the environment to soften his way of life. Certain specifications Francis made clearly show that ideas from his eremetic life molded and limited his allowances for acceptable habitations. For himself, he would accept a wooden cell "lined inside and out with gravel and branches" (*LP* 13). The "cells and houses of the brothers were to be constructed solely of earth and wood in order better to safeguard poverty and humility" (*LP* 13). These instructions, as well as the requirement that friaries must have a ditch and hedge rather than a wall around them (*LP* 16), reveal the clear influence of Francis' eremetic experiences. Further, they show how closely these experiences were connected with the desire to remain in humble intimacy with the natural environment—not to control or impose on it systematically. These conceptions thus not only contrasted with some Cistercian ideas, but led to a tension between early Franciscan experiences and the needs of the growing Order.

2

Traditional Elements in Francis' Interpretation of Creation

THE EREMETIC MODE OF LIFE

> It is important to realize that there was nothing, literally nothing, of a bright new dawn about Francis and his ideas; he was not the herald of salvation for whom the Church had eagerly been crying out. The roads to Rome had long been crowded with reformers of all sorts and conditions. Francis of Assisi was treading, metaphorically and even literally, in the footsteps of multitudes that had trod the same way before him. . . . Evangelical poverty, a life lived according to the gospel, the end of simony and abuses—they [the popes] had heard it all before.[1]

Mockler is speaking here of the Franciscan ideal in general, not particularly of Francis' attitude toward the natural environment. Yet since the latter developed out of the former, one should not be surprised to find it also included many unoriginal or traditional elements. For the Franciscan outlook was, just as much as the Cistercian, a part of an integrated unity—Francis' attitudes were inseparable from his experiences and ideals of ascetic life.

Francis was, as Omer Englebert says, "one of the greatest hermits in the history of the Church."[2] His experience with the eremetic life began very early in his career—in fact, even before he had a career, if one speaks in terms of a well-defined spiritual mission. Francis would have imbibed the ideals of the eremetic life and gained knowledge of Antony and other hermits from innumerable sermons at Mass, and by observing penitents and ascetics in his own time. His actions and expressions prove that he had extensive knowledge of the different modes of the ascetic life (see, e.g., *LP* 40; *LP* 114; *VP* 33). He made periodic retreats to a cave outside Assisi even before his formal "conversion" in 1206 (*VP* 6; *VS* 9; *ML* 2:5). His subsistence in caves and even, for a time, in a pit (*VP* 10), must have had a deep spiritual and psychological impact on him.[3] At this time came his full rejection of his former pampered city life for an ideal of total self-abnegation and austerity that had profound ramifications.[4] Francis and his first followers often lived in abandoned ovens, grottos, or caves (*VP* 39). Their habitation at the Rivo Torto was "a certain abandoned hovel in the shelter of which these most ardent despisers of great and beautiful homes lived; and there they kept themselves safe from the rains. For, as a certain saint once said, from a hovel one ascends more quickly to heaven than from a palace" (*VP* 42). The hovel was so tiny that Francis and his followers could not fit in at all without great cramping.[5] Later they even stayed in abandoned tombs.[6]

As Celano implies, the choice of habitation was deliberate and fitting for the ideals of the early Franciscans. Francis looked upon the eremetic life as a teacher of true Franciscan humility. Once he instructed his Order:

> Be humble and sincere. Keep silence from dawn until after Terce, praying to God in your hearts, and do not indulge in idle and unprofitable conversation. Although you are travelling, let your words be as humble and devout as in a hermitage or cell. (*MP* 65)

Even while friars were traveling, they were supposed to remember their cells and the ideals of humility and austerity they followed there.

Many of these ideals—living humbly and austerely, in purity and contemplation, working simply to support oneself—were those of the earlier ascetics, and reached back into the apostolic era.[7] Celano says of the Franciscan hermits:

> The norm for such hermits of the present time is to live as each one pleases. But this is not applicable to all, for we know some are living in a hermitage like saints in the flesh in accordance with the very best regulations. We know also that those fathers who were their predecessors bloomed as solitary flowers. Would that the hermits of our time would not fall away from that primitive beauty [*ab illa pulchritudine primitiva*], the praise of the righteousness of which remains forever. (*VS* 179)

Francis considered eremetic austerity of central importance for his Order and essentially apostolic. His defenses of it are directly Biblical, and show more clearly the sources of his attitudes that contrasted with some of the Cistercians'.

> He taught his brothers to make poor dwellings, of wood, not of stone, and to erect small "places" according to a humble plan. Often, indeed, speaking of poverty, he would propose to his brothers this saying of the gospel: The foxes have dens and the birds of the air have nests; but the Son of Man has nowhere to lay his head. (*VS* 56)
>
> The Lord . . . when he was in the desert where he prayed and fasted for forty days, did not set up a cell for himself there nor any house, but he lived beneath a rock of the mountain. (*VS* 59)

Francis' preferred type of eremetic habitation may best be seen from descriptions of those he actually lived in or made himself. Around the year 1211, Francis decided to spend a Lenten fast period on an uninhabited island of Lake Trasmene, near Assisi.

> As there was no building where he could take shelter, he went into a very dense thicket in which many thorn bushes and small trees had made a sort of little cabin or den. And there he began to pray and contemplate heavenly things in that place. (*F* 7)

Francis' motivations seem to have included opportunism and austerity: Since there was no habitation which might have provided him with temporary shelter (as in the Rivo Torto huts), he took advantage of a natural shelter and disturbed little in the area. Later, however, due to the fame of the location, people flocked to the area, a little village arose, and the Order established a "place" (*locus*) there for contemplation and prayer (*F* 7).

When Francis visited La Verna in 1224, nothing was there from previous visits of the brothers except "a very poor little hut made of tree-branches" (*F* II:1). Francis

> asked Count Orlando to have a poor little cell made for him at the foot of a very beautiful beech tree that was about a stone's throw from the friars' "place," because that spot seemed to him very suitable for devout prayer. And Count Orlando had it made without delay. (*F* II:2)

Several modern authors have described the settings and atmosphere of the early Franciscan *loci*.[8] The present author would add the following comments from his own visits to these Franciscan locales. The term "places" seems to be appropriate for several reasons. First, it applies simply because it is ambiguous enough to cover the range of habitations concerned—from modest rock hermitages (as in the Carceri outside Assisi) to tiny grottoes barely large enough to accommodate one person. Also, the term reflects a humility fitting the ideals of those involved and the common austerity of the habitations. To the early Franciscans these habitations were not conceived of as friaries or settlements, terms that would imply proprietary rights—a separation from the natural environment and a possessive imposition of human presence—but simply as special places amid creation which could accommodate friars when they wished to meditate in solitude.

Although these sites (which in their rusticity often call to mind early frontier sites in the Appalachians or the western United States) are ideal for meditation, they all share settings of sublime natural beauty. To take one example, the Carceri hermitage is far enough outside Assisi and well enough into rugged mountains to guarantee solitude, yet its position at the edge of a huge ravine allows a superb view of the hazy green and gold Spoleto valley far below. A forest filled with doves and other creatures shields from view the tiny caves used by Francis and his followers. As is shown by Francis' statement in the above quotation, the early Franciscans often purposefully selected "places" possessing both distant solitude and great natural beauty.

Francis' Eremetic Life as One Source of His Attitudes toward Creatures

The first incidents that demonstrate Francis' devotion to animals arise from his early eremetic experiences and very much resemble stories told of the first ascetics. Evidently when Francis visited the Isola Maggiore of Lake Trasmene around 1211, he discovered a rabbit which had been caught in a trap, and released it.[9] Life in hermitage retreats often brought Francis into direct contact with creation. He joined birds in praising God while at a "place" in the Venetian marshes (*ML* 8:9). He made his decision where to settle at La Verna when a flock of birds surrounded him and perched on his shoulders, which he took as a propitious greeting (*F* II:1). Obviously the animals living around these isolated retreats may have learned little fear of humans at the time. These intimate eremetic contacts with creatures gave Francis a love and sympathy for them typical of hermits before him. As the *Legend of Perugia* puts it, "He had so much love and sympathy for them that he was disturbed when they were treated without respect. He spoke to them with a great inner and exterior joy, as if they had been endowed by God with feeling, intelligence, and speech."[10] Many of these anecdotes are told with sentiments and language closely resembling those earlier medieval eremetic stories found in Short's study of *Saints in the World of Nature*.[11]

TABLE 1. Traditional Elements in Francis' Interpretation of Creation, as Reported by the Early Sources

Thaumaturgy: Control Over and Command of Creatures	Allegory in Creation	Creation Educates
Admonishes birds; gives permission: *VP* 58; *TM* 20; *ML* 12:3; *F* 16; *MNL* 5:6	*Moral allegory*	Swallows show obedience: *VP* 59; *TM* 21; *ML* 12:4; *F* 16
Swallows ordered to stop singing: *VP* 59; *TM* 21; *ML* 12:4; *F* 16	Doves: *F* 22	Useful lamb killed, sow dies: *VS* 111; *ML* 8:6
Command over fish: *VP* 61; *TM* 24; *ML* 8:8	Water: *MP* 118	Greedy bird dies: *VS* 47; *LP* 108; *MP* 107
Water to wine: *VP* 61; *TM* 17; *ML* 5:10; *MNL* 5:3	Lights and flame: *VP* 165	Bees and mysticism: *VS* 169
Water from rock: *VS* 46; *ML* 7:12; *F* II:1; *MNL* 5:3	Larks: *LP* 110; *MP* 113	Pious larks: *LP* 110; *MP* 113
Money changed to serpent: *VS* 68; *MP* 15; *ML* 7:5	*Mystical allegory*	Parable of drones and worker bees: *VS* 75; *LP* 62; *MP* 24
Bird's death from greed: *VS* 47; *LP* 108; *MP* 107	Lambs: *VP* 77; *ML* 8:6; *LaudHor*	Cuckoo: *MP* 122
Arezzo demons cast out: *VS* 108; *LP* 81; *ML* 6:9	Sun: *MP* 119	Ants as laying up for future: E. A. Armstrong, p. 154 (*Sayings of Brother Giles*)
Sow punished: *VS* 111; *ML* 8:6	Worms: *VP* 80; *Office of the Passion*	Lamb teaches respect for Eucharist: *ML* 8:7
Fire ordered: *VS* 166; *LP* 48; *MP* 115; *ML* 5:9; *MNL* 5:1	Stones: *VS* 165; *LP* 51	Birds show missions to take place: *F* 16
Bird ordered: *VS* 167; *ML* 8:10	Flowers: *MP* 118	All creation serves God better than man: *Admonition* 5
Pheasant ordered: *VS* 170; *ML* 8:10	Trees: *MP* 118	Mice as diabolic: *LP* 43; *MP* 100
Cricket ordered: *VS* 171; *LP* 84; *ML* 8:9		
Wine increased: *LP* 25; *MP* 104; *F* 19		
Others: F 21:1, 29; II:2; *New F* 55, 58, 61; *MNL* 5:9; 5:7; 5:4		

TABLE 2. Francis' Love for Animals and Concern Shown for Their Welfare

Pets	Francis Preserving or Caring for Animals, Restoring to Safety
Sheep: *VP* 78,79; *ML* 8:6	Rabbits and traps: *VP* 60; *ML* 8:8; *TM* 29–30
Falcon: *VS* 168; *ML* 8:10; *F* II:2	Returns fish to lake: *VP* 61; *ML* 8:8; *TM* 24
Pheasant: *VS* 170; *ML* 8:10	Sheep and general compassion: *VP* 77–80; *ML* 8:6
Cicada: *VS* 171; *LP* 84; *ML* 8:9	Saves worms: *VP* 80
Lady Jacoba's lamb: *ML* 8:7	Hay saved, animals cured: *VP* 87; *TM* 18
	Robins kept: *VS* 47; *LP* 108; *MP* 107
	Preserves wood, garden wild flowers, worms, bees get honey and wines: *LP* 51; *MP* 118; *VS* 165; *ML* 9:1
	Waterbird freed: *VS* 167; *ML* 8:10
	Birds and animals fed on Christmas: *VS* 200; *LP* 110; *MP* 114
	Fire preserved: *LP* 49–50

One may also suspect that the deep reverence for "Sister Earth, our mother" and the other very humble compliments given to various creatures in his *Canticle* reflect a life which was closely attached to the earth and deeply valued the simple experiences amid the natural world recounted in the documents. For example, on one occasion the *Fioretti* lovingly recounts a homely incident in which Francis and his followers spread out their modest dinner on a flat rock near a stream (*F* 13). Other incidents occur when the brothers are sitting around the campfire together, as they must often have done (*LP* 49–50). To those remembering and valuing such a simple experience, the praise of Brother Fire, "Through whom You brighten up the night" (as Francis says in the *Canticle*), would have special meaning. The simple and sincere appreciation of elements in the natural environment here resembles more the outlook of the aforementioned ninth-century Celtic hermit and nature poet than the Cistercian *Description of Clairvaux*. The experiences and outlook are distinctly eremetic in atmosphere and heritage, as opposed to monastic.

THE INTERPRETATION OF CREATURES AS DEMON-POSSESSED

Another distinctly traditional element in Francis' ascetic experience was his perception of a demonic presence within the environment, and his struggle with this presence. For even though Francis' view of creation was extremely positive and accepting, he still believed, in a very traditional way, that it was occasionally possible for the Devil to use creatures for his evil ends, subject to divine allowance. At one point, Francis lived in a cell near St. Damian's, where he was tormented by mice that prevented him from relaxing and sleeping. According to the *Legend of Perugia*,

> Not only at night but even by day they so tormented him that even when he ate they got up on to the table, so that his companions and he himself considered it must be a temptation of the devil, as indeed it was [*ut socii eius et ipsemet considerarent quod esset temptatio diabolica, sicut et fuit*]. (*LP* 43)

When Francis was on La Verna, his appreciation for his surroundings, thaumaturgy, and close relations with animals typified his encounters with the natural world. But so did struggle with the Devil, who had hidden himself amid this awesome unclaimed mountain fastness. On one occasion the Devil waylaid Francis near a precipice, so that the only way the saint could escape was to be miraculously received into the very rock. At other times he had to save Brother Leo and another companion from attacks by the Devil (*F* II:1). Here we see the reenactment of the eremetic conquest of the wilderness paradise, in which creation both aids the saint and is used against him.

Though the Temptation by Mice occurs in the *Legend of Perugia* (and thus the opinions there probably are truly reflective of the contemporary reactions), these other stories only occur in the *Actus-Fioretti*. Their authenticity is less certain. Nevertheless, the probably authentic *Letter* of Masseo, which contains Francis' Farewell to La Verna, includes Francis' remark, "Adieu, Adieu, rock that receivest me into thine entrails while thou mockest the demon! We shall never see each other again!"[12] The sentiments here are not at all contrary to early Franciscan conceptions. The *Fioretti* has probably here as usual remained true to the Franciscan ethos.[13] Celano also may allude to these incidents (*VP* 71–72).

Nevertheless, these incidents make up a very small segment of those left to us. The Temptation by Mice is the only incident linking specific creatures with temptation in a way seen in the earlier Dark Ages. Its special setting needs to be noted. It occurred during the winter of 1224–1225, when Francis himself was gravely ill and his followers were extremely distraught, and should be regarded as an aberration. In addition, Francis' temporary recovery produced one of his most enthusiastic praises of creatures—his *Canticle*. The *Actus-Fioretti* incidents are also unusual in that they were set down very late, and happened when the friars were in a new and at times terrifying mountainous environment. This gave ample room for exaggeration. Yet even the *Actus* incidents are interspersed with enthusiastically positive encounters with creatures and evidence of appreciation for the natural environment that Dark Age sources would be hard pressed to match (see *F* II:2). In general, the sheer number of anecdotes relating positive encounters with creatures dwarfs the number recorded in the masterpieces of hagiography from the ages before Francis. Without a doubt the number and consistency of these stories prove that Francis confronted creatures with preconceptions and associations that were unusually positive and full of spontaneous invention.

The Creature as Teacher

Francis often drew moral allegorical parallels from creation. For medieval people, creation was the "Book of Nature,"[14] which such ascetics as Antony had used,[15] inspired by Biblical passages such as Romans 1:20 and Jesus' exhortation to "consider the lilies."[16] Martin had seen gluttonous birds as a figure of demons.[17] To him, sheared sheep illustrated the New Testament command to give up a coat to someone who had none (the image here has a humorous pathos). A partly grazed meadow was symbolic of the states of virginity, marriage, and fornication.[18] Short[19] has collected many examples of saintly interactions with creation used as parables. Francis derived moral lessons from larks, as symbolic of devoted friars (*LP* 110); from a greedy baby robin, as warning given to greedy people (*LP* 108; *VS* 47); and from ants, as symbolic of those who worry too much about the future.[20]

Animals could instruct people more directly as well. As in examples we have seen earlier, creatures' responses to a saint are supposed to induce human awe and devotion.[21] Creation functions as an example to humanity. Martin of Tours once complained that snakes obeyed him, but people did not.[22] In Franciscan accounts, Lady Jacoba's lamb, a gift from Francis, taught adoration of the Eucharist by its example of piety (*ML* 8:7). The swallows' obedience to Francis' commands moves people to accept the saint's teaching (*VP* 59). Though Armstrong rejects the connection Celano makes between the animals' obedience and that of humankind, Francis makes this kind of linkage himself in an *Admonition*.

> Try to realize the dignity God has conferred on you. He created and formed your body in the image of his beloved Son, and your soul in his own likeness. And yet every creature under heaven serves and acknowledges and obeys its Creator in its own way better than you do.[23]

This *Admonition* shows that Francis' sentiments were not far from Martin's. After the Sermon to the Birds, Francis and his companions were raised to a new pitch of enthusiasm because the animals' reaction seemed to prefigure that of humans (*VP* 58; *F* 16). Thus the early Franciscans, in a manner typical of the medieval period, drew parallels from the lives of animals or from events in the natural environment for the purpose of allegory or instructive example to humankind.

SAINT AS THAUMATURGE: FRANCIS' CLASSIC DEMONSTRATIONS

The consistent appearance of thaumaturgy in Franciscan incidents undermines one researcher's claim that Francis "tried to depose man from his monarchy over creation and set up a democracy of all God's creatures."[24] The truth is more complex, and demands reconsideration of Francis' views within their medieval context instead of an idealized modern one. Francis' thaumaturgical actions prove most clearly that he considered himself a human agent of God, and he never lost the traditional concept of humankind's superior place in the hierarchy of creation. After his preaching to the birds, for example—an act which stressed hierarchy and community at the same time—Francis gave the birds permission to leave (*VP* 58). This is the gesture more of an abbot or priest than anything resembling a senator in a democracy. The Sermon to the Birds is not a minor incident; it is one of the most famous incidents reflecting the new Franciscan spirit. Its conclusion represented an ending which had characterized many previous encounters between saints and animals.[25] Other miraculous actions typified even more early patterns of interaction with the physical environment by saints through miracles. On one occasion, Francis turned water into wine (*VS* 61; *TM* 17; *ML* 5:10; *MNL* 5:2). At other times, he drew water from a rock (*VS* 46; *MP* 15; *F* II:1; *MNL* 5:3); he caused a boat to move (*MNL* 5:4); he "miraculously" increased a wine harvest (*LP* 25; *MP* 104; *F* 19); he cursed a sow and it died in infamy (*VS* 111; *ML* 8:6). A cicada sings upon his request (*VS* 171; *LP* 84; *ML* 8:9); swallows stop singing when he commands it (*VP* 59). Thus even if an incident reflects the authentic stamp of Franciscan innovation, it may yet hold a core of common medieval thought, or find itself among various other similar ones which seem typical of many medieval incidents. As we have said above, the "miraculous" elements in the stories need not invalidate them automatically. The reverse may be true: the "miraculous" elements and interpretations may serve to reveal even more clearly the powerful ideologies applied to nonmiraculous happenings (and, of course, to some Christians today, the events may be both believable *and* miraculous).

Francis' Affectionate Interactions with Animals

One may draw similar conclusions about traditional character of the many famous anecdotes that portray Francis befriending or making pets of animals.[26] Some strike the researcher as profoundly imbued with new Franciscan ideals, while others, though charming and still significant because of their unusual quantity, seem to reflect an outlook very much resembling that of earlier medieval ascetics. Few of them are extravagantly unbelievable, and in most of them the "miraculous" elements reveal the deeper beliefs present.

In a few cases, Francis evidently enjoyed meeting animals particularly because of the new special love he felt for them as part of the family of God's creation. For example, Francis enjoyed receiving a live fish as a gift on one occasion. He called the fish "brother" and released it. The fish, however, remained playing in the water beside Francis' boat until he gave it permission to leave—again an unexpectedly thaumaturgic finish to the story (*VP* 61). Some anecdotes show Francis treating creatures with special respect when he linked them with scriptural passages of mystical symbolism. As Celano says, "So, all things, especially those in which some allegorical similarity to the Son of God could be found, he would embrace more fondly and look upon more willingly" (*VP* 77). Thus Francis notices worms and spares them from being trodden upon, remembering the verse, "I am a worm, not a man" (*VP* 80—Psalm 21:7). Lambs also gain special attention for similar reasons (*VP* 77). None would deny this is quite a singular aesthetic. It was one of the results of the new Franciscan dedication to things imitating Christ in some way, and so is an excellent example of a general ideal of the Order bringing about a specific innovative response to the natural environment. Yet the classic medieval background of this practice should not be glossed over in attempts to modernize Francis' views. The sort of mystical symbolic association involved resembles those made in medieval bestiaries.[27] At other times Francis allegorized creation in typically medieval ways, as we have seen above.

Many other stories in which Francis shows concern or affection for animals would fit just as easily in a collection of Dark Age hagiography. The motivations involved remain faithful to traditional ascetic models. Francis often shows concern for animals' well-being, sheltering, protecting, or warning them of danger as did earlier saints such as Godric of Finchale.[28] This might appear a novelty to those familiar only with the monastic outlook, but in fact it is a typical product of the intimate association with creation that characterizes the eremetic life. If one wishes to salute Francis' thoughtfulness on this point, one should not forget that many Dark Age predecessors also possessed similar dedication and concern, though their actions are perhaps not recounted at such length or with such consistency.

Other interactions with creatures which seem especially charming do not necessarily reflect originality. On one occasion, Francis seems ready to accept some baby robins as fellow friars (*VS* 47; *LP* 108; *MP* 107). At other times, he joins in singing with a cicada or birds in order to give praise to God together with them (*VS* 171; *LP* 84; *ML* 8:9). These incidents have a charming humor and naiveté, yet are not strikingly original; there are earlier parallels.[29]

Likewise, other anecdotes show animals or elements aiding people and receiving respect and thanks for their efforts. One remembers Francis' great respect for fire and appreciation for its service (e.g., *LP* 49–50), as well as for the falcon which functioned as the ultimate in caring alarm clocks while Francis resided at La Verna (*F* II:2). When Francis was tired or ill, the bird would wake him up later than usual for Matins. Both the deed and the holy man's gratitude remind one of sentiments expressed in the Cistercian *Description*. While Francis' vision of the interdependence between humankind and animals was uniquely his own (as we shall see in our discussion of his *Canticle*), his basic values of respect and gratitude for creation's aid to humanity were not innovations.

Even Francis' qualms about attachments to creatures seem to be based on ascetic concerns. He renounced his pleasant friendship with an extroverted cicada due to a fear of self-indulgence or pride. One day he announced: "Let us give our sister cricket leave to go now, for it has made us sufficiently happy now; we do not want our flesh to glory vainly over things of this kind" (*VS* 171). Other motivations Francis may have had for not keeping pets may have involved a combination of ascetic values and the ideals of the Order. Francis, of course, would have eschewed the long-term possessions of pets because of his horror of possessing anything at all.[30] Besides, attachments to animals would be a nuisance to members of an Order which demanded a life of constant travel and a great deal of insecurity in such matters as regular food and housing. This is probably the motivation behind Francis' giving up of some prospective pets.[31] Yet even the extent of latitude Francis demonstrated in such matters may have led to abuses as the Order grew into the thousands, for in the *Rule* of 1221 (though not in that of 1223), the friars are forbidden to keep any animals.[32] One wonders if this prohibition was Francis' idea or if others had pressed it upon him, and he fought successfully to keep it out of the *Rule* of 1223. The friars were again forbidden to keep pets sometime after Francis' death.[33]

Early Reactions to Francis' Traditionality: Celano and Bonaventure

The unofficial sources of the Franciscan legends rarely step back from their detailed narrative presentation to interpret on an abstract level the significance of the incidents they recount. The *Legend of Perugia*, for instance, usually employs only the barest of transitions to separate its accounts. Only occasionally will it comment in a way that reveals that those present were aware of the deeper themes behind the incidents witnessed. After the long and detailed account of the Cauterization by Brother Fire, it allows itself one weighty sentence of commentary.

> It is not surprising that fire and other creatures at times showed their respect for him, since, as we who were with him have seen, he loved and respected them with such charity and affection, took so much joy in them, and was moved to such concern and pity over them, that if anyone did not treat them properly he was upset. (*LP* 49, Brooke's translation)

Such an illuminating remark demonstrates that Francis' expressions and experiences did not spring forth into a vacuum. He and his comrades were attentive to the deeper significances and relationships emerging around them. Their spirit lingered a moment to point out the reciprocality and concern that were seen to characterize Francis' relationships with creatures. But the Order in 1244 had called upon the friars for narratives, not for interpretations,[34] and narrative the Order evidently received. It is difficult to believe (but true) that the *Legend of Perugia*—closely based on the friars' work of 1244—moves through its remarkably detailed story of the *Canticle*, for instance, without a single line of abstract interpretation. That was left for Celano and Bonaventure, the official sources who organize, categorize, and interpret their accounts with great freedom.

What emerges in the official accounts is strange, at least to modern observers who concentrate only on the points they see as original in Francis' thought, for the early official biographers have exactly the opposite bias. Where moderns would see the innovation in Francis' expressions, the early official sources see Francis as the resurrector of all that was good in ancient Christian tradition. Both views illuminate a part of the truth and submerge another. Francis, while original in some thoughts and actions, also drew much from tradition. And while in some ways he did strive to revive older Biblical or ascetic attitudes and practices insofar as he understood them, his own limited understanding, different cultural context, and different personal outlook caused him to be genuinely innovative to an extent the early biographers could not fully recognize or appreciate. Yet understanding the real traditional base supporting many of Francis' expressions will allow modern critics to avoid simply classifying such unquestionably alert intellectuals as Celano and Bonaventure as naive when they insist upon seeing Francis in terms of earlier tradition. For there was an authentically traditional side to much of what Francis had to say.

The official biographers proclaim that Francis is a new spirit reviving the hallowed ancient beliefs and practices of Christianity. The *Sacrum Commercium*, the tale of a spiritual romance between Francis and Lady Poverty that Celano may have written in 1227,[35] asserts that Francis has recovered the ascetic life of poverty followed in Eden and by the apostles.[36] Celano's *Vita Prima*, written in 1228, declares:

> For when the teachings of the Gospel, not indeed in every respect, but taken generally, had everywhere failed to be put into practise, this man was sent by God to bear witness of the truth throughout the whole world in accordance with the example of the Apostles. . . . For in this last time [*novissimo tempore*] this new evangelist, like one of the rivers that flowed out of paradise, diffused the waters of the Gospel over the whole world by his tender watering. . . . Accordingly, in him and through him there arose throughout the world an unlooked for happiness and a holy newness and a shoot of the ancient religion suddenly brought a great renewal to those who had grown calloused and to the very old. A new spirit was born in the hearts of the elect. . . . Through him the miracles of ancient times [*antiqua miracula*] were renewed, while there was planted in the desert [*deserto*] of this world, by a new order but in an ancient way, a fruitful vine bearing flowers of sweetness. . . . (*VP* 89)

As we have seen, the "miracles of ancient times" were indeed renewed. And since Celano and Bonaventure consciously interpret Francis as the incarnation of ancient Christian traditions, many of their statements reveal, in a way not found before, the traditional assumptions behind a saint's unusual interactions with creation. The fervency and power of the new Franciscan movement spur more trenchant proclamations that Francis had achieved what ascetics in the past had sought. Old ascetic conceptions live again, in a new context. Thaumaturgic control over creation is strongly associated with a return to primordial, paradisal innocence. When Francis submitted to Brother Fire and was not harmed by him, Celano asserted, "I believe that he had returned to primitive innocence [*ad innocentiam primam*], for whom, when he wished it, cruel things were made gentle" (*VS* 166). Armstrong recognizes the ideal of harmony expressed here,[37] but cannot accept that in fact Francis' thaumaturgy is inseparable from it. Yet to a medieval observer, as we have seen in the case of Severus and Martin, thaumaturgical control over creation was just as sure a sign of the return to original harmony as such "milder" expressions as having pets.

Bonaventure expresses similar sentiments. "So it was," he says, "that by God's divine power the brute beasts felt drawn towards him and inanimate creation obeyed his will. It seemed as if he had returned to the state of primeval innocence, he was so good, so holy" (*MNL* 3:6). Several passages in Bonaventure's writings demonstrate he believed that Francis' unusual affectionate interactions with animals symbolized his return to the perfect relationship humankind had attained with creatures in Eden. Bonaventure postulates a link between Francis' possession of the virtue of compassion or sympathy and the restoration of cordial respect from animals.

> We should have the greatest reverence, therefore, for St. Francis' loving compassion which had such wonderful charm that it could bring savage animals into subjection and tame the beasts of the forest, training those which were tame already and claiming obedience from those which had rebelled against fallen mankind. (*ML* 8:11)

In one place Bonaventure used Francis to illustrate quite a detailed picture of how humans originally related to animals in paradise and reattained this ability with their increase in saintliness.

> If you ask what is the virtue which makes a person love creatures, because they come from God and exist for him, I reply that it is compassion and a sort of natural affection. For example, we see that even now a person can be very fond of a dog because it obeys him faithfully. In the same way, man in his original state had a natural inclination to love animals and even irrational creatures. Therefore, the greater the progress a man makes and the nearer he approaches to the state of innocence the more docile these creatures become towards him, and the greater the affection he feels for them. We see this in the case of St. Francis; he overflowed with tender compassion even for animals, because to some extent he had returned to the state of innocence. This was made clear by the way irrational creatures obeyed him.[38]

This is probably the most elaborate statement of the ascetic ideas intertwined around thaumaturgy involving animals and the significance of a saint's pets, as one will ever find. It was synthesized by a philosopher who could "intellectualize" them due to his Franciscan and ascetic ideals meeting and fertilizing his scholastic training in approaching this problem. Francis' kindness to animals is seen in a typical medieval manner, as a remaining vestige of humankind's paradisal state of innocence. Humanity's original relationships with animals are partially restored when the saint progresses toward greater purity and innocence before God, and God shows the saint's achievement by giving the saint thaumaturgical control over irrational creatures as a model of the primeval relationship between humans and other creatures.[39] Not that simple domination alone characterized this relationship—a mutual love and respect were involved also. Francis' accomplishment culminated in "restoring man's harmony with the whole of creation" (*ML* 8:1).

Celano gave the most moving expression of belief in this temporarily restored harmony. Francis' benevolence charms humanity and the physical universe for a brief space, and then the darkness of disharmony descends again.

> But after he had been taken away, the order of things was completely reversed and everything was changed; for wars and insurrections prevailed everywhere, and a carnage of many deaths suddenly passed through several kingdoms. The horror or famine too spread far and wide, and the cruelty of it, which exceeds the bitterness of everything else, consumed very many. Necessity then turned everything into food and compelled human teeth to chew things that were not even customarily eaten by animals. Bread was made from the shells of nuts and the bark of trees, and, to put it mildly, paternal piety, under the compulsion of famine, did not mourn the death of a child. (*VS* 53)

Celano's graphic picture, which refers to the wars and famine of 1227–1228, reveals the tragedy that befell central Italy when its protecting saint and restored harmony were taken away. The progress of history was interrupted and reversed, with a movement again toward chaos. Humanity returned to its evil ways, and even the physical universe resumed its rebellion against it again.

The classically trained Celano could not have been unaware that his description resembles that given of the primitive state of humanity by Roman authors such as Ovid and Lucretius.[40] Earlier hagiographers had also mourned the loss of their patron saints in such a moving way, though never in such an elaborate passage.[41] There is a strange conception of cyclicality that is implied here: In this progression and regression linked to the saint, humankind's fate in Genesis is acted out again and again, with the only escape from the worldly drama in a virtuous death and the final apocalypse. But for a moment humanity had attained a glimpse of a paradisal golden age, only to lose this vision and plunge into gloom again.

Some of the impetus for these more fervent statements may have derived from the influence of the writings of Joachim of Fiore, whose apocalyptic speculations heightened typical medieval yearning for the final restoration.[42] Joachim had predicted there would be a saintly leader of a great new Order in the coming Third Age. Joachim (died 1202) had a great influence on early members of the Franciscan Order. Bonaventure himself saw Francis as the Angel of the Sixth Seal in the Apocalypse—a very Joachimite idea.[43] The hope that Francis might be a prophesied spiritual leader may have been in the back of many Franciscans' minds, and could have stimulated more explicit statements about Francis' role in the universal order, as well as unleashed deeper manifestations of grief at his passing.

These "intellectualizations" of the official biographers, however, are not necessarily the views of Francis—though one must not underestimate here. Celano seems to prove fairly conclusively that Francis saw himself as personally staving off famine which might occur without his presence.[44] At other times Francis personally interceded to produce prosperity for righteous towns, or to predict (correctly) future civil strife for a foolish and ungrateful city.[45] Francis himself could link his presence or approval with prosperity (harmony with the environment) and civil peace (harmony between humans).[46] Thus there is no doubt that Francis shared his hagiographers' conceptions at least in a general way, and that his interpretation of creation was founded upon the same Christian ascetic basis as theirs. Francis did indeed interpret creatures' reactions to his orders and addresses as evidence of divine power bestowed in a gesture of favor toward him and for the instruction of observers. Creatures' responses to him demonstrated their respect for God's servant and the beginning of the restoration of harmony between God, humanity, and the rest of creation.[47] Francis thus saw himself inhabiting a natural realm that was constantly elevated and sublimated by divine grace—not one he saw in a heretical manner as somehow absorbed in a common soul. Yet even though one can see from the many elements of traditional ascetic thought in Francis' unoriginal reactions to creation that his beliefs arose from the common basis of Christian ascetic ideals, his ideas matured over the years until they gained their own unquestionable independence, originality, and profundity.

3

Francis' Transcendence of Tradition and Its First Major Impact on His Attitude Toward Creation: The Sermon to the Birds

Background: The Fusion of Wandering Evangelism With Eremetic Ideals

It is quite remarkable that we take for granted the multifaceted Francis of Assisi we know today when the early records show that not only strong ecclesiastical opposition to his plans, but also Francis' own predilections, could well have ensured that he became just one more of the legions of Italian hermits enjoying a contemplative life in the oblivion of natural solitude. Careful study of the brief early records suggests that Francis was strongly attracted to a life of solitude amid the beauty of creation. But Francis' positive attitude toward creation was one of his notable pre-"conversion" traits that was fortuitously enriched and rechanneled by both his psychological growth and the slow formation of his mature religious outlook, which grew to encompass much more than a life of solitude.

The anecdotes recounting the story of Francis' youth strongly imply that Francis constantly escaped to the sublime natural surroundings of Assisi as a joyful and necessary recourse. The first evidence of this comes from a passage in Celano which refers roughly to the period 1203–1204, when Francis was recovering from an illness.

> When he had recovered somewhat and had begun to walk about the house with the support of a cane to speed the recovery of his health, he went outside one day and began to look about at the surrounding landscape with great interest. But the beauty of the fields, the pleasantness of the vineyards,

> and whatever else was beautiful to look upon, could stir in him no delight. He wondered therefore at the sudden change that had come over him, and those who took delight in such things he considered very foolish. (*VP* 3)

Celano, who is the only source to report this event, has submerged psychological truth in moralizing platitude. Evidence from the following pages of his own account flatly contradicts any notion that Francis henceforth rejected his previous love of natural beauty. The hagiographer has generalized ineptly in his urge to prove Francis' rejection of all secular ideals and concerns. What actually seems to have happened is that Francis, who had often turned previously to the beauties of creation for consolation and refreshment, found himself in such a depth of depression and inner turmoil that not even his old habits of recourse could soothe his troubled mind. Celano has confused this temporary and very comprehensible psychological state with Francis' concurrent renunciation of secular goals and slow acceptance of the ascetic life in some vague form.[1]

The failure of Francis' next and last attempt at knightly success in war brought about another deep inner crisis (*VP* 5–6). After that, Francis again sought refuge amid the natural environment, this time with a companion, and seemingly in a typically ascetic way, frequenting "remote places, places well suited for counsel," or meditating in "a certain grotto near the city" (*VP* 6). When the crisis with his father erupted, Francis hid in a pit for a month (*VP* 10). But after this was resolved, we find him again at loose in the countryside, singing and joyful, for on an occasion when Francis was accosted by robbers, it was "as he passed through a certain woods singing praises to the Lord in the French language" (*VP* 16; *ML* 2:5).

Reviewing Francis' tumultuous early years, we can easily discern the emotional associations the young man would have had with city life as opposed to life in natural environs. The city was a place where he had experienced tensions, civil strife, war (Assisi's war with Perugia, 1201–1202),[2] crisis, humiliation, and rejection by friends and family. In contrast, life amid physical creation would have enticed Francis with its connotations of spiritual consolation and nourishment, beauty, solitude, and privacy. These associations are not limited to the medieval era, but to some extent are shared by many in the West even today. Leo Marx, in a masterful article, "Pastoral Ideals and City Troubles,"[3] explores in American novels the associations often made with a life of idyllic, contemplative, refreshing retreat amid the beauties of the natural environment, in contrast to the characters' active mission to be fulfilled in a troubling and threatening social environment. These modern presuppositions, while deeply affected by redefinitions and changes

TABLE 3. Chronology of the Important Early Contacts Between Francis, Creatures, and His Natural Surroundings

Date	Event	Sources
1203–1204	Vision of landscape after illness	*VP* 3; Englebert, p. 62
c.1205	Cave retreat outside Assisi	*VP* 6; *VS* 9; *ML* 2:5; *3 Comp.* 12, 16–17
1206–1207 spring	". . . as he passed through a certain wood singing praises to the Lord in the French language, robbers . . ."	*VP* 16; *ML* 2:5; Sabatier, pp. 62–63
1209	Rivo Torto life, huts	*VP* 42; *3 Comp.* 55; *ML* 4:3; Englebert, pp. 117ff.
1211 or 1212, Lent	Rabbit saved	*VP* 60; *TM* 30; *F* 7; Englebert, p. 473
May 8, 1213	La Verna hermitage area acquired from Count Orlando	*F*, Stigmata, 1; Englebert, pp. 185ff.
1213, summer	Sermon to the Birds, Pian dell'Arca, near Bevagna	*VP* 58; *ML* 12:3; *TM* 20; *F* 16; Englebert, pp. 185ff.
1213, later summer	Stilling of Swallows, Alviano	*VP* 59; *TM* 21; *ML* 12:4; *F* 16
1213	San Gemini chapel—altar antipendium has Francis' *Exhortation to the Praise of God*	Wadding, anno 1213; Esser, *Die Opuscula,* pp. 280ff.
1217, summer	"Dinner at Flat Rock"	*F* 13; *New F* 8 (context gives date)
1220, late	Marsh birds near Venice sing along with Francis	*ML* 8:9; Englebert, p. 247

in values since Francis' time,[4] still retain at their base a highly tensioned ideal of unity between two modes of life—withdrawn, peaceful contemplation and active, extroverted mission—that the Franciscan dream would attempt, as it emerged, to mold into one overarching ideal of life.

Francis' early followers joined him in a regimen of life that alternated between periods of retreat in hovels, caves, or grottoes (*VP* 34, 39, and elsewhere), and missions of preaching penance (*VP* 29, 36). Francis' growing experience in the ascetic life deepened his appreciation of creation's beauty and worth, and early incidents exhibit what would become characteristic Franciscan values. In 1211, Francis decided to spend a Lenten fast on the Isola Maggiore of Lake Trasmene. He faced conditions on the uninhabited island with tenacious and heroic austerity, taking cover in a sort of natural den created by a thicket, eating almost nothing over a forty-day span of time. Significantly, Celano relates that, evidently at this same early time, Francis discovered a rabbit caught in a trap on the island, released it, and became friends with it.[5] This is the earliest sign of the characteristic feeling of concern and affection toward specific creatures to be found often in Francis' later expressions, and its foundation in ascetic experience is undeniable.

During this same time Francis also asserts more strongly and coherently his new literalistic ideal of apostolic evangelism. He and his followers go to Rome and receive approval of their way of life (*VP* 32–33). That Francis recognized the need for his mode of life to incorporate both the eremetic and the apostolic evangelical ideals (in his interpretation) is seen from an incident that occurred while he and his followers were still based at the Rivo Torto. When a peasant with a donkey arrived at the place and intended to settle down there, Francis

> was considerably annoyed, especially because the commotion caused by the man and his donkey had disturbed the brothers intent upon silent prayer. So he turned to them: "Dear brothers, I know that God has not called me to entertain a donkey and live in the company of men, but to show men the way of salvation by preaching and counsel. We must, therefore, above all, make sure of being able to pray and give thanks for the graces we receive."[6]

Peaceful solitude is essential for Francis' prayer, contemplation, and thanksgiving—actions just as important as apostolic evangelism. The Franciscan friar must lead a life fulfilling the highest ideals of eremetic asceticism—solitary, introverted, austere, devoted to prayer, mysticism, and humble contemplation of God's creation—as well as devoting himself to a type of wandering evangelism requiring grueling extroversion, constant and perhaps aimless travel under the most variable and destitute of conditions, without any sense of security in possessions, money, or plans for the future. It is a cycle that moves between the extremes of the contemplative and the active lives, and thus heightens the tension between them to a most extraordinary degree—to a degree so challenging, in fact, that very few could relish it or endure all its demands.[7] It is no wonder that officials in the Catholic hierarchy urged Francis to become a monk or hermit instead (*VP* 33), and that when Pope Innocent III considered Francis' plans he warned: "My sons, your plan of life seems too hard and rough. We are convinced of your fervor, but we have to consider those who will follow you in the future, and who may find that this path is too harsh."[8]

Some of Francis' followers, even while he was alive, were unable to give themselves as he did to both aspects of the ideal. Bernard of Quintavalle and Giles valued the contemplative life, and became venerated hermits. Elias and John of Cappella became overinvolved with the temptations of secular affairs and reached their respective bad ends.[9] For Francis, the total ideal was exhilarating, driving, and challenging, but also daunting at times, and, toward the end of his life, impossible.[10]

This extraordinary union of two radically different modes of life,[11] with their contrasting and yet mutually supporting ideals, had an enormous impact upon Francis' attitudes toward the created world. The tension between the two modes of life fused in the Franciscan ideal was reflected in a dynamically developing and original conception of how humanity should relate to creatures and the physical universe.

The Sermon to the Birds and Its Relationship to the Emerging Franciscan Ideal

The first and most dramatic incident that illustrated the deeply productive effect of the interaction of ascetic and evangelical ideals on Francis' attitude toward creation occurred at a crucial moment. In 1213, Francis, daunted by the problems he saw and tempted by the peace of contemplative life, faltered in his commitment to the dual mode of life and seriously considered taking up the eremetic life exclusively.[12] In an agony of doubt, he turned to his trusted friends Brother Silvester and Sister Clare to advise him whether he should "preach sometimes or . . . devote [him]self only to prayer."[13] Francis was so inspired by their encouraging answers that "he set out like a bolt of lightning in his spiritual ardor, not paying any attention to road or path,"[14] henceforth rededicated to the preaching ideal as an integral part of the Franciscan life. In this state of extreme evangelical fervor, he encountered some birds in a field near Bevagna, and preached to them the famous Sermon to the Birds.[15]

Thus occurred one of the original and arresting incidents exemplifying what would become the typically Franciscan[16] attitude toward creation. Francis, the hermit who showed love and sympathy for animals in his ascetic life (as with the Isola Maggiore rabbit), had taken a new and original step inspired by the ideals of the missionary life which he now also reaffirmed. In an instant of overpowering fervor, he linked the ascetic respect for creation he had learned with his early love for creation and with his deeply felt mission at hand. The same passionate and literal mind which determined to follow those Biblical passages calling for evangelization remembered those Biblical and liturgical passages where (though in a merely literary context)[17] the psalmist and other followers of Yahweh had exhorted creation to praise its Creator. In a flash, all became clear: It was Francis' duty to preach to these birds, just as to humans, in his mission to restore apostolic harmony to the whole world. This synthesis and reapplication of previously unlinked ideas from different areas of Francis' experience in ascetic, secular, and liturgical life caused his dramatic and emotional response when he saw that the birds did not retreat before him, and is the reason he spontaneously preached to them. It was a burst of intuitive creativity[18] which permanently integrated Francis' general ideals for his Order with his interpretation of creation.

Before we discuss this subject in detail, however, it is best to turn to the different accounts of the Sermon itself in order to appreciate the earlier research done in the area, study the problems and questions raised by the accounts, and obtain an understanding of the specific ideas presented in the Sermon.

The Sermon Texts: Francis' First New Ideas

> Among the many things he spoke to them were these words that he added: "My brothers, birds, you should praise your Creator very much and always love him; he gave you feathers to clothe you, wings so that you can fly, and whatever else was necessary for you. God made you noble among his creatures, and he gave you a home in the purity of the air; though you neither sow nor reap, he nevertheless protects and governs you without any solicitude on your part" (*VP* 58, *Omnibus* trans.)

> The substance of St. Francis' sermon to those birds was this: "My little bird sisters, you owe much to God your Creator, and you must always and everywhere praise Him, because He has given you freedom to fly anywhere—also He has given you a double and triple covering, and your colorful and pretty clothing, and your food is ready without your working for it, and your singing that was taught to you by the Creator, and your numbers that have been multiplied by the blessing of God—and because He preserved your species in Noah's ark so that your race should not disappear from the earth. And you are also indebted to Him for the realm of the air which He assigned to you. Moreover, you neither sow nor reap, yet God nourishes you, and He gives you the rivers and springs to drink from. He gives you high mountains and hills, rocks and crags as refuges, and lofty trees in which to make your nests. And although you do not know how to spin or sew, God gives you and your little ones the clothing which you need. So the Creator loves you very much, since He gives you so many good things. Therefore, my little bird sisters, be careful not to be ungrateful, but strive always to praise God." (*Actus-Fioretti* 16, *Omnibus* trans.)

Both of the Sermon accounts above, the best we have remaining, are controversial. As usual, the *Fioretti* has been attacked for suspect elaboration. One author calls its retelling a "piece of bravura," a fantasy developed from Celano's version.[19] The historical setting the *Fioretti* establishes, however, has withstood the test of scholarly criticism, and provides the chronology for the incident we shall follow. (See Appendix III for a detailed analysis.)

Celano's account has its own problems. It was set down in Latin, and contains some Latinate rhetorical devices probably not present in Francis' actual address, which would have been given in Old Italian.[20] Nevertheless, Celano's version appeared in 1228, less than twenty years after the event and at a time when all those who were present at the Sermon, with the exception of Francis, would still have been alive to attest to its accuracy. One critic argues, however, that

> [f]or his part, Celano, being a stylist who liked to embellish, may have built on Francis' well-known attitudes toward Creation—that it was the privilege, duty, and pleasure of all things to praise the Lord—and thus put into his mouth words he might reasonably be supposed to have uttered.[21]

Here the stereotype of the embellishing hagiographer has conquered reality. Careful comparison of incidents proves that Celano hardly embellishes the accounts he receives; on the contrary, he cuts them down.[22] Research also shows that the *Fioretti* account is independent of Celano, making the obvious resemblances between the two accounts a source of support for Celano's, since both accounts state they are based on the same sources (or sources directly derived from them, in the case of the *Fioretti*). Celano's naming of his sources, a very unusual step for him, explicitly founds the authority of his account upon Francis and the followers who were present at the incident ("as he himself used to say and the brothers who were with him" are Celano's words in the middle of the tale).[23] Celano's claim seems to be borne out to quite a satisfying degree by his account, and makes up for our loss in not having an account of the incident from the *Legend of Perugia*. The Sermon to the Birds seems to represent Celano at his best, functioning as a reliable mouthpiece for Francis and his closest companions. The hagiographer makes a sophisticated analysis of the incident—one which reveals both an intimate understanding of what went on and a historical sense for the impact it had.

The structure of Celano's interpretation is built on a quintessentially Franciscan theme. Celano relates the Sermon encounter as yet another step in Francis' proclamation and restoration of the apostolic mode of life.

Francis, gathering disciples as Jesus did, preaches the true Christian way of life first to people and then to birds, and leaves rejoicing and praising God. Like Jesus, he has confronted creation and included it in his plans and outlook. It is the restored gospel ideal applied with assumed literalness and in a new setting, full of apostolic and ascetic spirit. There is every reason to believe that, in spite of its limitations, this is the interpretation that Francis himself wished to be made. He would have found myopic and unappreciative the modern view of the encounter as something radically new and bold.

Celano reveals his interpretive structure through a chain of allusions that create dynamic comparative interplay between the contemporary events and the New Testament record of early Christian evangelization. The incident occurs "while many were added [*appositi sunt*] to the brothers."[24] The unusual Vulgate phrases allude to the Biblical account of the time when many believers "were added to" the apostles in the early Church.[25] Celano describes Francis, after the Sermon, as "passing through their [the birds'] midst, (he) went on his way"—comparing by allusion Francis' preaching Christ's message to the birds to Christ's evangelization of the Jews.[26] Following this, Francis "went on his way rejoicing," as did the Ethiopean eunuch after being baptized by Philip (Acts 8:39). Francis then "gave thanks to God" as Paul did on the way to Malta (Acts 27:35). The saint, "calling on the name of the savior" (Acts 22:16), had applied Paul's missionary call to animals.

Celano's consistent quotation of the Acts of the Apostles cannot be a matter of chance. The hagiographer is showing the reader, in a very subtle and sophisticated way, that Francis is restoring and participating in the apostolic age, extending the Christian mission to its logical finality—to "preach the gospel to all creatures," as the Bible literally commanded.[27]

Celano's concluding remarks link Francis with the exemplification of ascetic ideals. Francis has attained anew, by divine grace, the state of primal simplicity, where creation obeys humanity: "But now that he had become simple by grace, not by nature [*gratia non natura*], he began to blame himself for negligence in not having preached to the birds before, seeing that they had listened to the word of God with such reverence" (*VP* 58). The hagiographer gives us intimate details which prove Francis as well thought of the event in terms of the ascetic thaumaturgic tradition at its core, even with the many Franciscan ideals superimposed. Celano's account states that Francis was surprised when he saw the birds did not fly away at his approach: "But, not a little surprised that the birds did not rise in flight, as they usually do, he was filled with great joy and humbly begged them to listen to the word of God" (*VP* 58). Francis did not expect the creatures of the natural world to react with such respect for a man, and he realized clearly that something distinctly unusual and abnormal was occurring in the situation. When he finished the Sermon, he gave the birds permission to leave, as an early saint might have done, and as he continued his journey, he, "from that day on," exhorted creatures "to praise and love their Creator, for daily, when the name of the Savior had been invoked [*invocato nomine Salvatoris*], he saw their obedience by personal experience."

The last remark, "for daily, when the name of the Savior had been invoked," proves that Celano accepted the traditional ideal of the relationship reestablished between the saint and creation by divine grace, as we have seen before. But is there any more evidence that Francis himself understood in a similar way what was occurring?

The answer lies in the determination of whether Francis himself actually invoked divine aid before he spoke to the birds, as Celano seems to assert. At first there seems no evidence of this action. But in fact another subtle hint, which Celano records only because he must have heard it directly from those involved, establishes that Francis did indeed call upon divine aid before he addressed the birds. Celano's account is unique in stating that as Francis ran up to the birds, he greeted them "in his usual way" [*more solito*], which means he said to them, "May the Lord give you peace"—which as a greeting functioned as a sort of trademark for Francis (see e.g., *VP* 23). The saint's surprise recorded by Celano evidently came from Francis' realization that his call upon the Lord had in fact produced a divine intervention which allowed the birds to respond to their saintly leader. His greeting had transformed the encounter into one of thaumaturgical influence over creation,[28] thus making it in its core an incident typical for the ascetic tradition.

On other occasions described at length, we can demonstrate that Francis understood an incident with obvious original elements to be based upon this same traditional ascetic thaumaturgic paradigm. Before Francis underwent the Cauterization by Brother Fire, for example, he invoked divine aid. According to the *Legend of Perugia* 48 (which closely resembles Celano VS 166 here), he said, "'I beseech our Creator who made you to temper your heat so that I may be able to bear it.' His prayer finished, he made the sign of the cross over the fire." The *Legend* rightly terms the address a prayer (*oratione*). Francis' expressions show not only that he considered he had, through God, a reciprocal relationship of respect and love with this element of creation, but even more, that he expected divine intervention to sustain this gentle and chivalrous[29] relationship in the trial. Creation was then "sanctified" through the sign of the cross, and, guided by divine will, it related respectfully to the saint. All present thought it was a miracle.

Celano completed his account of the Cauterization with a comment aptly reflecting the view of the previous ascetic tradition when he remarked, "I believe that he had returned to primitive innocence [*ad innocentiam primam*], for whom, when he wished it, cruel things were made gentle" (*VS* 166).

Francis' Specific New Conceptions in the Sermon

The traditional medieval ideas at the base of the encounter with the birds allow the expression of new elements within their context. Not the least of these is the fact of the Sermon itself. Armstrong claims boldly that "Francis was by no means the first preacher to birds,"[30] but in fact it seems he was. All the earlier incidents which somewhat parallel this may be divided into three groups: (a) purely literary exhortations, like Psalm 148 and the Hymn of the Three Children in Daniel 3, both of which probably inspired Francis, (b) addresses to birds not as birds but as spiritual beings—examples of which, as we have seen in the *Voyage of Brendan*, are represented in Irish hagiography, and (c) incidents in which a saint commands, befriends, or allegorizes about birds.[31] No saint before Francis, it appears, had addressed birds as creatures in the sustained homiletic manner he did. This idea arose in Francis' mind, as we have seen, from the uniting of ascetic experience with his new evangelical fervor.

The Sermon itself contains expressions originally derived from earlier Christian sources, but which undergo major alterations very Franciscan in spirit, or which fit within a context of new ideas extending or complementing them in innovative ways. As his early biographers and many modern researchers have noted,[32] Francis drew some of his inspiration for the Sermon from the Psalms and Canticles he would have recited frequently in the course of the liturgical offices.[33] Their exhortations to creation would have been at hand, ready for his prodigious memory to draw on.[34] Similar liturgical sources are used in Francis' *Exhortation to Praise God*, also dating from 1213.[35]

Francis took the liturgical and purely literary exhortations at face value and built on them in order to present an actual address to creation. His opening lines contain sentiments centering on two ideas found in the

Biblical sources. It is the duty of creatures to praise the Lord: He created them and they are dependent on him for their essential characteristics in the hierarchy of creation, and for their continued existence. Compare Francis' ". . . you should praise your Creator very much . . . he gave you feathers to clothe you, wings so you can fly, and whatever was necessary for you," and the following phrases from Scripture:

> Bless the Lord, all the works of the Lord,
> sing praise to him and highly exalt him for ever. . . .
> Bless the Lord, all birds of the air,
> sing praise to him and highly exalt him for ever. . . .[36]
>
> Praise him, sun and moon,
> Praise him, all you shining stars!
> Praise him, you highest heavens. . . .
> For he commanded and they were created.
> And he established them for ever and ever;
> He fixed their bounds which cannot be passed.[37]

The *Actus-Fioretti* account expands along the same lines as Celano, using related arguments and other Biblical references to strengthen the ideas of the birds' debt to their Creator. His gifts include the birds' liberty (*libertà*), and "your singing that was taught you by the Creator." Furthermore, "your numbers . . . have been multiplied by the blessing of God. . . . He preserved your species in Noah's ark so that your race should not disappear from the earth. . . . He gives you high mountains and hills, rocks and crags as refuges, and lofty trees in which to make your nests" (*F* 16). Though the elaboration has less authority than Celano's account, it still seems appropriate to the spirit of the speech recorded in Celano. Both Sermons proclaim the same message: The birds should give thanks to God and love him in return for his provision for and preservation of them.

In Celano, Francis' speech concludes with Francis' use of either Matthew 6:25 or Luke 12:24 ("Consider the ravens . . ."). But the saint's consistent concern with God's respectful care of creatures gives the allusion an entirely different meaning in the new context. Jesus had wished to emphasize God's care for humanity, since humankind was so far above the birds God protected and cared for. Francis, however, uses the phrases to stress instead the birds' status in creation and God's special favor that they enjoyed. It is a sign of the birds' prestige and position that they are taken care of without working. They have their own niche ("a home in the purity of the air"), and their own special status before God.

This subtle change highlights another new element in the Sermon. Francis calls the birds "noble," and compliments them. This does not occur at all in the Sermon's Biblical parallels, and only rarely in pre-Franciscan Christian literature, but it is a common element in the saint's later sayings. It underlines Francis' increased respect for his fellow creatures. Each creature has its special worth, its special character of which it should be proud.[38] The nearest parallel to this is perhaps Jesus' praise of the lilies: "Not even Solomon in all his glory was arrayed like one of these."[39]

We begin to see that Francis' encounter and speech reveal some conceptions of horizontal relationships and reciprocity which complement the hierarchical, vertical relationships amid creation stressed in Francis' liturgical sources. There is the mutual respect and love between God and creatures (". . . you should always . . . love Him"), and the feelings of mutual esteem and familial affection between creatures and humanity ("My brothers, birds!"). Francis esteems creatures since he preaches the word of God to them and compliments them, while they in turn listen with intense respect. The *Fioretti* states:

> Now at these words of St. Francis, all those birds began to open their beaks, stretch out their necks, spread their wings, and reverently bow their heads to the ground, showing by their movements and their songs that the words which St. Francis was saying gave them great pleasure. (*F* 16)

He thinks of them as his "brothers," not because they are in his Order, but because, after the loss of his first human family, his present family is "the family of those who serve God." The birds evidently recognize and return his affection, as do other creatures in later accounts (*VP* 60–61; *VS* 167–71).

These dynamic expressions of Francis', which also appear in another of his lengthy exhortations, the *Canticle* (where we shall study them in more detail), have a curious dual character. While they are strikingly original and have a complexity which is uniquely Francis', seen from the perspective of the ascetic tradition, they are the apotheosis of the subtle and often merely implicit precepts of mutual affection and harmony which lay at the root of the saint's concept of the reattainment of humanity's state in paradise by divine grace. Francis' values of mutual love, respect, and family feeling neatly superimpose themselves upon, and fittingly extend, earlier and more inchoate medieval conceptions. They are a fusion of individual innovation with collective tradition.

THE EFFECTS OF THE ENCOUNTER UPON FRANCIS

Though the *Actus-Fioretti* reveals more of the historical setting leading up to the Sermon, Celano here proves his analytical ability and historical knowledge by gauging more than the other biographers the exact effect this incident had on Francis. He sees that this incident provided the crucial central transformation in Francis' attitude toward creation. Henceforth, Francis would extend his evangelical mission to all creation, not just to humans; he would preach to other creatures the word of God so they might participate as well in the world of apostolic harmony Francis hoped to restore among humankind. Celano describes Francis' change of outlook thus:

> But the blessed father went his way with his companions, rejoicing and giving thanks to God, whom all creatures venerate with humble acknowledgement. But now that he had become simple by grace, not by nature, he began to blame himself for negligence in not having preached to the birds before, seeing that they had listened to the word of God with such great reverence. And so it happened that, from that day on, he solicitously admonished all birds, all animals and reptiles, and even creatures that have no feeling, to praise and love their Creator, for daily, when the name of the Savior had been invoked, he saw their obedience by personal experience. (*VP* 58)

The Sermon encounter was the factor that integrated Francis' assumptions about creation with his general apostolic ideals. The dynamic interplay between them produced a new synthesis, a new outlook upon creation, which at the same time reinforced the more general Franciscan aims. Examining the process more deeply, one finds that the Sermon encounter consisted of a series of ideational steps. First, Francis' ascetic and evangelical ideals coincided to produce Francis' genuinely creative reaction. This is expressed in his Sermon, which crystallizes a new and complex attitude faithful to both Francis' ascetic and evangelical goals, though also going far beyond their bases. The birds' seemingly reverent response to the proclamation of this new complex of thought had a double impact. It at once encouraged Francis to sustain his new perspective, and (if we can believe there is a kernel of truth behind *Fioretti* elaboration)[40] it increased his already-high pitch of enthusiasm for evangelization because it appeared to predict that people as well as birds would heed his message. Thus Francis' spontaneous original view of creation promptly reinforced his general Franciscan ideals: the two became integrated and mutually supportive.

The Stilling of the Swallows at Alviano, which Celano relates directly after the Sermon (and which Bonaventure reports occurred later in the same evangelical tour),[41] seems to reflect Francis' new attitude. Francis, preparing to address a crowd, first addresses his "sisters" the swallows, who were chattering loudly. They obey his gentle command to be silent, as it is his turn to speak, whereupon the impressed observers also heed and venerate him. The incident reveals the new feelings of mutual love and respect between the saint and creatures, the thaumaturgic, hierarchic core of these feelings, and the parallel human reaction (this time, more concrete)—all of which reflect the influence of the earlier incident. The Sermon has provided a new paradigm for the relationship between the saint and creation—a paradigm that will remain consistent through the many encounters Francis has with creatures until it reaches its greatest formulation in Francis' *Canticle*. Celano witnesses to Francis' consistent attitude toward creatures henceforth when he says in wonder:

> When he found an abundance of flowers, he preached to them and invited them to praise the Lord as though they were endowed with reason. In the same way he exhorted with the sincerest purity cornfields and vineyards, stones and forests and all the beautiful things of the fields, fountains of water and the green things of the gardens, earth and fire, air and wind, to love God and serve him willingly. Finally, he called all creatures "brother," and in a most extraordinary manner, a manner never experienced by others, he discerned the secrets of creatures with his sensitive heart. . . . (*VP* 81)

This perceptive passage brings together all the innovative ideas we have discussed—preaching, exhortation, love, service, familial affection, and sensitive care. It proves that because of their continuous expression, they deserve to be seen as uniquely characteristic of the Francis whom the world would come to know and love after the Sermon to the Birds.

4

Francis' Special Regard for Creation

Although it would be tempting to move immediately from Francis' remarkable Sermon to consideration of his greatest expression of love and joy toward creation, the *Canticle of Brother Sun*, this would ignore other ways in which the early anecdotes reveal Francis' characteristic special regard for creation. For Francis not only showed his high regard for creatures through his preaching to them and his sincere affection for them. He showed how much he valued them in the way he applied standards of chivalric behavior to them, in his beliefs about the proper use of creation's bounty as food, and in his contemplative experiences amid the glories of creation.

Chivalry: Courtly Relationships and Creation

The era which saw the birth of the Franciscan Order was also the dawn of the age of chivalry. The young Francis had spent many an hour listening to troubadour poetry, and had yearned to become a knight.[1] The saint's early and modern biographers have recognized his admiration for the life and ideals of chivalry.[2] Nor did Francis lose his respect for chivalric ideals when he underwent his conversion. "[A]s with all his natural gifts, he vitalized this, in his later life, by the force and intensity of his spiritual longings."[3] Early sources dub him the "doughty knight of Christ" (*VS* 21), and say that he was "as though by nature chivalrous."[4] He called his brothers his "companions of the Round Table,"[5] and seems to have been familiar with even esoteric sections of Arthurian legends.[6]

Francis' inner circle shared his values, but his official biographers clearly did not. They display an ecclesiastical bias against the secular ideals of chivalry. Both Celano and Bonaventure evidently downplay this side of Francis, and some notable incidents concerning it come to light only with the *Fioretti*.[7] Celano "found it difficult to reconcile his hero's gaiety with his austerity"[8] in these and similar matters. Celano's tactful displeasure comes out in his attitude toward Brother Pacifico's past life, as compared with the reaction of the *Legend of Perugia*. Pacifico was a famous troubadour who joined the Order and became very holy.[9] The writers of the *Legend of Perugia* unequivocally praise Pacifico's talents and honor his secular reputation.

> For his spirit [Francis] was then in such sweetness and comfort that he wanted Brother Pacifico, who in the world had been known as the King of Verses [*qui in seculo vocabatur rex versuum*] and who had been a really chivalric doctor of songs [*valde curialis doctor cantorum*], to be sent for and given some good and holy friars that they might go through the world preaching and praising God . . . as minstrels of the Lord [*joculatores Domini*]. (*LP* 43)

At another time, Francis travels with Pacifico, "a native of the March of Ancona, who formerly in the world had been dubbed 'the King of Verses,' a noble and chivalric doctor of song [*nobilis et curialis doctor cantorum*]" (*LP* 23). But Celano's introduction of Brother Pacifico turns out somewhat differently.

> In the Marches of Ancona there was a certain secular person who, forgetful of himself and not knowing God, gave himself completely to vanity [*sui oblitus et Dei nescius, qui se totum prostituerat vanitati*]. He was called the King of Verses because he was the chief of those who sang impure songs and was a composer of worldly songs [*princeps foret lasciva cantantum et inventor saecularium cantionum*]. To put it briefly, so high had worldly glory raised him, that he had been crowned with the greatest pomp by the emperor. While he was thus walking in darkness and drawing iniquity with the cords of vanity [*in tenebris ambulans iniquitatem traheret in finiculis vanitatis*] the merciful kindness of God thought to call him back. . . . (*VS* 106)

To Celano, Pacifico was a proud and iniquitous prince (*princeps*) of scurrilous ditties.[10] But to Francis and his inner circle, Pacifico was a noble and courtly master of song, whose status (*doctor*) was worthy of comparison to the teachers of Paris.

Francis knew troubadour poetry by heart and quoted it to advantage on occasion. Once he was drawn to attend a dubbing ceremony, and gave a sermon based on the chivalric couplet, "I aspire to so great a treasure/ That all pain for me is pleasure"[11]—thoughts that succinctly describe the atmosphere of his early religious life (in which he sought a secret treasure),[12] and reveal a process of reinterpretation he must often have applied to the lyrics he knew and loved. On this particular night, Francis and Orlando, a count at the gathering, were so impressed with one another that Orlando offered Francis a retreat he owned at La Verna. The date was 1213.[13]

Probably during that same summer, Francis greeted the birds with the unusual tribute, "God made you noble among his creatures [*nobiles . . . inter creaturas suas*], and he gave you a palace [or manor—*mansionem*] in the purity of the air" (*VP* 58). This praise must have resulted from the connection Francis made with the birds' way of life (they were supported, he thought, without work)[14] and their habitations (nests in towering trees and cliffs) with the elegant, carefree nobility who possessed hill castles or city tower fortresses. The links not only demonstrate poetic ability; they represent the beginning of a characteristic practice—that of employing the graceful, courtly mode of address while speaking to creatures. The effect of this style of chivalric compliment would reach its height in Francis' praise of the honorable "Sir brother Sun" (*messer lo frate sole*) in the *Canticle*. In the Sermon and *Canticle*, then, the ideals of chivalry were also incorporated into the synthesis of old and new that was Francis' interpretation of creation. The chivalric address was not an affectation.[15] Rather, it was part of Francis' unique way of showing his high regard for creatures by giving them the same type of chivalric honors he also gave to his human "companions of the Round Table."[16]

Chivalry influenced Francis' attitudes toward creatures in many other ways. Many of the ways in which Francis infused the ideals of chivalry into his view of creation may remain forever lost to us, for the sources we have today provide only glimmerings from which we may deduce, tentatively, various ramifications. Yet enough evidence survives to show that Francis made use of the potential in chivalric values to express his unique conceptions of spiritual honor and deference between all the levels of creation. We might almost call it the "honor code" followed by God and creation. In envisioning it, Francis was not only a theological innovator—again he elevated creatures by seeing them as common participants in the code of noble behavior. In this area, one incident (if authentic)[17] is of special value to us, since it allows us to deduce from Francis' general statements views that illuminate some of his specific responses to creatures. Francis and his followers arrive at an aristocratic household. A nobleman greets them cordially, and offers to provide for all their needs and give to the poor.

> Consequently St. Francis, when he saw his great courtliness [*cortesia-curialitate*] and affection and when he heard his generous offer, felt such love in his heart for him that later when he was going away with his companion he said: "That gentleman certainly would make a good member of our Order: he is so grateful to God, so kind to his neighbor, so generous to the poor, and so cheerful and courtly [*courtèse-curialis*] to guests. For, dear Brother, chivalry [*cortesia-curialitas*] is one of the qualities [*proprietà*] of God, who chivalrously [*curialiter*] gives his sun and his rain and everything to the just and to the unjust. And chivalry [*curialitas*] is a sister of charity. It extinguishes hatred and keeps love alive. (*F* 37)

The central portion of the passage, Francis' praise of chivalry,[18] possesses a special claim to authenticity since it seems to resemble strongly a statement of Francis' in the *Legend of Perugia*.

> For St. Francis held that to beg alms for the love of the Lord God was of the highest nobility, dignity, and chivalry [*curialitate*] in the sight of God and even of the world, since all that the heavenly Father created for the use of man he conceded after sin [*concessa sunt post peccatum*] to the worthy and unworthy free as alms for the love of his dear Son. (*LP* 60)

These two passages put forth a uniquely Franciscan theological conception of *cortesia*. The essential ideals integrated here signify far more than "courtesy" in our devalued modern understanding. They "spiritualize" the chivalric values of largesse[19] and noblesse oblige: beneficent magnanimity and special consideration or deference to others, especially those lower in station.

The ideal implicitly recognized differences in status while promoting and emphasizing horizontal relationships of mutual respect and deference. Thus it fitted well with Francis' values in his Sermon to the Birds. Francis sees it working between three levels of the cosmic hierarchy: between God and humanity, between humans, and between humankind and the rest of creation.

Cortesia with God involved a magnanimous, self-denying effusion and bounty, a form of condescending love to those both just and unjust, chosen and unchosen. Thus it merits being "the sister of charity." God's *cortesia*, his largesse and special consideration for creation, allows humanity to take freely and with self-respect from God's bounty, whether it be in gaining provision directly from creation, or in honorably requesting others to share their excess from the divine bountifulness. This is a chivalric justification of the medieval belief that almsgiving reflected well upon both the donor and the receiver,[20] as well as being a legitimation of the proper human use of creation.

The aristocrat Francis met in the *Fioretti* anecdote exhibited the highest human form of *cortesia* when he deigned to give magnanimously and considerately from his superabundance to God's poor—the friars and the needy. The higher gives to the lower, with both preserving their self-respect. This is the attitude which impressed Francis and led him to comment on its social usefulness: "And *cortesia* is a sister to charity. It extinguishes hatred and keeps love alive" (*F* 37). His observation seems astute enough, not only for interactions between rich and poor, but also for interactions within Francis' own Order. One can observe the value of Francis' magnanimity and noblesse oblige on several occasions. Once when at the Rivo Torto, Francis deigned to eat with a very hungry brother, although Francis would have been able to deny himself the food, so that the brother would not feel guilty or inferior (*LP* 1). At another time, Francis has to ask his minister-supervisor to grant him a favor, and so he requests, "Brother guardian, you have always been chivalrous [*curialis*] to me, and I beg of you to show me the same chivalry [*curialitatem*] now" (*VS* 92). The term's meaning here seems to center on being obliging, magnanimous, or deferential. In another instance, the virtue solved a conflict between religious and social rank (*LP* 30). The ideal incorporated a tremendously useful method of face-saving deference or yielding in a religious community with rigid standards and volatile personalities. Thus while chivalry was the sister of charity, it seems also to have been the daughter of humility.

The phrase "you have always been chivalrous to me" in the example above suggests that Francis believed the virtue formed a part of his consistent and expected relationships with others. It was part of a contract or code of mutual respect and consideration established between two individuals who had known each other for a long time. Interestingly, Francis applied this idea of a chivalric code between two parties of long acquaintance to his relationships with nonhuman creatures. Several incidents demonstrate Francis' chivalrous deference to Brother Fire, for example (see e.g., *LP* 49–50). At the Cauterization, most surprisingly, Francis refers to his customary relationship with Brother Fire when he makes a request of it: "Be kind to me in this hour, be chivalrous [*curialis*]. For I have loved you in the past in the Lord."[21] Francis wishes the Fire to acknowledge now the deferential *cortesia* he had shown to it in the past, to respect him, and, through divine grace,[22] to condescend to renounce the strength of its character and status so that he not be hurt by it. The whole interaction here (from Francis' point of view, of course) is governed by two conceptions: a divinely established relationship, and chivalric *noblesse oblige* which creates a mutual regard and honorable deference between brothers serving God together, even though they are on different levels of the divine hierarchy. The first conception produced Francis' invocation of divine aid and his expectation of a miraculous alteration of the fire's properties; the second led to his kind and respectful address to the fire and his expectation of deference to him also.[23] Thus in this incident we can see most clearly the code of honor uniting humanity and the rest of creation.

Francis' consistent attitude of deference to creation explains another statement considered "almost Buddhist."[24] In his *Salute to the Virtues*, Francis proclaims:

> Holy obedience [in man] puts to shame
> all natural and selfish desires.
> It mortifies our lower nature
> and makes it obey the spirit
> and our fellow men.
> Obedience subjects a man
> to everyone on earth.
> And not only to men,
> but to all the beasts as well
> and to the wild animals,
> So that they can do what they like with him,
> as far as God allows them.[25]

Francis' condescension and submission, here stated in a theological context, represent one facet of the relationship of mutual deference established between humanity and other creatures in common service to the divine will.

Francis certainly practiced what he preached. In the Temptation by Mice (*LP* 43), Francis endured without resistance the depredations and distractions of animals—not because he was attaining Buddhistic transcendence through self-denial, but because he considered he was undergoing a demonic temptation with fortitude and divine protection. Francis' ideals of humility and deference, even to creatures, went very deep indeed.

Francis' chivalric ideals were a part of his unique way of showing special regard for creation. Even though some of their ramifications probably remain imperceptible to us, the strands of thought we can see seem to show that courtly ideals were well integrated into different areas of the saint's beliefs about God and creation. Chivalric values clearly supported the traditional basis for Francis' new expressions concerning creatures, in that they deepened his conception of mutually respectful relationships, divinely established, between humanity and the rest of creation. They also lend a new poetry and charm to his statements, and demonstrate how his originality could arise out of his contemporary milieu through adaptation and reinterpretation of the chivalric standards of the time.

THE USE OF CREATION'S BOUNTY: FRANCIS' ATTITUDES TOWARD FOOD

Francis' attitudes toward food illustrate another area in which he showed his special regard for creation. His views here are complex, and reveal a struggle to value creation in his unique way while dealing with difficult issues of his time: how to live the apostolic life while avoiding or countering negative beliefs about nonhuman creation that were prevalent in his time and region. Specifically, it involved Francis balancing himself among Biblical injunctions that humans should have dominion over creation and accept its fruits, traditional medieval ascetic ideals which included dietary restrictions, Francis' own love for creatures, and the (more implicit) wish to counter Cathar ascetic extremes.[26]

First, Francis struggled to show his high valuation of creation by following the letter of the Gospel in eating (or at least tasting) meats, even those considered delicacies, when offered or necessary, and he often depended on evangelical providence to supply food of any type, especially through begging.[27] In Francis' *Rule* of 1221 it is carefully stated, "In obedience to the Gospel, they (the friars) may eat of any food put before them."[28]

It may seem strange to us today that this should have represented Francis' respect for creation, yet in the context of his own time, Francis' opinions would have been striking and daring. They were an attempt to return to an evangelical standard that valued food as a part of God's creation and thus as good and worthy for humanity to eat. The Gospel passage Francis probably refers to in his *Rule* (1 Timothy 4:4–5) affirms: "For everything created by God is good, and nothing is to be rejected if it is received with thanksgiving; for then it is consecrated by the word of God and prayer." This positive injunction which Francis accepted as the pattern for his revival of apostolic life harmonized well with his belief in creation's goodness and with his conception of creation as an expression of divine largesse dispensed for humanity's needs. A modern statement that affirms creation in this way comes from Henry David Thoreau, who

TABLE 4. Francis and Creation's Bounty: Food and Various Standards

Old Ascetic	Evangelical	Compared to Catharism	Luxuries/ Confessions
RNB 22	*RB* 3 (evangelical rule)	*VS* 78 (capon)	*VS* 44; *MP* 110 (lobster)
Admonition. 10,14; *VP* 51–52; *3 Comp.* 15; *ML* 5:1; *MNL* 3:1 (rigor, chicken)	*RNB* 3:9, 14	*RNB* 3; 9; 14; 17; 22 (attitude to fasts; lower nature)	*VS* 52 (chicken)
VS 22; *ML* 5:7; *LP* 1; *MP* 27 (eats with brother, lectures vs. excess)	*VS* 78 (capon)	*Admonition* 27, *Letter to the faithful, Admonition* 14 (against excess, pride in fast, respect clergy)	*VS* 131; *LP* 40; *MP* 61–62; *LP* 39 (lard, etc.)
VS 131; *LP* 40; *MP* 61–62; *LP* 96	*VS* 199 (meat at Christmas)	*RB* 3 (no fasts when in need)	*LP* 29; *MP* 111 (fish and lobster)
VS 175 (mercy)	*VS* 175 (compassion)	Rule of 3rd Order, 2 (diet)	*LP* 101; *MP* 29 (sweets)
New F 10 (too much food)	*VP* 51; 3 *Comp.* 15; *ML* 5:1	*RB* 3 (evangelical rule)	*VS* 22; *ML* 5:7; *LP* 1; *MP* 27 (eats with starving brother, lectures vs. excess)
	VS 75–7; *LP* 62; *MP* 23; *LP* 63; *MP* 25; *LP* 59; *MP* 22; *ML* 7:10 (begging)	*3 Comp.* 58–60, (Chapter injunctions)	
	F 18 (food at Chapter of Mats)	*LP* 80; *MP* 65; 96; *VS* 117 (attitude toward the body)	
	F 26 (food and robbers)		

shared many of Francis' values and experiences: "As a mother loves to see her child imbibe nourishment and expand, so God loves to see his children thrive on the nutriment he has furnished them. . . ."[29]

Francis' opinions in this area were noteworthy and daring in his own time for two major reasons. While Christian laity were normally allowed to eat various kinds of foods, including meats, Francis' allowance to himself and his followers would have been considered a very liberal one for ascetics. The Cistercians, for example, practiced rigorous dietary abstinence,[30] and some of Francis' own followers wished more rigorous rules.[31] Francis was well aware of the tension between the harsh ascetic standards of the old saintly and monastic ideal that he still wished to follow, and his new evangelical standard. As a holy man he felt his standards here exposed to public view, and thus he often stated clear justifications for his actions (as with the *Rule*) or confessed publicly when he could not live up to a standard. As he once said when discussing his failings in matters of food, "I want to live before God [that is, privately] in hermitages and other places in the same way that men know and see me in public. For if they believe me to be a holy man and I do not live the life which befits holy men, I would be a hypocrite" (*LP* 40). But when Francis publicly confessed any dietary failing, he was not rejecting his evangelical standards. Rather, he was admitting that he had not kept a fast, or had temporarily fallen from those still-respected ascetic standards expected of holy men.[32] In deference to those standards he sometimes mixed ashes with his food to conform to practices of austerity (*VP* 51). Francis' challenge here seems to have been to show that following the apostolic standard in accepting a diversity of food did not mean one became indulgent or discarded revered examples of saintly self-denial. It was a difficult balance for him to maintain.

The second reason Francis' standards represent a positive valuation of nonhuman creation in the context of his own time is that they presented a contrast to a competing view of material creation present in his region and propounded by the Cathars. The Cathars were an essentially non-Christian religious group considered in Francis' time to be heretics. They believed the spiritual world had been created by a beneficent divine power, and the material world by an evil one.[33] The austere Cathar elite, the *perfecti*, practiced almost total vegetarianism, in that they would not eat anything they considered had been born of coition (which to them was an impure mixing of the spiritual with the material).[34] Within this context, Francis' new standards assume a special importance: They may be seen as a positive and Catholic response affirming the worth of material creation against the Cathar beliefs and practices. Cajetan Esser notes how often Francis' values provided a Catholic counterexample to Cathar ideas: ". . . Francis in word and writing, but above all through his example and his spiritual attitude gave a reply to so many questions which pertained to the inner life of the Church and were raised by Catharism."[35]

Thus we may see why Francis disagreed with some of his own followers' more rigorous views about food. They may have wanted to compete with the Cathars' asceticism, but this would have violated Francis' evangelical standard and validated the very beliefs that Francis wanted to contradict. Francis instead urged all to be Catholic in their eating habits,[36] and he listed the specific Catholic fasts to be observed by the friars (as opposed to Cathar nonobservance or observance of different fast schedules than the Catholic).[37] He countered the mystique of Cathar vegetarian ascetism with a direct appeal to the Bible's own positive view of creation, and with his own well-known, though modified, ascetic austerities. In these ways he provided a counterexample.

The Cathars challenged this counterexample in a bold face-to-face encounter with Francis (*VS* 78). While visiting a Christian's house in Lombardy (a district known for heretics at that time),[38] Francis was invited to eat chicken, following the Biblical standard, and did so. A "son of Belial," a Cathar or Cathar sympathizer scheming to embarrass the holy man, begged for food at the door of the house, and Francis gave him some of the chicken. The next day, the false beggar attempted to oppose Francis' preaching to a crowd by exhibiting the meat and scoffing at Francis' holiness. Instead, the crowd laughed at the Cathar because the chicken seemed to have turned into fish. Why the laughter? The crowd obviously knew the Cathar opposing beliefs. The Cathar *perfecti*, who called themselves the true Christians,[39] and who would have been the Cathar equivalent of saints, abstained from almost all meats, but were allowed to eat fish, since they believed fish were born of water, not coition.[40] Thus the crowd's delight and the Cathar's humiliation when the chicken appeared to be fish: the tables had been turned on him! God had intervened to defend Francis' new evangelical, apostolic standard and *simplicitas* by changing the food into a kind acceptable even to the Cathar "saints."

In other anecdotes, Francis shows his respect for creatures when, out of love and pity, he refuses to eat living creatures given him as food. For example, he makes a pet out of a pheasant presumably sent to him for his gustatory rather than spiritual delight (*VS* 170). Here again, Francis set an example of special regard for creatures by refusing to kill them needlessly; at the same time his attitude was extremely useful as a strongly positive Catholic assertion expressing the value and worth of creation, equalling and excelling the Cathar example commonly known at the time. Ladurie relates a tale spread by the Cathars which surprisingly resembles Franciscan stories.

> Another very well-known exemplum was that of the two goodmen [Cathars] and the animal caught in a snare. Two *parfaits* [*perfecti*] were going through a forest when they came upon [in one version] a squirrel or [in another version] a pheasant caught in a trap. Instead of taking the animal and killing it in order to sell it or eat it just for pleasure, they set it free, out of reverence for the human soul which might be shut in the animal's body. They placed the equivalent in money beside the snare so that the hunter, who had to earn his living, would not lose by their action.[41]

Even though this story is recorded sometime later, it evidently was widely known and springs from a fundamental tenet of the Cathars—that animal souls could be those of reincarnated humans—which probably would have produced such stories anywhere the Cathars were present. How many stories about Francis it resembles! He saves not only pheasants, but fish, hares, and lambs (*VS* 170; *VP* 60–61; *VP* 79), exhibiting a Catholic counterexample in his reasoning and actions.

Thus Francis' regard for creation in matters relating to food emphasizes a more positive evangelical standard, rejects Cathar beliefs and austerities, and correlates well with his chivalric values applied to the relationship between humanity and the rest of creation. Though the differences between Francis' own historical context and ours may make it difficult to see at first, Francis has his own special and positive view of food and creation.

Francis' Most Untraditional Reaction to Creation: Nature Mysticism

Francis' beliefs about creation and food included a new attempt to return to Biblical standards and a forbearance of unnecessary violence to creatures out of love for them. Another of Francis' characteristic expressions of regard for nonhuman creation—his nature mysticism—arose out of his deep love for creatures. His hagiographers attributed it to a further return to earlier Christian tradition, but it was nothing of the sort. Francis' nature mysticism was his most untraditional positive reaction to creation.*

---

*The reader may assume that nature mysticism, being an interesting issue, has been much studied, and that Edward A. Armstrong's book, *St. Francis: Nature Mystic*, must have already dealt with the topic adequately (see especially his pp. 12–17). Both of these assumptions are, unfortunately, quite incorrect. Research on nature mysticism per se is still at the groundbreaking level. The subject of mysticism in general, however, has generated much research and controversy over the last fifty years. W. James' *The Varieties of Religious Experience* (New York, 1929); and J. Leuba's *The Psychology of Religious Mysticism* (London, 1925), are early masterpieces. A. Huxley's *The Doors of Perception* (London, 1954), and R. Zaehner's *Mysticism, Sacred and Profane* (Oxford, 1957) have embroiled the field in controversy over the essence and value of the mystical state. For early philosophical analysis see W. Stace, *Mysticism and Philosophy* (London, 1960). C. Tart's *Altered States of Consciousness* (New York, 1969), sets mystical experiences within psychological research into other related mental states. A. Greeley's *Ecstasy: A Way of Knowing* (New Jersey, 1974) is a good popular introduction to the new research. Most penetrating in terms of astute criticism of the various arguments in the field are two excellent recent volumes of essays edited by Stephen Katz. *Mysticism and Philosophical Analysis* (New York, 1978) includes his own fundamentally important article: "Language, Epistemology, and Mysticism." *Mysticism and Religious Traditions* (Oxford, 1983) includes the fundamental "Francis of Assisi: Christian Mysticism at the Crossroads," by Ewert Cousins. I shall often refer to these sources in the following pages.

While few of the volumes of research on mysticism say anything specifically about nature mysticism per se, they do provide thorough examinations of various mystical states and associated phenomena. Yet even when some works touch on our subject, it is only too apparent that they approach an area which has its own history and problems, where even the most basic questions of outlook are at issue. For example, how is one to define "nature mysticism"? Zaehner and Knowles approach the subject from the Christian theological perspective, distinguishing that mysticism which concerns experiences of "all as one and one as all" ("natural mysticism")[42] from that "in which the soul feels itself to be united with God by love" ("supernatural mysticism").[43] Armstrong, who approaches the subject from the perspective of a layperson and historian, provides quite a different definition.

> The points of importance [in Christian nature mysticism] are the degree to which a religious mystic's experiences of enlightenment or exaltation is inspired by or dependent upon his attitude toward nature and the extent to which he regards nature as a manifestation of the divine. . . . A Christian nature mystic is therefore one whose mystical experience, whatever form it may take, is based on Christian beliefs and involves an appreciation of Creation as God's handiwork.[44]

Zaehner, though providing a rigorous analysis and many useful examples, concludes that the "natural" mystical experience is an aberrant mental state similar to the manic excitement of manic-depressive psychosis,[45] and would include under his definition of "natural" mysticism Huxley's contemplation of a chair while under the influence of mescaline. Both Zaehner and Knowles intend to separate all Christian mystical experience from those of "natural mystics." Neither writer mentions St. Francis in this regard, and it is extremely difficult to imagine how they would account for his experiences, given their conceptual framework.

Armstrong's definition more nearly relates to the popular conception rather than that of abstruse theological concerns. It puts the focus where it should be: on the role of the natural environment in the experience, instead of the spiritual value of different mental states. Knowles and Zaehner would subsume any idea of "nature mysticism" under their category of "natural mysticism." This step, however, would make it impossible to appreciate Franciscan nature mysticism, which would have to be either dismissed as an aberration or ignored. Once one accepts a definition of nature mysticism more similar to Armstrong's—one which includes no reference to a questionable and artificial standard of Catholicity—one finds it easy to understand Francis' experiences in a broad conceptual manner. Francis' experiences began with phenomena of the natural world and finished with a vision of God. In Zaehner's analysis, this would be impossible, for "natural" mystical experiences by definition are achieved without divine grace, nor do there seem to be any "supernatural" experiences in which the natural world plays an important part.

Yet Armstrong's enthusiasm leads him toward some questionable conclusions also. He contends that there were many Christian nature mystics. Basing his argument on the extreme difficulty of identifying the "lower rungs" of the mystical experience, Armstrong argues for "democratization" of definition to include "those who would not claim more than—to use John Wesley's phrase—to have felt their hearts 'strangely moved' on perceiving some beautiful scene, sound, or scent. . . ."[46] This statement is ambiguous, albeit well-intentioned. Also vague is Armstrong's attempt at a historical overview of the phenomenon.[47] But most important, Armstrong does not use reasonable criteria to establish that there actually were any nature mystics, Christian or otherwise, before Francis. I believe it is impossible to prove his contention. While I wish to accept Armstrong's implicit assumption that nature mystics can arise from different philosophical or religious systems (including Christianity), I believe he has given too little attention to the careful explanation of the phenomenon of nature mysticism, and the understanding of why the Western world has generally proven inimical to its expression.

Before one may establish the occurrence of any mystical experience, one must define the particular mystical experience and provide proper evidence to prove its occurrence. Katz's recent articles criticize Zaehner and others for attempting to divorce mysticism from the mystic's conceptual background. The mystic is, according to Katz,

> a shaper of his experience . . . he is not a *tabula rasa* on which the "ultimate" or the "given" simply impinges itself—whatever ultimate he happens to be seeking and happens to find. This much is certain: the mystical experience must be mediated by the kind of beings we are. And the kind of beings we are require that experience be not only instantaneous and discontinuous, but that it also involve memory, apprehension, expectation, language, accumulation of prior experience, concepts and expectations, with each experience being built on the back of all these elements and being shaped anew by each fresh experience. Thus experience of *x*—be *x* God or nirvana—is conditioned both linguistically and cognitively by a variety of factors including the expectation of what will be experienced. Related to these expectations are also future-

> directed activities such as meditation, fasting, ritual ablutions, self-mortification, and so on, which create further expectations about what the future and future states of consciousness will be like. There is obviously a self-fulfilling prophetic aspect to this sort of activity.[48]
>
> [M]ystical experience is "over-determined" by its socio-religious milieu: as a result of his process of intellectual acculturation in its broadest sense, the mystic brings to his experience a world of concepts, images, symbols, and values which shape as well as colour the experience he eventually and actually has.[49]

Katz's very valid point is that any mystical experience is affected by the interaction of several factors: cultural environment, individual beliefs, the setting and experience itself, and the individual's interpretation of these in terms of cultural environment. Katz's attitude toward mysticism harmoniously combines such issues as individuality and cultural or religious norms, allowing for different experiences even within similar general systems of thought. In Katz's essay, "The Conservative Character of Mysticism" (from his *Mysticism and Religious Traditions*), he specifically examines the dynamic between innovation and conservatism in many mystical experiences. He maintains that mysticism is "a dialectic that oscillates between the innovative and traditional poles of religious life," and that in both mystics' experiences and their new symbolic readings of traditional texts, they "function to maintain the authority" of the tradition while expanding it.[50]

Mysticism, of course, is one of the most inherently elusive and ineffable of human experiences. Armstrong believes that clear distinctions here are demanded only of the "theologian or psychologist,"[51] yet a middle ground of useful clarity may be found between Armstrong's generous vagueness and theological or psychological subtlety. A nature mystical experience is one which arises when a positive conception of the beauty and worth of creation and its intimate relationship with a spiritual force of some sort catalyzes profound personal reactions of wonder or exhilaration. In the face of an overwhelming encounter with the sublimity of the natural world, whether in general (a landscape, the stars at night) or specific (a flower), the mystic progresses directly toward a vision of, contact with, or participation with, that spiritual force. This description remains faithful to the modern popular conception of a nature mystic, while avoiding complex and irrelevant issues such as the spiritual value of the experience, or its psychological or emotional foundations.

Following Katz's reasoning, evidence proving that a particular figure was a nature mystic must consist of two general parts: conceptual and experiential. That is, proof must exist that the person indeed held deeply positive views of creation, and actually underwent a mystical experience. These distinctions are crucial. For example, one may have an extremely positive conception of creation, yet never undergo any mystical experience directly associated with this. One may write poetry demonstrating fervent lyrical appreciation for creation, yet never actually experience nature mysticism. One may reach a state of ecstatic possession or intoxication while amid the natural environment, alone or in a primitive communal ritual (such as the bacchanals, or the rites of modern primitive societies), without having a conception of mystical rapture stemming from a sublime vision of the natural world and leading to the contemplation of God. Sabatelli implicitly accepts this careful approach in his discussion of Francis' *Canticle*,[52] where he assumes that Francis' work is the product of a nature mystic only because we know indisputably the character of Francis' mystical experiences from the supporting evidence. David Knowles also makes the distinction between conceptual and experiential evidence in these statements about Bonaventure.

> St. Bonaventure is often described as a mystic. If by this it is implied that he himself was in the fullest theological sense an experiential mystic and that this influenced his doctrine and method of presentation, it can only be replied that nowhere in his writings does he claim this or give clear evidence of such experiences. If, on the other hand, all that is meant is that St. Bonaventure regarded the mystical experience as a foretaste of the vision of God to which every Christian must aspire, and as given to some souls here on earth, and that, writing for religious and regarding theology as primarily the science of a holy life, he includes in his teaching much that now would be called "mystical" as distinct from "dogmatic" theology, the title may be allowed, though perhaps it would be better to call him a mystical theologian than a mystic.[53]

I agree with Knowles' conclusions both with regard to Bonaventure (in contrast to Francis) and in wishing to stress the careful sorts of distinctions which should be made in the area of mysticism and the possible mystic.

No strong evidence for nature mysticism exists in Hebrew, classical, or Christian culture up to the thirteenth century. If one accepts Katz's arguments, one should attempt to explain what factors in the "intellectual acculturation" of Western society held back or steered away the devout from an experience which linked the natural environment with mystical rapture. It is indeed possible to point to some factors.

Some Psalms reflect a remarkably unusual view of creation, both in terms of many modern conceptions and some Biblical ones.

The Mighty One, God the Lord,
speaks and summons the earth from the rising of the sun to its setting.
Out of Zion, the perfection of beauty,
God shines forth.[54]

The pastures of the wilderness drip,
the hills gird themselves with joy,
The meadows clothe themselves with flocks,
the valleys deck themselves with grain,
they shout and sing together for joy.[55]

Praise him, sun and moon,
praise him, all you shining stars!
Praise him, you highest heavens,
and you waters above the heavens![56]

But these passages seem to describe the impact of a mighty God exploding upon the world,[57] or to urge the praise of this God, rather than to pertain to a mystical phenomenon experienced by the poet. The early Hebrew Scriptures portray a transcendent divinity who governs creation according to his will and whose jealousy demands that religious devotion be rendered to him, not to his creation.[58] Such a religious viewpoint does not provide a conceptual foundation for nature mysticism as we have described it, however much it may establish the spiritual value and usefulness of creation. Later portions of Scripture, such as Ecclesiastes and Ecclesiasticus, exhibit a view of the physical world much more imbued with philosophical reasoning, but not with mysticism.

The Greco-Roman world provided a general conceptual context which could have produced a nature-mystical experience, but also exhibited other conflicting attitudes. Many works, such as those of Theocritus or Vergil,[59] as well as Pompeian paintings, reflect the classical world's idealization of the idyllic and pastoral aspects of the natural environment. The expression of intense reactions to the natural world, however (with the exception of fear or awe),[60] seems to have been rare. Ecstasy in any form tended to be explained in terms of "madness" or possession, which produced a deep ambivalence.[61]

Plato's *Phaedrus*, which alone of his dialogues takes place in a sublime natural setting, contains another example of possession within this context. Socrates walks with a disciple through a landscape of idyllic beauty, dominated by a sacred shrine. The philosopher seems to come under the influence of a spirit which pervades the spot. He says to Phaedrus, "Then listen to me in silence. For truly there seems to be a divine presence in this spot, so that you must not be surprised if, as my speech proceeds, I become as one possessed; already my style is not far from dithyrambic."[62] Socrates is carried away and loses control of his thoughts—a situation which he finds transcending, but also disconcerting and worth examination.[63]

Classical authors considered all these experiences to be examples of possession, not mysticism. Mysticism played very little part in the classical world, where religion often involved more a loyalty to traditional practice, and ritual than emotional fervor.[64] It was left to Plotinus and the Christian tradition to establish fully the value and authority of a refined mystical experience.

Plotinus built upon Plato's advice to the initiate: "Starting from individual beauties, the quest for the universal beauty must find him ever mounting the heavenly ladder, stepping from rung to rung" toward "that wondrous vision which is the very soul of the beauty he has toiled so long for. It is an everlasting loveliness which neither flowers nor fades."[65] But for Plotinus, Plato's quest for the vision of the highest love is transformed into the mystic's journey through creation's beauty to the divine vision and the height of the mystical experience.

> Now, if the sight of Beauty excellently reproduced upon a face hurries the mind to that other Sphere, surely no one seeing the loveliness lavish in the world of sense—this universal symmetry, this vast orderliness, the Form which the stars even in their remoteness display—no one could be so dull-witted, so immovable, as not to be carried by all this to recollection, and gripped by reverent awe in the thought of all this, so great, sprung from that greatness. . . .[66]
>
> Material forms containing light incorporated in them need still a light apart from them that their own light may be manifest; just so the Beings of that sphere, all lightsome, need another and a lordlier light or then even they would not be visible to themselves and beyond. . . . That light known, then indeed we are stirred towards those Beings in longing and rejoicing over the radiance about them, just as earthly love is not for the material form but for the Beauty manifested upon it. . . . The soul taking that outflow from the divine is stirred; seized with a Bacchic passion, goaded by these goads, it becomes Love.[67]

Note that earthly beauty is supposed to gain the observer's attention only to direct the person immediately toward the hidden divine Beauty. No indication exists suggesting that Plotinus' mystical experiences were ever inspired by immediate direct observation of the natural world; rather, they result from abstract contemplation. Yet his linkage of the environment with divine beauty provided a possible conceptual foundation for nature mysticism, even though his other ideas undercut this.

Augustine, drawing in addition upon a Christian tradition which justified the goodness of creation through its utility, providential purpose, and evangelism (in that it proclaimed the goodness, power, and beauty of the Creator),[68] evinced an attitude which at times resembled Plotinus'.

> Ask the loveliness of the earth, ask the loveliness of the sea, ask the loveliness of the wide airy spaces, ask the loveliness of the sky, ask the order of the stars, ask the sun making the day light with its beams, ask the moon tempering the darkness of the night that follows, ask the living things which move in the waters, which tarry on the land, which fly in the air; ask the souls that are hidden, the bodies that are perceptive; the visible things which must be governed, the invisible things which govern—ask all these things, and they will all answer thee, Lo, see we are lovely. Their loveliness is their confession. And these lovely but mutable things, who has made them, save Beauty immutable?[69]

All creation participates intimately in the beauty given it by Immutable Beauty, and confesses its Maker with the display of its own beauty. These ideas could easily be the basis for a Christian nature mysticism. Yet the general tenor of Augustine's works suggests instead a more ambivalent view, as exemplified in the following two passages.

> Let us not seek in this [earthly] beauty that which it has not received, for because it has not received that which we seek it is on that account in the lowest place. But for that which it has received let us praise God, since even to this that is lowest He has given also the great good of outward fairness.[70]

> Though I say this [the praise of beauty in light and art] and see that it is true, my feet are still caught in the toils of this world's beauty. But you will free me, O Lord. . . . I am caught and need your mercy, and by your mercy you will save me from the snare. Sometimes, if I have not fallen deep into the trap, I shall feel nothing when you rescue me; but at other times, when I am fast ensnared, I shall suffer the pain of it.[71]

These passages reveal a profound sense of guilt, an unease with the beauty of the created world characteristic of "the converted Manichee Augustine, who throughout his life remained ambivalent towards matter"[72]—hardly an attitude which would give rise to nature mysticism. Augustine feared absorption of the observer in the natural world as a tendency to forsake the Creator for the creation.

Thus it is interesting that Augustine's first successful mystical experience, the vision of Ostia, took place in a natural setting.[73]

> . . . [M]y mother and I were alone, leaning from a window which overlooked the garden in the courtyard of the house where we were staying at Ostia. . . . As the flame of love burned stronger in us and raised us higher towards the eternal God, our thoughts ranged over the whole compass of material things in their various degrees, up to the heavens themselves, from which the sun and the moon and the stars shine down upon the earth. Higher still we climbed, thinking and speaking all the while in wonder at all that you have made. At length we came to our own souls and passed beyond them to that place of everlasting plenty. . . .[74]

Although I believe this is the closest the West ever came to a nature-mystical experience before Francis, it seems the physical environment here was not so much the primary catalyst for the experience, but rather a fitting setting for the abstract conversation Augustine and his mother had which led them to mystical rapture. Augustine's ambivalence toward creation and his concentration upon the soul's inner journey would not have enabled him to have a nature-mystical experience. As Katz says, the religious and individual background forms the character of mystical experience, and in this case, while certain factors in Augustine's religious and philosophical background could have stimulated such an experience, his deep sense of sin and desire to escape the natural world militated against the possibility.

Possible Ascetic Examples of Nature Mysticism

Edward Armstrong believes that

> from the Desert Fathers to the present time there has been a succession, albeit intermittent, of Christian nature mystics; but because their biographers—when they had any—did not recognize the authenticity of the tradition to which they belonged, some without recognizing their lineage, little has been recorded of them.[75]

Yet when one calls to mind passages from the major Christian authors in the aforementioned early medieval period, such as Sulpicius Severus, Gregory the Great, John Moschus, Bede, and many others who might provide evidence, one finds a strange lack of convincing incidents. Instead of a dynamically positive view of the natural environment, one sees in the medieval ascetic view of creation a deeply ambivalent moral perspective which, as with Augustine's reactions, would act to prohibit such an absorbing experience in the natural world as nature mysticism. Gregory the Great told the wonderful story of Florentius and his pet bear,[76] but he also related the disturbing incident in which Benedict was tempted by a blackbird.[77] Even in the *Voyage of St. Brendan*, undoubtedly one of the most enthusiastic examples of Dark Age hagiography in its reaction to creation, the ambivalence seems heightened instead of being resolved. Brendan constantly watches for temptation from the natural world, and sternly warns his men to be on their guard.[78] Incidents which might have turned into nature mysticism take another direction entirely. On one occasion, the sailor and his wizened companions discover a mysterious iceberg.[79] The Biblical phrases in the hagiographical description heighten the feeling of divine mystery in creation. However, the explorers seem not so much overcome by mystical rapture as by something infinitely more comprehensible to us: the beginnings of scientific curiosity. They proceed to examine the phenomenon, explore around it, and measure it assiduously. Here Dark Age hagiography more clearly reveals the beginnings of science than nature mysticism. One is again aware of the deep and many-sided potential residing in medieval reactions to the natural environment.

It is possible to trace the inheritance of Augustine's ambivalent reaction to creation as it moved through the sophisticated Christian theologians and mystics of later ages. The following quotation is from Bonaventure's *Soliloquy*:

> O soul, you should now direct the beam of contemplation upon the things that are around you, that is, upon the sensible world, in order that you may disdain it and everything in it, and thus burn with a more ardent love for the Spouse. . . . "May all creatures appear worthless to you, so that the Creator alone may gladden your heart." (Augustine, *In Psalmum* 30:3–8)[80]
>
> "But beware, my soul, lest you be called adulteress instead of bride, for having valued the gifts of the Giver above the love of the Lover" (Hugh of St. Victor, *De arrha animae*). "Woe to you if you wander about His traces, if you love his signs instead of Him and seek temporal gains, never understanding the message of that blessed light which is intelligence in the cleansed soul, and of which the splendor of all creatures is but a trace and symbol." (Augustine, *De libero arbitrio* 16:43)[81]

And these are from a collection made years after Francis' time, by a great Franciscan![82]

Thus it appears that evidence does not support as much as expected the assumption that there were many early nature mystics. It is not just a matter of the possibility of some sort of "hidden tradition" of nature mystics we can no longer get at. The medieval ascetic ambivalence to creation seems to have prevented nature mysticism's emergence, though the medieval tradition could expand its expressive range in other directions. It would take a new, more thoroughly positive point of view outside these currents to allow a clear example of a Christian nature-mystical experience to arise.

Francis' Nature Mysticism

Francis' innovative nature mysticism should first briefly be situated within the context of the generally original character of his mystical experiences, most of which were not nature-mystical. Cousin's study places Francis at the crossroads of Christian mysticism.

> Francis represents a watershed in the history of Western Christianity. After him Western religious experience flows in two currents: speculative Neoplatonic mysticism gains vigour, reaching a culmination in the Rhineland mystics. But the devotional current flowing from Francis—with its focus on the humanity and passion of Christ—spreads throughout the people at large and becomes the characteristic form of Western sensibility for centuries to come.[83]

Francis' "mysticism of the historical event," in which "one recalls a significant event in the past, enters into its drama and draws from it spiritual energy, eventually moving beyond the event towards union with God,"[84] is compared by Cousins with Francis' nature mysticism.

> If Francis was innovative in evoking the mysticism of the historical event, it should not be surprising that he is equally innovative in nature mysticism. Considered the prime example of a nature mystic in the history of Christianity, he took spontaneous joy in the material world, singing its praises like a troubadour poet in his "Canticle of Brother Sun." With a disarming sense of immediacy, he felt himself part of the family of creation. . . . As is the case with the mysticism of the historical event, this is a far cry from Neoplatonic speculative mysticism, which focuses on an abstract cosmological structure and which turns quickly from the material world and its individual creatures to scale the metaphysical ladder to the spiritual and divine realms by means of universal concepts.[85]

Francis entered into a mystical experience when he meditated on and extended his depth of feeling for events such as Jesus' birth and death; he did so also when he meditated on God's creatures and deepened his feelings for them. Historical mysticism leads to communication with God through identification with a religious event, while in nature mysticism, "our union with nature becomes a mode of God's communication of himself to us through his creation and of our union with him by perceiving his presence in the physical world."[86] The similarities between the two involve an intense identification with something spiritual seen in concrete reality.

As we turn to Francis' nature mysticism specifically, we observe that the early Franciscan sources amply document Francis' unusually high regard for creatures and his intense, immediate positive reactions to them. Out of the many relevant anecdotes in all the early Franciscan sources, only a very few stories link creatures with temptation in a way seen in the earlier Dark Ages. The sheer number of anecdotes relating positive encounters with creatures overwhelms the reader and dwarfs the amount recorded about any earlier saint. Without a doubt, the number and consistency of these stories prove that Francis confronted creatures with preconceptions and associations in his mind that were unusually positive and full of spontaneous invention. We have already examined many of these in earlier chapters. Some of them would have been particularly and uniquely favorable to incidents of nature mysticism—for example, Francis' expressions of deep respect, affection, praise, and love for creatures. These expressions show a willingness to go beyond tradition, to draw upon such unexpected sources as evangelical and chivalric ideals to enrich and enlarge his conceptions and reactions. The same inventive mind would turn itself to its beloved mysticism and draw upon that area to produce new reactions to creation which would reveal deeper experiences of love and exhilaration when Francis was confronted with something he thought wonderful in the natural environment.

Another factor—a negative one—is of immense importance. Francis had not been trained as an intellectual in his youth, and, as Cousins hints, had never absorbed the Christian Neoplatonic attitude toward creation—one which led to careful categorization of the levels of creation, their different significances, and the "intellectualization" and internalization of the mystical experience. It is ironic that both Celano and Bonaventure make use of their Christian Neoplatonic intellectual training to attempt to explain Francis' nature-mystical experience (*VS* 165; *ML* 9:1). They ignore the fact that their mystical outlook and training had nothing to do with the natural environment catalyzing a mystical experience in a direct manner, and, in fact, their training probably would have prevented the occurrence of nature mysticism. For all their enthusiasm here, no one can prove that either of them were nature mystics!

TABLE 5. Franciscan Nature Mysticism:
Specific and Related References

Background or General Theory in Sources	Specific Experiences Alluded to or Recounted
Basis in new view of creation orginated: *VP* 58	Ineffable joy described: *VP* 80; *MP* 119; *F* II:2 (walking in the moonlight)
Mystical allegory governs affections: *VP* 77	Specific experiences in mind or recounted: *LP* 49, 51; *MP* 118; *VS* 167; *ML* 8:8; *VP* 61
Other helpful passages: *VP* 61; *ML* 12:3; *TM* 20; *F* 16; *ML* 8:8; 8:6; *TM* 24	
Francis prays in hidden places, "drawing external things into himself": *VS* 94–5; compare to *VS* 165	
Platonic theory used to explain Francis' reactions: *VS* 165; *LP* 51; *MP* 118; *ML* 5:9 (correlates)	
More theory *MP* 115–120	
Francis; emotional reactions to landscape: *F* II:1–2 (link of beautiful place to prayer/mysticism)	

Yet Francis' hagiographers were impressed with his experiences because they believed he was applying in a more concrete, literalistic way the same ideals they had found in their intellectual training. Just as they had focused earlier on the literalism and traditionalism in Francis' ascetic standards and Sermon to the Birds, so now they discuss with admiration Francis' nature mystical experiences in terms of Augustinian Platonism. From Celano's perspective, it would have seemed in all these cases that Francis had seized upon something Christians had taken for granted and given it a new meaning or applied it in a striking new way still faithful to ancient Christian tradition. But Celano's reaction in this case produced some bizarre results. Consider the passage from Celano which introduces a short discussion of Francis' nature mysticism.

> In every work of the artist he praised the Artist; whatever he found in the things made he referred to the Maker. He rejoiced in all the works of the hands of the Lord and saw behind things pleasant to behold their life-giving reason and cause. In beautiful things he saw Beauty itself; all things were to him good. "He who made us is the best," they cried out to him. Through his footprints impressed upon things he followed the Beloved everywhere; he made for himself from all things a ladder by which to come even to his throne. (*VS* 165)

Any intellectual of Celano's time would instantly have recognized the hackneyed Augustinianism of these comments.

But their effect is quite significant. Placed before Francis' experiences, as a sort of commentary upon them, they cause the reader to interpret Francis' actions as typical and even conservatively literalistic expressions of a well-known tradition. Even if the reader were to realize the distinction between Francis' experiences and Augustinian mysticism, he probably would react all the more favorably to Francis—not because Francis was an innovator, but because the saint had the faith to take Augustinian teachings in a simple, literal way. Celano does not consciously intend to cover up the originality in Francis' actions; he exhibits no reticence at all in discussing them. Yet his interpretation of them, which sets them in the context of sophisticated Christian mystical tradition, makes their originality be seen in a manner that emphasizes their conservative and literal (rather than radically innovative) character.

Cousins points out the tasks that hagiographers like Celano and Bonaventure were performing here—tasks which are common in assimilating innovative mysticism with tradition: "(1) to situate Francis' experience within the mainstream speculative, metaphysical, cosmological Neoplatonic tradition; and (2) at the same time to extend this tradition to encompass"[87] Francis' original strain of mysticism.

THE ANECDOTES

Sometimes the sources are general and vague, but their expressions still leave no doubt that they were referring to something unusual and rapturous which was happening to Francis.

> He embraced all things with a feeling of unheard of devotion [*inauditae devotionis affectu*], speaking to them of the Lord and admonishing them to praise him. (*VS* 165)

Though this chapter of Celano trails off into incidents which are not examples of nature mysticism, it does serve warning that often Francis' spontaneous reactions to creatures went far beyond what Celano considered usual. The phrase "feeling of unheard of devotion" seems especially unparalleled in describing a saint's reactions to creation. This state seems to have produced the instances of deep reverence and respect for creatures that Celano notes, as well as Francis' *Canticle* and nature mysticism. In another passage, Celano terms this state one of exhilaration or exultation.

> How great an exhilaration [*exhilarationem*] do you think the beauty of the flowers brought to his mind when he saw the shape of their beauty and

> perceived the odor of their sweetness? He used to turn the eye of consideration immediately to the beauty of that flower that comes from the root of Jesse and gives light in the days of spring and by its fragrance has raised innumerable thousands from the dead. (*VP* 81)

Celano's writing is filled here with sensual mystical imagery that makes it some of his best. For example, the complex levels of symbolism here create earthly and spiritual equivalents: flowers, odor, and spring parallel, on a spiritual level, Christ (the flower of Jesse's root), spiritual power (odor), and Christ's saving message to humanity (light of spring). This leads the paragraph, following its implicit logic, to illustrations of Francis' preaching to creatures.

A passage of Bonaventure's uses the words "delight" and "exultation" to describe Francis' state, but makes clear that something is occurring beyond Francis' discovery of mystical symbolism in creatures.

> Francis sought occasion to love God in everything. He delighted in all the works of God's hands and from the vision of joy on earth his mind soared aloft to the life-giving source and cause of all [*Ut autem ex omnibus excitaretur ad amorem divinum, exsultabat in cunctis operibus manuum Domini et per jocunditatis spectacula in vivicam consurgebat rationem et causam*]. (*ML* 9:1)

This passage relates exactly, though in a general way, what our definition of nature mysticism centered on: a vision of sublime creation catalyzing a mystical experience with the divine. Another of Celano's passages specifically uses the word "contemplation" to describe Francis' reactions, and talks of the experiences in terms of being "ineffable."

> Who would be able to narrate the sweet delight [*dulcedinem*] he enjoyed while contemplating [*contemplans*] in creatures the wisdom of their creator, his power and his goodness? Indeed, he was very often filled with a wonderful and ineffable joy [*miro atque ineffabili gaudio*] while he looked upon the sun, while he beheld the moon, and while he gazed upon the stars and the firmament. (*VP* 80)

One last passage from Celano employs the technical language of the Christian Neoplatonic mystical experience to describe carefully what was happening in these cases. It is the epitome of the attempt to understand Francis' nature mysticism in terms of the traditional mystical experience, even though, as we have seen above, his expressions were totally original and had nothing to do with Christian Neoplatonism.

> When he prayed in the woods and solitary places [*in silvis vero et solitudinibus orans*], he would fill the wood with sighs and water the places with his tears. . . . Often, without moving his lips, he would meditate within himself and drawing external things within himself [*et introrsum extrinseca trahens spiritum subtrahebat in superos*], he would lift his spirit to higher things. (*VS* 95)

Francis "took in" a vision of creation—the opposite of the usual Neoplatonic withdrawal from the sensual world—and, meditating on this vision, he drew himself unto the heights of mystical contemplation. Celano states this process happened "often" (*saepe*), when Francis was away from others. It perhaps was his primary form of contemplation when he was alone in the midst of creation, and thus would have made up quite a significant portion of his contemplative life. The process led to a vision of God.

> All his attention and affection he directed with his whole being to the one thing which he was asking of the Lord, not so much praying as becoming himself a prayer. . . . Thus, filled with a glowing fervor of spirit and his whole appearance and his whole soul melted, he dwelt already in the highest realms of the heavenly kingdom. (*VS* 95)

The *Legend of Perugia* supports Celano without employing Neoplatonism or grandiloquence. What emerges seems refreshingly concrete. One chapter, which tells of Francis' deep love and respect for creatures, adds this remark.

> He chatted to them with inward and outward joy, just as if they felt, understood, and could talk about God, so that many times in this way he was rapt in contemplation of God [*multotiens illa occasione rapiebatur in contemplatione Dei*]. (*LP* 49)

The *Legend*'s language could not be more plain. Francis often entered a state of mystical rapture while delighting in an affectionate interaction with various creatures. The encounter began with the establishment of Francis' usual relationship of love and respect for the animal. As Francis deeply delighted in this interaction, he began to converse with the creature about spiritual subjects, and thus attained a state of divine contemplation. The description in the *Legend* again matches our description of a possible nature-mystical experience.

Very occasionally one may find in the sources an incident involving nature mysticism that the hagiographers left in its modest Franciscan simplicity. These incidents reflect an aura of mystery and elusive, understated significance, and occur when Francis is away from the crowd, in magnificent surroundings. Once Francis was in the middle of the lake of Rieti, crossing to go to the hermitage of Greccio, when the fisherman whose boat he occupied gave him a waterfowl, "that he might rejoice over it in the Lord."

> The blessed father accepted it joyfully [*gaudenter*] and opening his hands, he gently told it that it was free to fly away. But when it did not wish to leave, but wanted to rest there in his hands as in a nest, the saint raised his eyes and remained in prayer [*in oratione*]. And returning to himself as from another place after a long while [*quasi aliunde post longam moram ad se reversus*], he gently commanded the bird to go back to its former freedom. (*VS* 167; *ML* 8:8)

Those who are aware of the language of Christian mysticism will immediately call to mind that Celano's phrases "in prayer" and "returning to himself as from another place after a long while" denote a mystical experience. In fact, Celano's "returning to himself" (*ad se reversus*) is a Biblical quotation alluding to Peter's miraculous rapture as he was led from prison.[88] Celano's language and Francis' experiences are best understood in terms of this passage from Bonaventure's *Legenda Maior*.

> [Francis] tried to keep his spirit always in the presence of God, by praying to him without intermission [*sine intermissione orans*], so that he might not be without some comfort from his Beloved. Prayer was his chief comfort in this life of contemplation [*oratio contemplanti solatium*] in which he became a fellow-citizen of the angels, as he penetrated the dwelling places of heaven in his eager search for his Beloved. . . . (*ML* 10:1)

This reads like a gloss on Celano's "prayer" which took Francis to "another place" and then returned him to himself.

Celano's *Vita Prima* recounts with more helpful detail what happened when Francis, again on the Lake of Rieti, was presented with a fish.

> He accepted it joyfully and kindly and began to call it brother; then placing it in the water outside the boat, he began devoutly to bless the name of the Lord [*devotus benedicere nomen Domini*]. And while he continued in prayer for some time [*Sicque aliquamdiu, dum in oratione persisteret*], the fish played in the water beside the boat and did not go away from the place where it had been put until his prayer was finished [*oratione completa*] and the holy man of God gave it permission to leave. (*VP* 61)[89]

This gives a fuller sense of the delicacy and charm present in the ethos of these Franciscan stories. Francis and the little fish seem to enter an enchanted world of their own, a world filled with joy, respect, kindness, and unity, where they share a mysterious and sacred sort of communication. There is an indefinable and elusive feeling of transcendence in the image of the saint and the fish who have entered together the realm of the sacred and share there an ineffable rapport for a short time. They enter a world of archetypal unity where Francis' ideal, for a brief moment, becomes reality. Their interaction is characterized by the pattern we have sketched before. Feelings of mutual love, respect, and joy lead Francis to accept a new member of his spiritual family as brother. The fish replies by showing its joy and obedience as it plays beside Francis' boat until he finishes his ecstasy and gives it permission to depart. Francis praises the Lord and thanks him, perhaps as in the *Canticle*, for the beauty and usefulness of his creature. Contemplating the unity of creation and Creator, Francis enters a state of mystical transcendence.

Let us go deeper for a moment to understand what Francis' nature-mystical experiences may have been like for him personally. Although one does not usually employ the word "feeling" in describing a mystical experience, which is certainly more than a "feeling," the hagiographers and Francis himself leave no doubt that feelings for creatures were an extremely important element in his nature mysticism. The sources positively light up with emotional phrases when they come to this subject. Celano delights in telling about Francis' "feeling of unheard of devotion" for creatures—his joy, love, rapture, and adoration of the divine in creation. This emphasis on the honest, simple, human sensual and emotional beginning of the mystical experience is the quintessential path taken by Francis. It is the exact nature-mystical counterpart of his other "historical" mystical experiences so well described by Cousins, where Francis in opening his human emotions to a historical religious event, such as the birth of Christ or the crucifixion, is led to a mystical experience.[90] Those who would fear to link senses and emotions with Francis' mysticism are living in a world more Augustinian than Franciscan. They have forgotten the Francis whose tongue licked his lips when he spoke the name "Jesus" (*VP* 86), and who "was very often filled with a wonderful and ineffable joy" (*VP* 80) when he gazed up at the sun or moon or stars, and entered a mystical experience. Francis' mystical experiences, especially his nature-mystical ones, occurred because he was unusually open to his senses and emotions which led him into ecstasy—not because he avoided or feared these human reactions to experience. One gets the impression that Francis' emotions on these occasions sweep him completely off his feet. When he focuses his emotional attention on a flower, a fish, or another creature, he is so overwhelmed with exquisite joy and love that he enters the abandonment, the spiritual intoxication, of mystical ecstasy. Francis' own writing, the *Canticle*, probably attests to this in lines which, in describing beloved qualities of a creature, shine with a barely-controlled, intoxicated delight. Especially behind such phrases as "Be praised, my Lord, for Brother Wind/ And for Air, for Cloud, and Clear, and all weather. . . . Be praised, my Lord, for Sister Water/ She is very useful, and humble, and precious, and pure. . .", we can sense the deep emotions preceding or accompanying a mystical experience—emotions that unite with the sensual rhythm of the text. The feelings are like those of a child. They bounce along with ecstatic, free joy, and reveal a mystic absorbed in the ineffable, timeless wonder of the experience. These are the same reactions Celano reports in awe: "How great an exultation[91] do you think the beauty of the flowers brought to his mind when he saw the shape of their beauty and perceived the odor of their sweetness" (*VP* 81)? At this point, we touch the height of Francis' special regard for creation, and see the radical originality stemming from his feelings for creatures—an originality, however, consistent with the character of Francis' other mystical experiences.

5

Tradition and Its Impact on the Canticle

Our next three chapters will examine Francis' *Canticle of Brother Sun* in terms of its bases in Christian tradition, the controversy over its meaning, and the vision of creation it presents. The *Canticle* is without a doubt "the best known and most appreciated of all the written work" of the saint,[1] and it would be impossible to do justice to the many appraisals of it in the most diverse fields. Not only is it important to the fields of theology and philosophy,[2] but it "can lay legitimate claim to an important and lasting place in the history of the literature of the Western world"[3] due to its stature as one of the first great Italian poems, and in terms of its later literary influence. As Lawrence Cunningham observes, it should be understood in the context of Francis' actions and related writings.[4] It represents the final expression, the final synthesis, of Francis' thought in the area of relationships between humanity, creation, and Creator. The Italian text and my English translation appear on pages 100–101.

The recent controversy among several Italian authors over exactly where the *Canticle* was composed has been resolved in favor of the account in the *Legend of Perugia*.[5] This account states that the main section of the *Canticle*, the "nature-segments" (strophes 1–25) came into existence at San Damiano, while Francis resided there over the winter of 1224–25.[6] Strophes 26–30 were composed sometime later, to halt a feud between the bishop and *podestà* at Assisi.[7] The strophes on "Sister Death" were added a few days before Francis' death, which occurred October 3, 1226.[8]

This composition in stages raises one of the many questions concerning the *Canticle*. Is the poem's literary unity maintained through this process? The first section discusses various creatures; the latter seems to relate more to humanity. Of course, the incidents that gave rise to the second portion make it comprehensible on that level, but is there a literary explanation of the poem's unity which would successfully deal with the problems of the poem's contrasts and composition in stages? Did the poem's models, for instance, justify its completion in this way, rather than by Francis' composition of a new poem?

It is possible to see the poem as a literary unity. In order to discuss this literary question in its proper context, however, we must first consider the general problem of traditional influence and originality in the poem.

In Chapter 1 we discussed the many different attitudes toward creation present in the Middle Ages. Some of the manifestations of these different views, for example, poems of Paulinus, Ausonius, Fortunatus, Alcuin, an anonymous Celtic poet, and others, demonstrate a sincere appreciation for creation. But none of these is known to have influenced Francis directly. Direct sources, in fact, seem to have stemmed from a fairly circumscribed area: the Biblical texts and liturgical passages which Francis reacted to and modified through the years.

Several researchers have noted that Francis' writings on creation—and indeed, his whole attitude toward it—were profoundly influenced by the liturgical Psalms and Canticles.[9] Some specify particular Psalms, (e.g., 148), or Canticles (e.g., the Canticum of the Three Young Men), as especially influential. However, researchers may be more exact in analysing the possible influence of specific Psalms and other passages on Francis' attitudes because his own breviary has survived as one of the treasures of Assisi and one of the rarest discoveries in the history of the liturgy.[10] We know from its inscription by Brother Leo that Francis possessed this breviary from 1223, and he would have followed its instructions devotedly during the last years of his life, if not earlier.[11]

When one examines the breviary instructions, one is immediately struck with the sheer number of times the Psalms of praise are to be repeated. Such famous ones as *Caeli enarrant* (Psalm 19) and *Jubilate Deo omnis terra* (Psalm 66) appear. Lauds, said at daybreak, is especially noteworthy. Psalm 148 is to be repeated every morning of the week; on Sundays and feast days, it is joined with two other works which call on creation to praise the Lord: Psalm 99 and the Canticum of the Three Young Men. Without question, Psalm 148 and the Canticum must have ranked near the Pater Noster and Ave Maria as texts that were extremely familiar to Francis. He quotes from them, and themes from them dominate several of his works: the *Exhortation*, the *Praises before the Hours*, and the *Canticle*.[12] The links between the Psalm, Canticum, and *Canticle* bear careful examination.

Il Cantico di Frate Sole[13]

1 Altissimo omnipotente bon Signore,
2 tue so le laude la gloria e l'onore e onne benedizione.

3 A te solo, Altissimo, se confano
4 e nullo omo è digno te mentovare.

5 Laudato sie, mi Signore, cun tutte le tue creature,
6 spezialmente messer lo frate Sole,
7 lo qual è iorno, e allumini noi per lui.

8 Ed ello è bello e radiante cun grande splendore:
9 de te, Altissimo, porta significazione.

10 Laudato si, mi Signore, per sora Luna e le Stelle:
11 im cielo l'hai formate clarite e preziose e belle.

12 Laudato si, mi Signore, per frate Vento,
13 e per Aere e Nubilo e Sereno e onne tempo
14 per lo quale a le tue creature dai sustentamento.

15 Laudato si, mi Signore, per sor Aqua,
16 la quale è molto utile e umile e preziosa e casta.

17 Laudato si, mi Signore, per frate Foco,
18 per lo quale enn' allumini la nocte:
19 ed ello è bello e iocundo e robustoso e forte.

20 Laudato si, mi Signore, per sora nostra matre Terra,
21 la quale ne sostenta e governa,
22 e produce diversi fructi con coloriti flori ed erba.

23 Laudato si, mi Signore, per quelli che perdonano per lo tuo amore
24 e sostengo infirmitate e tribulazione.

25 Beati quelli che 'l sosterrano in pace,
26 ca da te, Altissimo, sirano incoranti.

27 Laudato si, mi Signore, per sora nostra Morte corporale,
28 de la quale nullo omo vivente po' scampare.

29 Guai a quelli che morrano ne le peccata mortali!
30 Beati quelli che trovarà ne le tue sanctissime voluntati,
31 ca la morte seconda no li farra male.

32 Laudate e benedicite mi Signore,
33 e rengraziate e serviteli cun grande umilitate.

The Canticle of Brother Sun[14]

1 Most High, omnipotent, good Lord,
2 All praise, glory, honor, and blessing are yours.

3 To you alone, Most High, do they belong,
4 And no man is worthy to pronounce your name.

5 Be praised, my Lord, with all your creatures,
6 Especially Sir Brother Sun,
7 Who brings the day, and you give light to us through him.

8 How handsome he is, how radiant, with great splendor!
9 Of you, Most High, he bears the likeness.

10 Be praised, my Lord, for Sister Moon and the Stars.
11 In heaven you have formed them, bright, and precious, and beautiful.

12 Be praised, my Lord, for Brother Wind,
13 And for Air, for Cloud, and Clear, and all weather,
14 By which you give your creatures nourishment.

15 Be praised, my Lord, for Sister Water,
16 She is very useful, and humble, and precious, and pure.

17 Be praised, my Lord, for Brother Fire,
18 By whom you light up the night.
19 How handsome he is, how happy, how powerful and strong!

20 Be praised, my Lord, for our Sister, Mother Earth.
21 Who nourishes and governs us,
22 And produces various fruits with many-colored flowers and herbs.

23 Be praised, my Lord, for those who grant pardon for love of you
24 And endure infirmity and tribulation.

25 Blessed are those who endure them in peace,
26 For by you, Most High, they will be crowned.

27 Be praised, my Lord, for our Sister, Bodily Death,
28 From whom no man living can escape.

29 Woe to those who die in mortal sin!
30 Blessed are those whom she shall find in your most holy will,
31 The second death shall do them no evil.

32 Praise and bless the Lord,
33 And give thanks and serve him with great humility.

A comparison of the three works will prove that Francis' *Canticle* unquestionably depends on the two liturgical texts, using them as storehouses from which to draw ideas and amplify upon them in original ways. The most relevant connections between the texts are shown by the parallel passages given in Table 6.

As is quite apparent, the "scripture is the alphabet and the language of the saint."[15] "The vulgar of the Canticle in its lexicon . . . appears clearly modeled on the Latin most familiar to the saint," according to Branca,[16] who points out specific word choices in the *Canticle* demonstrating the "ennobling" of the early Italian with Latinate diction deriving from the Psalms and other liturgical texts. Francis' choice of the name *Cantico* itself probably arose from the liturgical canticles.[17] Many phrases such as *gloria e l'onore*, *Laudate e benedicite*, *Beati quelli che*; words such as *aere*, *voluntati*, *jocondo*, and *flori*, provide the deep influence of Biblical and liturgical passages. Esser and Branca provide indices of all the scriptural allusions in the *Canticle*.[18]

The structure of the liturgical passages seems to have furnished a model for the *Canticle*. The three poems all follow a noticeable step-like progression. They begin with an address to the Lord in thanksgiving, and then turn to creation. In the Canticum and *Canticle*, a general address to or mention of creation in general precedes mention of specific creatures. Then they turn to the ranks of people, using a recurring refrain-address (*Laudate enm*, *Benedicite Domino*, *Laudato si, mi Signore*) until the conclusion of a cycle or sequence has been reached. Table 7 shows parallel texts of the poems' passages relating to people.

If one accepts the hypothesis that these liturgical passages may have furnished models for Francis' work, one can begin to understand why Francis felt at liberty to add to the *Canticle* the later stanzas relating to people. As his models incorporated references to humankind after their stanzas on creatures, Francis may well have considered his later additions quite fitting in that context.

The *Canticle*, while dependent on its models to some degree, also reveals many significant departures from them. The Psalm and the Canticum, through the use of a recurring refrain, address all levels of creation as if they were endowed with reason: sun, moon, stars, wind, as well as human beings. Francis, as we have seen, also addressed different creatures in various anecdotes remaining to us,[19] as well as in other Latin praises he composed.[20] But does he intend to address creatures in the *Canticle*? The Benedicite address of the Canticum (*Benedicite, omnia opera Domini, Domino*) seems to compare well to Francis' *Laudato si*. . . . Yet one cannot conclude immediately that similar form entails

TABLE 6. Textual Relationships between Psalm 148, the Canticum, and the *Canticle*

Psalm 148	Canticum	*Canticle*
	57 Benedicite, omnia opera Domini, Domino; *Laudate* . . .	5 *Laudato* Sie, mi Signore, cun tutte le tue creature
3 Laudate eum, *sol* et *luna*; Laudate eum omnes *stellae* et lumen	62 Benedicite, *sol* et *luna*, Domino; *Laudate* . . .	6 spezialmente messer lo frate *Sole* . . .
	63 Benedicite, *stellae* caeli . . .	10 *Laudato* Sie, mi Signore, per sora *Luna* e le *Stelle* . . .
8 Ignis, grando, nix, glacies, *spiritus procellarum*, Quae faciunt verbum eius . . .	65 Benedicite, omnes *spiritus* Dei, Domino . . .	12 Laudato . . . per frate *Vento*
	64 Benedicite, omnis imber et ros	13 e per Aere e *Nubilo* e sereno e *onne tempo*
	68 . . . rores et pruina	14 Per lo quale a le tue creature dai sustent–amento . . .
	70 . . . glacies et nives	
	73 . . . fulgura et *nubes*	
4 et *aquae* omnes quae super caelos sunt . . .	77 . . . *fontes* . . .	15 . . . per sor *Aqua*
	78 maria et flumina	
8 *Ignis* . . .	66 *ignis* et aestus	17 . . . per sor *Foco*
7 Luadate . . . de *terra*	74 *terra*	20 . . . per sora nostra matre *Terra*,/ la quale ne sostenta e governa,/ e produce diversi fructi con coloriti flori ed erba
9 . . . ligna fructifera, et omnes cedri	76 universa germinantia in terra	

similar meaning. Francis' phrasing is passive; that of the Canticum, active imperative. If Francis' purpose was to exhort all creatures to praise God, as the Canticum does, one must explain this unnecessary passive form and also the reasons Francis chooses to omit the Canticum's references, directly following the general exhortation, to the angels and powers of heaven praising God. Why would Francis include physical elements of creation and leave out others?[21]

There are other instances in which Francis' *Canticle* at first appears to resemble the Psalm or Canticum, yet upon closer inspection seems subtly to metamorphose into something quite different and distinct. For example, Francis' progression of sun, moon, and stars parallels both liturgical works. But when Francis next moves to the wind and air, clouds and

TABLE 7. Parallel Texts of Psalm 148, the Canticum, and the *Canticle* Relating to People

Psalm 148	Canticum	*Canticle*
11 Reges terrae et omnes populi,/ Principes et omnes judices terrae	82 Benedicite, filii Dominum, Domino, . . .	23 Laudato si, mi Signore, per quelli che perdonano per lo tuo amore . . .
12 Juvenes et virgines, senes cum junioribus laudent nomen Domini, Quia exaltatum est nomen eius solius. Confessio eius super caelum et terram/ Et exaltavit cornu populi sui./ Hymnus omnibus sanctis eius/ Filiis Israel, popolo appropinquanti sibi	85 Benedicite, servii Domini, Domino . . .	Beati quelli che
	86 Benedicite, spiritus et animae justorum . . .	25 'l sosterrano in pace,/ ca da te, Altissimo, sirano incoronati
	87 Benedicite, sancti et humiles corde, Domino . . .	

weather, in a passage which abbreviates several from the Canticum, the expressions in the *Canticle* diverge from the liturgical passages. Francis devotes much more time to description of creatures, whereas the other works seem most often merely to list them. Further, even when Francis' descriptions do link up with some in the two other texts—both the Psalm and *Canticle* associate the earth with fruits, for example—the *Canticle*'s descriptions commonly go far beyond the Biblical passages' neutral phrases by lyrically praising the creatures' admirable qualities. The Psalm's mere listing of *ligna fructifera* (fruit trees) as being one of the earth's products cannot begin to compare to Francis' ". . . our Sister, Mother Earth./ Who nourishes and governs us,/ And produces various fruits with many-colored flowers and herbs." Or for Sister Water: "She is very useful, and humble, and precious, and pure."

Further, in Francis' descriptions one begins to discover themes which move far beyond the liturgical works' simpler ideas of creatures merely praising their Creator. For instance, Francis' comments about the winds, air, and weather ("By which You give Your creatures nourishment," or his mention of the water's usefulness, seem to hint at more profound assumptions about the interlinkages between creatures and their relationships with humans and God.

Differences in style between the works also exist. While there are obvious similarities in stylistic devices, such as anaphora, the *Canticle* possesses a greater poetic complexity in its use of rhythm, alliteration, and evocation of emotion through expressive word choice. For example, compare these several factors in just two lines of the *Canticle*: *Altissimo omnipotente bon Signore* (the majestic opening invocation) and . . . *è molto utile e umile e preziosa e casta* (the charming gentle lyricism of Sister Water's claim to glory).

Can we account for the *Canticle*'s divergences in terms of other sources Francis knew and which might have influenced him? Or are these steps purely his own, purely original? How do these manifestations in the *Canticle* compare with what Francis had already achieved in his earlier poetry? And as far as the *Canticle*'s ideas and assumptions, just how much are these derived from its major liturgical sources, and how far are Francis' intentions different from these and from his earlier expressions? These are questions we shall explore further in the sections of the chapter ahead.

OTHER INFLUENCES ON THE *CANTICLE*

Other sources within the liturgy may have influenced Francis. One, mentioned by a few scholars[22] but not analysed in print, is the eleventh-century *prosa* (shown on p. 106 with Shepherd's translation) found in Roman-French missals, *Jubilemus omnes*.

This *prosa*, while obviously derived from Biblical sources similar to those in Francis' *Canticle*, goes beyond them in important ways. Like them it moves down through creation in a progression, ending with humankind. It addresses creation as if all its different parts were rational. But, unlike the Psalms and Canticum, it also has a clear poetic rhythm, it rhymes, and it compliments creation: "The sun, the ornament of the world," "The moon, the night's beauty." All these devices are found in Francis' *Canticle*, though Francis' complimentary description of creatures is less literary, more mystical and emotional. The midline pauses in some of its stanzas resemble the rhythms of medieval liturgical sequences that may have been in the "humus"[23] which produced the *Canticle*. The benedictory ending also bears a slight resemblance to both liturgical examples and the *Canticle*. Nevertheless, the influences of *Jubilemus omnes* and the sequences in relation to the *Canticle* must remain conjectural, since it is impossible to prove that Francis actually knew *Jubilemus omnes* or specific sequences.

Jubilemus omnes una, Deo nostro qui creavit omnia;
Per quem condita sunt saecula
Coelum quod plurima luce coruscat, et diversa sidera;
Sol mundi schema, noctium decus luna, cunctaque splendentia;
Mare, solum, alta, plana, et profunda flumina;
Aeris ampla spatia; quae discurrunt aves, venti atque pluvia.
Haec simul cuncta tibi soli Deo Patri militant.
Nunc et in aevum, sine fine per saecula:
Laus eorum tua gloria:
Qui pro salute nostra prolem unicam,
Pati in terra misisti sine culpa, sed ob nostra delicta.
Te, sancta Trinitas, precamur, ut corpora nostra
Et corda regas et protegas, et dones peccatorum veniam. Amen.[24]

Let us sing together to our God who created all things;
By whom all the ages were made;
The firmament, which shines with much light, and the various stars;
The sun, the ornament of the world; the moon, which is the night's beauty;
  and all shining things;
The sea, the land, the hills, the plains, and the deep rivers;
The wide space of the air, through which pass birds, and wind, and rain;
All these serve and obey thee alone, O God.
Now and ever more, for endless ages;
Their praise is thy glory;
Who for our salvation didst sent thine only-begotten Son,
In whom could be no sin, to suffer on earth for our sins.
We beseech thee, O holy Trinity, to govern and protect our
Hearts and bodies, and grant us forgiveness of our sins. Amen.

Similarly conjectural, though very intriguing, are possible influences on Francis from troubadour lyrics, some of which Francis undoubtedly loved and could recite.[25] Some troubadour poems are especially striking because of their *Natureingang*, an initial invocation of nature to set the tone for subjective emotional expressions. Consider the following examples.

When the new grass and the leaves come forth
and the flower burgeons on the branch,
and the nightingale lifts its high
pure voice and begins its song,
I have joy in it, and joy in the flower,
and joy in myself, and in my lady most of all;
on every side I am enclosed and girded with joy
and a joy that overwhelms all other joys.[26]

True God, in your name and Saint Mary's
I shall be wakeful from this day forth, for the morning star
rises toward Jerusalem and teaches me to say:
Arise, stand
you lords who love God,
day has come,
night passes on:
now let us praise
God and adore him;
and pray Him give us peace
all our days.
Night passes, day comes.
the heaven is calm and bright,
the dawn does not hold back,
it rises fair and full.[27]

These not-untypical Provençal lyrics, the first of which could have been reinterpreted to praise the Church or Lady Poverty,[28] and the second of which is openly religious,[29] combine a feeling for the natural environment with inner joy and a sense of mission that clearly fits the associations Francis made between French songs and creation. For example, one early incident in Francis' religious life occurred "as he went through a certain woods singing praises to the Lord in the French language."[30] These same themes of joy and mission occur directly connected with the *Canticle*'s origin, and in the *Legend of Perugia* and *Mirror of Perfection* accounts.[31] The *Legend of Perugia*, which the *Mirror of Perfection* follows closely,[32] relates that Francis

> wanted brother Pacifico, who in the world had been known as the king of verses and who had been a really courtly doctor of singers, to be sent for and given some good and holy friars that they might go through the world preaching and praising God. He said he wanted it that first one of them who knew how to preach should preach to the people and after the sermon they were to sing the Praises of God [the *Canticle*] as minstrels of the Lord. After the Praises he wanted the preacher to say to the people: "We are the Lord's minstrels and as our reward we want you to live in true penitence." He said: "For who are servants of the Lord unless in some measure they are his minstrels who ought to move the hearts of men and rouse them to spiritual joy?"[33]

According to this account, Francis conceived of his *Canticle* as a sort of Franciscan spiritualization of the type of poetry a troubadour minstrel might sing. God's troubadour, Francis, would give his verses to be sung by the former court poet, Pacifico. The friars would become the minstrels of the Lord (*joculatores Domini*).

Certain themes in the *Canticle* do indeed bear some similarity to popular lyrics of the time. For Francis, as well as for the troubadour poets, there was a subtle interplay, usually positive, between the natural setting and human experience. With these poets, in a different way than in Biblical sources, one senses that it is fitting for humans to be in the midst of creation, and to be happy there. Whereas Psalm 148 and the Canticum link humankind and creation together only through common praise of God, Francis and the troubadours link people to creation directly and emotionally—with love and joy. Creation's beauty inspires people to respond with joy to it and toward the poet's beloved, whatever that is conceived to be. In Francis' case, this is yet another aspect of his chivalric spirit, which bears on the *Canticle* particularly.

It would be narrow to believe that such poetry as these Provençal lyrics had no influence on the *Canticle*. The sense of joy and love pervading that work, the interest in and flattery of creation, probably reflect a debt to troubadour poetry, however much Francis' spontaneity and emotional range transcend the sometimes-plodding stylization of the troubadours. Since no certain sources here are evident, however, we should concentrate instead on more aspects of the relationship among some of Francis' works, their indisputable liturgical sources, and the *Canticle*.

Vicinelli: The Progression in Francis' Poetry

Vicinelli[34] has conducted a most interesting and intensive stylistic analysis of Francis' early writings, relating them to both liturgical sources and the later *Canticle*. He notes the similarity of theme and style even between certain passages of Francis' *Rules* and *Letters*, and *Canticle*, but concentrates especially on the literary evolution of Francis' poetry. According to Vicinelli, "From the Bible to the Laudes to the Laudi—it is an instinctive movement in Francis the poet."[35] He arrays Francis' works in a succession, moving from the *Exhortation* (1213), to the *Office*, to the *Salute to the Virtues*, the *Salute to the Virgin Mary*, the *Praise of God*, and the *Praises before the Office (LH)*. He sees in this succession a gradual development in style and rhythmic verse toward the *Canticle* and the later Italian *laudi*.

Though chronologically unverifiable, Vicinelli's conception of stylistic development is compelling and leads to important insights on that level.

It provides an intriguing microcosmic thematic study of custom and innovation in Francis' own works—thus allowing us to measure the growth of his originality.

Three of Francis' compositions prior to the *Canticle* have especially noteworthy similarities to it in terms of themes and source background. Deeper analysis of these works will provide a better perspective by which the *Canticle* may be considered in regard to the multifaceted originality present, Francis' intentions, and the historical setting.

The *Exhortation to the Praise of God*, which Vicinelli calls a sketch for Francis' *Canticle*,[36] is an early Latin work, probably written in 1213,[37] and is also known as the San Gemini Lauds. Its style is rough and awkward, and its Italianisms show that Francis had not fully mastered Latin.[38] It is a collection of excerpted and adapted texts from the Scriptures and the liturgy, which was inscribed on the altar cloth of a tiny hermitage chapel. Evidently, the altar also contained stylized representations of creatures. The whole unfortunately perished, being last seen during the Renaissance. As the *Exhortation* has remained obscure until the present, a translation of it follows.[39]

The Exhortation to the Praise of God

1 Fear the Lord and give him honor (Revelation 14:7)
2 Worthy is the Lord to receive praise and honor (Revelation 4:11)
3 All who fear the Lord, praise him (Psalm 21:24)
4 Hail Mary, full of grace, the Lord be with you! (Luke 1:28)
5 Praise him, heaven and earth! (Psalm 68:35)[40]
6 Praise the Lord, all rivers! (Daniel 3:78)
7 Bless the Lord, ye sons of God! (Daniel 3:82)[41]
8 This day hath the Lord made: let us rejoice and be happy in it. (Psalm 117:24)[42]
Alleluia, Alleluia, Alleluia, King of Israel! (John 12:13)
9 Let everything that breathes praise the Lord! (Psalm 150:6)
10 Praise the Lord, since it is good (Psalm 146.1); all who read this, Bless the Lord! (Psalm 102:21)[43]
11 All creatures, bless the Lord! (Psalm 102:22)
12 All birds of the air, praise the Lord! (Daniel 3:80)
13 All ye servants, praise the Lord! (Psalm 112:1)
14 Young men and maidens, praise the Lord! (Psalm 148:12)
15 Worthy is the Lamb which was slain to receive praise, glory, and honor (Revelation 5:12)
16 Blessed be the holy Trinity and the Unity Indivisible![44]
17 Holy Michael Archangel, defend us in battle![45]

The verses of the *Exhortation* manifest a deeply felt sense of vocation and mission. This very much fits the situation around the summer of 1213, as recorded by Celano and the *Fioretti*,[46] when Francis, after a period of doubt and hesitation, returned to his preaching mission with tremendous fervor, especially after his encounter with the birds. The composition may specifically reflect the effect of this transforming encounter for its particularly stresses, "All creatures bless the Lord/ All birds of the air praise the Lord."[47]

While the verses of the *Exhortation* are highly derivative in one sense, in that they mostly are a collage of Bible or missal passages, they often reflect something distinct, original, and representative of Francis' thought. That Francis selected the passages from the liturgy instead of inventing his own expressions should not make one averse to understanding the originality which actually is revealed by his particular selection. What if Francis had chosen the following verses instead?

> O that thou wouldst slay the wicked, O God,
> and that men of blood would depart from me. . . .
> As a rock which one cleaves and shatters on the land,
> so shall their bones be strewn at the mouth of Sheol.[48]

Some of the verses Francis selected have a formulaic creedal resonance, such as lines 4 and 16. But the impact of the praise Psalms is quite discernible, with selections proclaiming the Franciscan ideal that all humankind and all creation should humbly join in the praise and veneration of their Creator. Though clearly Francis' primary intentions in the *Exhortation* were consecratory and dedicatory, they also were proclamatory and directive. The verbs show constant repetition of the imperative or monitory subjunctive: *timete, laudate, benedicite, exultemus, laudet*. Further, the literal intent of the admonitions to praise God was underscored by the actual representations of creatures in conjunction with the *Exhortation*. None can doubt that the Francis who wrote the *Exhortation* was the Francis who preached to the birds, and that by this inscription he shows his desire that all his Order should admonish creatures similarly and praise the Lord with them. Nevertheless, he does not exactly address creation as directly with this expression as he would have done in his Sermon to the Birds: the *Exhortation*'s initial placement on the hermitage chapel's altar cloth would make it instead normative, confessional, and inspirational to the friars who would see it there.[49] Creation is addressed and told of its duty at second remove, so that the friar who reads the *Exhortation* will go forth and achieve the ideal described in the verses, that is, the exhortation to all creation to join him in praise of God.

Francis' *Salute to the Virtues* and *Praises before the Office (LH)* show many advances on the way from the *Exhortation* to the *Canticle*. Neither the *Salute* nor the *Praises* can be dated, though both must be later than the *Exhortation* because they are far more sophisticated and unified. The *Salute* moves from a Psalmic background toward the *Canticle* in several ways: It is more obviously morally didactic; its focus clearly alters from the invocations of the first lines to the elaborations and justifications of the inner sections; and it transcends Psalmic parallelism and attains a rhythmic form in lines broken into members by "et," resembling the Isidorean style of medieval poetry.[50] Its anaphora finds analogues both in the Psalms and the *Canticle*, and is a consistent device of Francis, appearing, for example, in the *Rules*,[51] and in the rapturous *Praises of God*, which resembles the *Canticle* also in its strong rhythms and end rhymes.[52]

Francis' *Praises before the Office*, though still linked to the Biblical Psalms and Canticles in form, phrasing, repeating refrain, and parallelism, has a somewhat broken rhythmic structure, verse sections of different lengths, and rhythmic echoes at verse beginnings, with assonances instead of exact psalmic repetition.[53] The *Praises* maintains an especially close relationship with the *Exhortation*—no less than four stanzas show very close resemblances and common Biblical sources.[54] Both begin with grave intonations, serene and austere addresses to God. But the *Exhortation*'s phrases cannot match the impressive accomplishment of the *Praises*. Even though its words are still highly derivative, the selection and flow are much more sophisticated and powerful in their expression of genuine religious devotion. The central sections of both contain references to creation and its praise of God, but the *Praises* emphasizes the duty of creation to reverence its Creator through the skillful expedient of a response refrain, a repeated "Let us praise him and glorify him for ever,"[55] which encloses such phrases as a much more apt and grander expression than some awkward ones in the *Exhortation*. The reference to birds has been dropped, and instead one finds the more all-embracing, "And every creature that is in heaven and on the earth and under the earth and such as are on the sea and all that are in them."[56] The end of both compositions leads out of the realm of creatures into the spiritual world again. One has gone cyclically from high to low and back again.

It should not be concluded, simply because Francis' expressions are derivative in these cases, that they were less impressive to his contemporaries. Rather, Francis' choice of liturgical formulae and Biblical passages

Salute to the Virtues[57]

Hail Queen Wisdom! The Lord save you,
  with your sister, pure, holy Simplicity.
Lady Holy Poverty, God keep you,
  with your sister, holy Humility.
Lady Holy Love, God keep you,
  with your sister, holy Obedience.
All holy virtues,
  God keep you
  God, from whom you proceed and come.
In all the world there is not a man
  who can possess any one of you
  without first dying to himself.
The man who practises one and does not offend against the others
  possesses all;
The man who offends against one,
  possesses none and violates all.
Each and every one of you puts
  vice and sin to shame.
Holy Wisdom puts satan and
  all his wiles to shame.
Pure and holy Simplicity puts
  all the learning of this world,
  all natural wisdom, to shame.
Holy Poverty puts to shame
  all greed, avarice,
  and all the anxieties of this life.
Holy Humility puts pride to shame,
  and all the inhabitants of this world
  and all that is in the world.
Holy Love puts to shame all the temptations
  of the devil and all the flesh
  and all natural fear.
Holy Obedience puts to shame
  all natural and selfish desires.
It mortifies our lower nature
  and makes it obey the spirit
  and our fellow men.
Obedience subjects a man
  to everyone on earth.
And not only to men,
  but to all the beasts as well
  and to the wild animals,
So that they can do what they like with him,
  as far as God allows them.

Praises Before the Office[58]

"Holy, holy, holy, the Lord God almighty,
Who was, and who is, and who is coming."[59]
Let us praise and glorify him for ever.

"Worthy art thou, O Lord our God,
to receive power and divinity
and wisdom and strength
and honour and glory and blessing."[60]
Let us praise and glorify him for ever.

Let us bless the Father and the Son and the Holy Spirit.
Let us praise and glorify him for ever.

"Bless the Lord, all the works of the Lord."[61]
Let us praise and glorify him for ever.

"Praise our God, all you his servants,
and you who fear him, the small and the great."[62]
Let us praise and glorify him for ever.

Praise him in his glory, heaven and earth, "and every creature
that is in heaven and on the earth and under the earth,
and such as are on the sea, and all that are in them."[63]
Let us praise and glorify him for ever.

Glory be to the Father, and to the Son, and to the Holy Spirit.
Let us praise and glorify him for ever.

As it was in the beginning, is now, and ever shall be,
world without end. Amen.
Let us praise and glorify him for ever.

PRAYER

All-powerful, all holy, most high and supreme God, sovereign good, all good, every good, you who alone are good, it is to you we must give all praise, all glory, all thanks, all honor, all blessing; to you we must refer all good always.[64]

allowed him to expound his ideas by using a vehicle that possessed the legitimacy and authority of unquestionable and traditional Christian sources. As Benz has proven in the cases of Christian visionary images, those expressions that are most traditional and best known are also quite moving and powerful in their emotional effect.[65]

Francis' *Canticle* contains many elements similar to these other works. Its general structure resembles those of the *Exhortation* and the *Praises* in that it begins with an address to God, then concerns itself with creation, and concludes by moving back again to spiritual matters and the mystery of divinity. Its liturgical background is evidenced not only by this structure, but by its anaphora and Latinate vocabulary, as we have seen earlier.

Nevertheless, the contrasts with Francis' earlier works, especially with the *Exhortation*, are striking. Originality in the *Canticle* is not a matter of selection and modification of sources, but of language, expressions, and intent. Its fresh and rustic Umbrian creates the same effect of vivid originality as that in Caedmon's hymn in Bede[66]—both works initiate Christian poetic expression in their respective vernaculars with a hymn of praise to God the Creator. Its expressions, while at times drawing effectively from liturgical passages,[67] demonstrate for the most part a striking independence from other sources and a refreshing inventiveness that is a new and true expression of the early Franciscan ideal.

The choice of language and expression, however, is important in another respect: Francis' intention in writing the *Canticle*. The *Exhortation* was written to dedicate and consecrate an obscure wayside chapel; the *Canticle*'s language and expression reveal entirely different purposes. As Vicinelli notes, the *Canticle*, while given by Francis to his Order, was clearly meant not only for the Order, but for all the faithful, since it broke with the saint's usual practice by appearing in Italian—thus linking it with the vernacular troubadour poetry and allowing a more widespread transmission. The most detailed accounts of its creation, found in the *Legend of Perugia* and the *Mirror of Perfection*, consistently link it with troubadour poetry and with Francis' conception of the friars as troubadours or jongleurs of God, as we have seen. The poem's popular characteristics are essential to its end. Its specific expressions eschew the more stylized and formalized literary modes, instead emphasizing simplicity, humility, and spontaneous emotional utterances, along with easy rhythm to facilitate memorization and understanding.[68] While its "ennobling"[69] Latinate terms and phrases raise its eloquence above common speech, they stem from common liturgical formulae well known to the faithful. The *Canticle* is clearly not meant to be obscure, esoteric, or literary, but, rather, popular and oral. It is a medieval attempt to propagandize.

6

The Controversy over the Canticle's *Meaning*

Given that the *Canticle* is an attempt to propagandize, what interpretation of creation did Francis intend to disseminate? What happens in the poem compared with Francis' earlier works and with the liturgical sources from which the *Canticle* arose?

To answer these questions, we will need to look at some crucial sections of the poem which have aroused a controversy with roots that go back as far as the thirteenth century. The controversy concerns the famous central stanzas of the poem which refer to various creatures, and especially lines 10, 12, 15, 17, 20, 23, and 27, which all contain a key phrase, *Laudato si . . . per*. For example, line 10 of the *Canticle*'s Italian text is *Laudato si, mi signore, per sora Luna e le Stelle*. The dispute focuses on how the lines with *per* in them should be understood. Of the several conflicting interpretations, we shall consider at length the two that have by far the greatest support in the early sources.[1] The older but currently less favored one interprets the *per* of the important lines as the Latin *propter*: because of, or for, as in "Be praised, my Lord, *for* Sister Moon and the Stars" (line 10). This has been termed the "causal" interpretation, and essentially envisages Francis exhorting humankind to join him in praise of God because of his creation's beauty and usefulness. The other, newer, interpretation sees the *per* as denoting the French *par* (by): "Be praised, my Lord, *by* Sister Moon and the Stars." This view suggests that creation itself be seen as an agent,[2] and pictures Francis looking upon creation and urging it to join him in a chorus of praise to God.

Some critics have seen the poem as essentially "polyvalent," with the *per* having both possible meanings. As Cunningham says, "both the idea of cosmic praise and constant thanksgiving occur in the writings of the saint. . . . My own inclination is to admit that double sense in light of the different readings that were given to the *Canticle* in the time of Francis himself."[3] This is a justifiable and reasonable position, since the arguments are delicate, and the assertion of essential ambiguity allows both interpretations full play and gives the poem a rich significance. Yet it is difficult to believe that Francis would consciously have inserted such an ambiguity into a poem of clearly spontaneous origin. Therefore, which idea was foremost in his mind at the time of the composition's origin?

CREATURES AS PRAISING GOD IN THE *CANTICLE*

This interpretation has many different sources of support. The two most important models for the *Canticle*, Psalm 148 and the Canticum of the Three Young Men, both exhort different creatures to praise God. Any other explanation must clearly show why Francis would have had a different intent in his *Canticle*, especially since on several other occasions he certainly did enjoin various things of creation to praise the Lord with him. For example, in his *Exhortation*, as we have seen, Francis incorporated the same liturgical texts' exhortations into his composition. Several well-known stories, not the least of which is the Sermon to the Birds, relate how he personally urged various things in creation, whether animate or inanimate, to praise the Creator.[4]

Certain passages in Celano and Bonaventure would seem to support this interpretation. The *Vita Prima* appears to allude to the *Canticle* in the following passages.

> He used to praise in public the perfection of their works and excellence of their [bees'] skill for the glory of God, with such encomiums [*praeconio*] that he would often spend a whole day praising them and the rest of creatures by lauds [*laudibus*]. For as of old the three youths in the fiery furnace invited all the elements to praise and glorify the Creator of the universe [*ad laudandum et glorificandum creatorem universitatis, elementa omnia invitabant*], so also this man never ceased to glorify, praise, and bless the Creator and ruler of all things in all elements and creatures [*in omnibus elementis et creaturis creatorem omnium ac gubernatorem glorificare, laudare, ac benedicere non cessabat*]. (*VP* 80)
>
> When he found an abundance of flowers, he preached to them and invited them to praise the Lord [*ita praedicabat eis et ad laudem eos dominicam invitabat*]. . . . In the same way he exhorted earth, fire, air, and wind, to love God and serve him willingly [*Sic et . . . terram et ignem, aerem et ventum sincerissima puritate ad divinum monebat amorem et libens obsequium hortabatur*]. (*VP* 81)

These passages clearly seem to support the interpretation of the *Canticle*, if they indeed do allude to it, in a way favoring the *per*-as-by argument. Much later, Celano, in his *Vita Secunda*, again refers to the *Canticle* as if it was intended to exhort creation to praise the Lord.

> He also invited all creatures to praise God, and by means of the words he had composed earlier, he exhorted them to love God. He exhorted death itself, terrible and hateful to all, to give praise [*Invitabat etiam omnes creaturas ad laudem Dei, et per verba quaedam quae olim composuerat, ipse eas ad divinum hortabatur amorem. . .*].[5]

If one accepts this interpretation, which has some support in the early documents, what should one then conclude about Francis' originality in this central issue of the *Canticle*? In modern eyes, this interpretation would be more striking than to medieval analysts, for to us it is unusual to see creation envisioned in an active rather than a passive, abstract, objectified sense ("the laws of nature"). It strikes us as romantic or pantheistic in derivation. Thus it is not surprising to see modern authors mistaking the *Canticle* as an essentially un-Christian expression.[6] Yet this modern reaction receives absolutely no confirmation in any early source. Those who interpret the *Canticle* seeing *per* as agent (Celano and Bonaventure, among others) react very positively to it and seem to consider it authentically Christian. The reason is not at all that they saw something *new* in it—on the contrary, they saw it (yet again) as affirming and putting into practice an ancient Christian concept superbly similar to other Franciscan efforts to revive authentically Christian beliefs in a more literal manner of statement and practice. They saw it not as something new, but as tradition restored. Thus they compared it either to the Canticum or to Psalm 148. Moderns would respond, "But these two expressions are quite rare and untraditional ones, only uncommonly seen in the Christian community,"[7] and perhaps (with the Canticum especially) even of somewhat dubious orthodoxy in origin.

This view is extremely unmedieval. The medieval response would rather have been that these expressions have been established in such a commonplace way that they have instead been completely taken for granted. Moderns must realize that Francis, along with huge numbers of his devout contemporaries, would have recited Psalm 148 at Lauds as a regular (and perhaps tedious) custom countless mornings of his religious life, and would have recited the Canticum every Sunday for the same part of the Office. Furthermore, we have seen that other liturgical hymns or "proses," with which Francis may have been familiar, echo the same sentiments. Seen in this context, Francis' *Canticle* would have been noteworthy as a restatement and reaffirmation of ancient and well-known Christian precepts that, although found in the everyday liturgy, were not imitated or put into practice as often as Francis' particular way of life permitted. This is exactly the context in which one should see the statements of Celano (*VP* 80–81) and Bonaventure (*ML* 9:1), both of which seem to refer to the *Canticle* and compare it as a matter of course with the Canticum or liturgical Psalms.

Thus the central part of the *Canticle* relating to creation may have been seen in its own time as nontraditional, only in a very limited sense, if at all. The originality would be seen in the fact that Francis chose what had been old and commonly known ideas to restate well and follow with success in a literal and practical way. The rest of Francis' life was obviously devoted to other expressions which demonstrated his love for created things—and it is precisely this context in which the hagiographers place their positive references to the *Canticle*. I would maintain that these hagiographers may not have focused on it at great length because, with the liturgical statements well in mind, they had no need to stress a startling originality that in fact they could not see, except in the context of Francis' other actions showing that he literally and concretely adhered to the sentiments expressed in the *Canticle*. A re-reading of *VP* 80–81, *VS* 217, and *ML* 9:1 will confirm that this is their actual viewpoint. Although their view possessed a truth of its own, it also neglected some of the essential originality in Francis' expressions, including the *Canticle*. Its special synthesis of Francis' thought was too easily glossed over or ignored.

THE *CANTICLE* AS THANKSGIVING FOR AND APPRECIATION OF CREATURES

Other early sources found quite a different interpretation of the *Canticle* (and many modern scholars would agree with this), in which the *per* is understood as causal (as in "Be praised, my Lord, because of all you have made"). At first this might seem to lessen the apparent originality of the *Canticle* by seeing it merely as another Christian prayer of thanksgiving to God for creation. However, if one accepts the setting given in the other early sources, then the *Canticle* is much more radical and original than this—and indeed much more radical in essence than the interpretation which would see *per* as agent. For the interpretation of *per* as causal implies a view of the *Canticle* that few have considered at length and that possesses a striking power of its own. It depicts the *Canticle* as the positive, injunctive form of an extremely unusual and forceful accusation by Francis—that medieval society does not appreciate creation and is not grateful for creatures' benefits to humanity.[8] Such a direct, outspoken criticism coupled with a positive injunction is, so far as I know, unique for Francis' time and perhaps unparalleled in medieval history before him.

We have already seen that through arguments concerning the places and times of the *Canticle*'s composition, the authority of the accounts of *LP* 43 and *LP* 119 has been substantially validated.

Here again is an instance where Celano's account cannot stand as final authority against the more detailed and informative *Legend*. Early secondary authors such as Ubertino da Casale[9] strongly associate the *Legend* chapters with Brother Leo and Francis' inner circle, and many researchers believe that these segments are among those that go back directly or indirectly to the *rotuli* of Leo and the other brothers compiled before Celano's *Vita Secunda* in 1244.[10] Some analysts even believe that at least one manuscript of the *Legend* chapters may date from c. 1250.[11] If these chapters do stem early from the inner circle (and in my opinion, the arguments here are compelling), its evidence is of crucial importance, and deserves careful study.

According to *LP* 43, Francis received a vision in the night, which informed him that he should "be glad and joyful in the midst of your infirmities and tribulations: as of now, live in peace as if you were already sharing my kingdom." The morning after this vision (called the *certificatio*), Francis awoke and joyfully told his companions about it. Then he said:

> Therefore, for His glory, for my consolation, and the edification of my neighbor [*ad laudem eius et ad nostram consolationem et ad hedificationem proximi*] I wish to compose a new "Praises of the Lord" concerning his creatures [*novam laudem Domini de suis creaturis*]. These creatures minister to our needs every day; without them we could not live; and through them the human race greatly offends the Creator. Every day we fail to appreciate so great a blessing by not praising as we should the Creator and Dispenser of all these gifts. He sat down, concentrated a minute, and then cried out: "Most High, all-powerful, and good Lord . . . [*quibus cotidie utimur et sine quibus vivere non possumus et in quibus humanum genus multum offendit Creatoreum et cotidie sumus ingrati tante gratie, quia inde nostrum Creatorem et datorem omnium bonorum sicut deberemus non laudamus. . .*]. (*LP* 43)

The *Mirror of Perfection* chapters that discuss the composition of the *Canticle* relate the story using, quite often, exactly the same phrases (*MP*

100–101). The *Mirror* account clearly derives from the *Legend*. A later *Mirror* chapter refers back to the circumstances of the *Canticle*'s origin, discussing Francis' attitudes and circumstances surrounding the event with internal consistency.

> Above all creatures unendowed with reason he had a particular love for the sun and for fire. He used to say, "At dawn, when the sun rises, all men should praise God, who created him for our use, and through him gives light to our eyes by day. And at nightfall every man should praise God for Brother Fire, by whom He gives light to our eyes in the darkness. For we are all blind, and by these two brothers of ours God gives light to our eyes, so we should give special praise to our Creator for these and other creatures that serve us day by day. . . ." And since in Holy Scripture the Lord Himself is called The Sun of Justice, and because blessed Francis thought the sun the loveliest of God's creatures and most worthy of comparison with Him, he gave its name to the Praises of God concerning His creatures *which he had written when the Lord had assured him of his kingdom*. (*MP* 119) [emphasis added]

Both accounts, then, describe the same attitude of thankfulness associated with the *Canticle*'s purpose, and hark back to the same event—the *certificatio*—as being responsible for its creation.

The only instance (*VS* 213) in which Celano specifically mentions the *Canticle* relates also the same story of Francis' illness and dream, as the *Legend* does, clearly setting it near the approximate time of Francis' death. But when Celano discusses the *Canticle*, he says only, "It was at this time that he composed the Praises of the Creatures, and inflamed them as much as he could to praise their Creator" (*Laudes de creaturis tunc quasdam composuit, et eas utcumque ad Creatorem laudandum accendit*). The account omits how Francis came to compose the *Canticle*, as the information is clearly irrelevant to Celano's chapter, which concerns itself with what Francis was promised for his infirmities. But in attaching the *Canticle*'s origin to the *certificatio* incident, he unwittingly undercuts his own interpretation of the *Canticle* here, in *VS* 217, and in *VP* 80–81, for he ties it to the *LP* account that gives its own very detailed explanation in careful sequence, deriving thus its different interpretation. Nowhere can Celano or Bonaventure match the *Legend*'s thoroughness. One is tempted to conclude that, at least in this sequence of events, the *Legend* is simply more complete and more correct than Celano's account because Celano often abbreviated his earlier sources.

Accepting the *Legend-Mirror* view of *per* as causal not only systematically defines *per* as for, or because of. It also accounts for Francis' striking use of a curious verb form, *laudato si*, the passive imperative, as opposed to his other expressions, unquestionably meant to exhort creation to praise God, in which he uses the normal imperative. For if Francis wished the sun to praise God, why did he not simply speak directly to it, in the form he had used so many times before: "Praise God, O Brother Sun . . ."? Similar direct exhortations occur in the *Exhortation* and the *Praises before the Office*, which obviously envision an ideal situation in which humankind and the rest of creation unite in praise of God. As far as specific actions are concerned, when Francis on one occasion found a cicada at the Portiuncula, he said to it, "Sing, my sister cricket, and praise your Creator with a joyful song" (*VS* 171). The cricket obeyed, and Francis joined in with his own *laud* (*suam laudem interserens*). His Sermon to the Birds represents, of course, another notable parallel.

However, if one accepts the *Legend* interpretation, one overcomes this difficulty easily. For it is not primarily creation that would be exhorted to praise God, but *people*, because of their offensive ingratitude to God. Thus the *per* would be interpreted as "Be praised, my Lord, (*by humankind*) for (because of) Sister Moon and the stars."

Further support for this interpretation may be found in the anecdotes. Readers of the early Franciscan sources should remember the line would signify, "Be praised, my Lord, *together with* all your creatures" by *humanity*. This is exactly what the poem would mean: an exhortation to humankind to praise God and his creatures along with him.

Further, this motive would explain in a very direct way several original elements of the poem not present in its models and not accounted for with the *per*-as-by argument. Francis, unlike the authors of the Canticum and Psalm 148, flatters the elements of creation. The sun is "Sir Brother Sun," the fire is "handsome . . . how happy, how powerful and strong." Also, the elements' *usefulness to humankind is* emphasized. The sun "brings the day and you give light to us through him." Water is "so useful and humble"; earth "sustains and governs us." These two kinds of comments, vitally original to the poem, simply have no intrinsic purpose if the poem's point is to exhort creation to praise God. On the other hand, if one accepts the *Legend-Mirror* account of Francis' intentions in the poem, their presence is absolutely essential. They justify the worth of creation and express its value, opposing those who "fail to appreciate so great a blessing" (*LP* 43). The elements and creatures are beautiful, useful, and symbolic (the sun, for example, signifies God).

The *per*-for interpretation, with the aid of the *Legend* account, well explains why Francis composed the *Canticle* in his native Umbrian, rather than the Latin of its models. If Francis wished to exhort creatures to praise

God, why would he alter his normal poetic expression from Latin to Umbrian? One assumes that divine will could have allowed the creatures addressed to understand Latin just as well as Italian. On the other hand, if Francis wished his friars to disseminate the *Canticle* as troubadours of God, the saint's choice of Umbrian represents a thoughtful step taken to popularize his opinions, in the same manner that troubadour songs were spread, by using the vernacular to reach his fellow townspeople and peasants. The *Legend* account, and the *per*-as-for interpretation, are the only ones to make full sense of Francis' decision here.

Finally, this interpretation explains another problem—why Francis would have thought it fitting to add to the *Canticle* his later stanzas relating to people who grant pardon and live in peace (lines 23–26). The stanzas on creatures and on forgiving reflect the same pattern of thought and response on Francis' part. In both cases, people have been neglectful, and Francis feels pain when he thinks of their actions (for the story of the later stanzas' origin, see *LP* 44). In the first case, humankind has neglected to respect and appreciate creatures. Francis does not choose to upbraid humankind (as he might have by writing another letter), but instead urges it to make up for its lack by imitating his praise of the creatures' virtues before God. He leads by example. Similarly, when Francis hears that the bishop and *podestà* of Assisi have quarreled, he feels pain. All have forgotten the greatness of those who are forgiving. But again, instead of upbraiding the bishop and *podestà* directly, he follows the pattern set earlier in the *Canticle*: he personally gives praise to God for the virtues of those who are forgiving, and thus aims to motivate the neglectful to follow him in putting these virtues into play. Again a negative criticism leads to a positive injunction. Interestingly enough, those involved in the conflict got Francis' message clearly. They do not perceive that the *Canticle* is intended to make them praise God (as it is not intended to exhort creatures to praise God), and they do not praise him. Rather, they take the *Canticle* as we have interpreted its meaning, and follow Francis in appreciating the virtues of those who forgive. Bishop and *podestà* are reconciled.

Conclusions

In this case, our study supports the explanations of motivation that arise from the *Legend*'s detailed, continuous narrative rather than from the edifying, philosophizing, or generalizing accounts in Celano. I believe that for Francis and his intimates, the *Legend of Perugia* account of the *Canticle*'s origin gives the intended meaning. But Celano's more distanced mind—one more trained than Francis in abstraction, generalization, and recognition of earlier sources—classified the poem differently, and led him to see a more traditional origin and interpretation, one that every devout Christian could relate to because of its obvious links with daily liturgical passages. This was (and is) a legitimate interpretation, which presumably gained much currency after the proliferation of Celano's text. Later, Bonaventure's *Legenda Maior* supported Celano's interpretation and perpetuated it after the 1266 prohibition of all other writings about Francis save Bonaventure's.

Both interpretations were current in the thirteenth century, and both are indisputably Christian, as well as Franciscan. That view which saw the *Canticle* as an invocation to creation would not have considered that invocation itself as original, except insofar as it had been produced by a recent author whose life demonstrated that he took Biblical pronouncements seriously and literally. That Francis also flattered the elements of creation and showed why people should appreciate them in the *Canticle* is something moderns would see as striking and new. However, those who interpreted the *Canticle* as an invocation did not see this as especially significant though they might point out that Francis did only what he was reported to have done according to other stories.

On the other hand, those who were intimates of Francis believed that the *Canticle* was not an invocation to creation, but an exhortation to humanity, intended (*LP* 43) *ad hedificationem proximi*—for the spiritual instruction of those around Francis, as well as for dissemination by the friars as Umbrian troubadours of God. In gratitude to God, Francis had composed a *Canticle* to thank him and his creatures who ministered to human needs. This account makes the message of the *Canticle* appreciative and ecological.[12] It is appreciative in that people are instructed to value creation on at least three levels: the symbolic (the sun as signifying God), the aesthetic (Brother Fire as beautiful), and the utilitarian (the sun gives light, the earth feeds people). It is ecological in that it explicitly rejects a view of creation that would objectify it and take it for granted as being worthless and irrelevant unless it proves serviceable to humanity. Francis' answer to this view is a vision of creation that emphasizes not only its usefulness to people, but also its intrinsic qualities—its worth apart from humanity's needs, a worth gained from its specific divine endowment, which merits notice and respect. As Doyle says,

> We are in nature's debt, a debt we must acknowledge in order to cooperate with her and to be able to recognize the inherent value of all creatures. . . . Nature has a meaning-in-itself because it is created by God, it does not have its value or meaning purely from man.[13]

Even this, however, sounds distant and abstract compared to the intimacy and individual emphasis of Francis' "Be praised, my Lord, for Brother Fire. . . . How handsome he is, how happy!" Any abstract analysis takes away the qualities of loving closeness and sincere individual appreciation Francis showed to creatures.

This sense of intimacy with, dependence on, and appreciation for the things in creation stemmed from Francis' new synthesis of ascetic ideals, evangelical fervor, and poetic talent first expressed many years earlier. The *Canticle* represents the final and greatest expression of this complex vision of the universe, and we shall examine it as such in our next chapter. The *Canticle* did not simply spring from Francis' "sadness at man's misuse of creatures"[14] at the time of its composition. Its roots went very deep. Many earlier incidents show that Francis was indeed concerned about humanity's misuse of creatures, and the *Canticle* provides proper justification for human concern for animals. Creation's humble service to people would surely merit reciprocation; its independent beauty, good qualities, and symbolic significance added to its value and gave solid grounds for humanity's respect. From this perspective the *Canticle* may rightly be seen as a very rare medieval document, in that its main purpose is to inspire people and teach them how to think of creation with gratitude, appreciation, and respect. That is a part of its essential originality, and to some extent it merits Doyle's daring when he asserts, "I will be forgiven the rather gross anachronism in saying that the ecological problem had its influence on the composition of the Canticle of Brother Sun."[15]

7

The Canticle*: Francis' Ideal Vision of Creation*

LEVELS OF APPRECIATION IN THE *CANTICLE* NATURE-SEGMENTS

Whether or not one accepts the conclusion presented in Chapter 6, one cannot deny that the segments of the *Canticle* relating to physical creation reveal a deep appreciation of the natural environment. In the *Canticle* may be seen one of the subtlest and most beautiful of developments—that of an aesthetic appreciation for the things of creation delicately unfolding itself, born from the womb of the sacred. This is one of the most moving of Francis' achievements, not because it is unparalleled in Christian thought, but rather because Francis, unschooled and unintellectual, did it himself. It arose from the joy he felt amid the things of creation even as a youth and from his sure grasp of Christian doctrine and modes of expression. It was his own achievement, a product of his personal experiences[1] and his grasp of the potential to enhance old forms and expressions. Fully accepting traditional Christian doctrine, Francis emphasized that creation's author was God, and that its duty was to serve him and his highest creation, humankind.[2] Francis' praise of creation also revealed his conception of creation's autonomous beauty and worth. In addition, the *Canticle* provides a detailed sketch of the complex relationship he saw among God, humankind, and other creatures. Let us examine Francis' assumptions in these areas, along with the several different levels on which he chose to appreciate creatures in the *Canticle*: the levels of ontogeny, utility, beauty, fraternity, symbolism, and the sacraments.

Biblical Links and Traditional Attitudes Found in the Poem

Francis' observations of and appreciation for creation were nurtured by the Biblical passages we have seen—passages which, more than any other sources, directed his attention to creatures, enhanced their value, sensitized his perception of them, and gave justification for their essential goodness. The other levels of insight found in the *Canticle* rest on this base.

Francis' first reference to creation in the *Canticle* occurs in the stirring line 5, which alludes to Genesis and the Psalms: "Be praised, my Lord, with all your creatures"—an invocation of God which accents the splendid panoply of his creation. The positive attitude of the statement, assuming that the universe of creatures is a valuable, good, and glorious thing for which God should be thanked and praised, sets the tone for all the following lines. The Scriptures provide the justification for seeing creation as essentially good due to its divine origin. In an allusion to Genesis directly after (line 7), Francis connects the sun with divine providence, when he describes it as the one "who brings the day, and you give light to us through him." He thus stresses from the first the creature's origin in God and duty to humankind. This Biblical appreciation of creation in terms of its divinely allotted function and usefulness to men recurs in several other instances. Brothers Wind and Air, "Cloud, and Clear, and all weather" are useful in that by them, "you give your creatures nourishment." Sister Water is "very useful, and humble, and precious, and pure." The theme reaches a climax with "Our Sister, Mother Earth, who nourishes and governs us, and produces various fruits with many-colored flowers and herbs."

Francis links creatures with the Bible in another manner. Often Francis tends to connect creatures with scriptural passages which refer to them specifically, in much the same fashion as moderns might call to mind Shelley's poetic description of clouds while musing on the subject. This is another reflection of what one might call the "specificity" in Francis' view of creation. For instance, Francis' "Sister Moon and the Stars, in heaven you have formed them," alludes to their specific mention in Genesis 1:14. This is similar to the incident in Francis' Sermon to the Birds, when Francis addressed the fowl and cited the famous Matthew 6:26: "Consider the birds of the air."

Likewise, Francis could show his esteem for various creatures by thinking of them in terms of Biblical symbolism. Celano maintains that this was Francis' way of showing special respect and appreciation for them

(*VP* 77). In the *Canticle*, this occurs when Francis notes that the sun "bears the likeness" of the Lord; this mystical symbolism harks back to Malachi 4:2 (*MP* 119). Anecdotes show Francis treating creatures with special respect when he linked them with scriptural passages of mystical symbolism.[3] Francis even conserves trees, remembering the wood of the cross (*MP* 119; *VS* 165), and spares flowers "out of love for Him who is called 'The Rose on the plain and the Lily on the mountain slopes'" (*MP* 119).

But the medieval background of this practice should not be glossed over in attempts to see Francis' views only in a modern light. The symbolic association Francis made here resembles those made in medieval bestiaries,[4] even though there is a new and characteristically Franciscan stress on allegories of Christ. It was a level of appreciation long supported by Christian tradition, however foreign it seems today.

In another pattern which clearly relates to the medieval setting, Francis seems to connect the elements with the sacraments. Water is "useful, and humble, and precious, and pure"—a description presumably referring on one level to its connection with baptism and penitence.[5]

Flattery and "Enfraternization"

Francis most certainly breaks new ground in his appreciation of creatures by giving them flattering titles, as we have seen. One researcher believes that the fraternal or familial titles (as opposed to the chivalric) reflects Francis' view of creation as a huge religious order.[6] But this probably limits the connotations of the words too strictly. What seems more likely is that Francis, uniquely, "enfraternizes all creation in God"[7]—accepting the creatures into his spiritual family as brothers and sisters. Thus he introduces us to "Brother Fire" and "Sister Water." The tenderness and feeling in this action should not be doubted, since Francis, in a very emotional and final way, had given up his first family (*VP* 10–15), and reached out in turn to his friends, followers, and fellow creatures to find his second family. It is this emotional background which assures us that Francis' salutations meant more than a simple reflection of creation as a gigantic Franciscan Order. Thus Francis can see the earth as both sister (connoting affection), and mother (reverence and fertility).[8] Similar reverence combined with affection underlie the title "Sir brother Sun." Francis' feeling of brotherly love for the sun is united with a sort of spiritualized chivalric deference to the orb which signifies Christ. Such familial acceptance and chivalric titles or flattery given in deference to creatures are classic and consistent expressions of Francis' original additions to Christian spirituality.[9]

The titles "brother," "sister," or "mother" do not imply any pantheistic or pan-psychic view of creatures, since Francis' conceptions of them were rooted soundly in Christian doctrine. They are rather a way of showing in a poetic and emotional way Francis' affection for and affinity with creatures.

Other descriptive themes in these lines also fulfill the same purposes. When Francis calls Sister Water humble and pure, or Brother Fire happy, he does not mean (as Doyle aptly points out) to "romanticize nature by reading human reactions and qualities into non-rational creatures."[10] Such implicit personifications instead serve to link humankind with creatures in a positive emotional manner, aiding people to identify with them and feel their kinship with them. Francis' point is the opposite of romanticization or mystification: By implicitly humanizing creatures through these affective links, he makes it easier for others to share his bond with creatures. One might compare this process to Francis' attempt to recreate the Nativity physically at Christmas through the crèche. Such humanizing produced a powerful effect on observers and strengthened their human sympathy for the infant Christ (*VP* 84–85).

Structure as a Vehicle for Emotional Originality in the Poem

The poem's introduction acknowledges God's greatness and ineffability in a grand proclamation, ending with "And no man is worthy to pronounce Your name." The bridge passage, "Be praised, my Lord, with all your creatures," begins to shift the emphasis to creation, at first to express Francis' appreciation to God *for* it. But the description of creatures that follows swiftly turns into a passionate justification *for their appreciation*. The awe and deep reverence at the beginning change to expressions of delight and rapturous enjoyment—a characteristic emotional reaction of Francis to the environment, as his biographers witness (*LP* 49; *VP* 80). The measured rhythm and careful structure of the poem break down, yielding to a long, lyrical outburst in praise of the sun: "Especially Sir Brother Sun,/ Who brings the day; and you give light to us through him./ How handsome he is, how radiant, with great splendor!/ Of you, Most High, he bears the likeness." The last phrase allows a reduction of emotion and neatly reconnects the creature with the exalted Creator addressed at the poem's beginning.

The next lines (10–19) follow the same pattern in discussing various creatures. The repeating bridge passage ("Be praised . . .") voicing appreciation *for* creatures leads into rapturous praise *of* creatures. The special spontaneous joy of these lines shows itself several times where the Italian is marked by short descriptions punctuated by "and"—producing a vivid impression of the breathless wonder Francis felt when looking upon the creatures. Often these same lines are accentuated further by beautiful inner rhymes, producing a remarkable effect: *sora Luna e le Stelle . . . formate clarite e preziose e belle*; *frate Vento,/ e per Aere e Nubilo e Sereno e onne tempo*; *sor Aqua . . . utile e umile a preziosa e casta*; *frate Foco . . . ed ello è bello e iocondo e robustoso e forte*.[11] Rarely has simple spontaneous joy been so well rendered. The lightness of the short, often monosyllabic nouns or adjectives reveals an attitude of childlike delight and sincerity worlds away from the more literary and stylized descriptions of creation common in many earlier secular or liturgical Latin antecedents of the *Canticle*. These lines are the expression of that joy and mystical exultation Francis experienced when he contemplated creatures or the natural environment.[12] The *Canticle*'s early grandeur and solemnity begins to return only with the Mother Earth stanzas (20–22), in which the "and . . . and" (*e . . . e* in the Italian) pattern is lost—a stylistic transition which allows for the mood change of the darker last verses.

In these crucial lines (10–22), one sees Francis' appreciation of creatures growing from the more traditional expressions in medieval spirituality (the appreciation of creation in Biblical, symbolic, and sacramental terms) to his very personal spiritual view of creation: the "enfraternization" of creatures and the honoring of them with titles in spiritualized chivalric deference. This enriched spiritual appreciation, involving Francis' deeper personal appreciation of creation's autonomous physical beauty and worth, leads to an original mode of poetic expression when Francis reveals the emotions of joy, exhilaration, and admiration he feels when he thinks of various creatures. In a simple and childlike way, each creature is praised—its best physical qualities are described with wonder and enthusiasm. It is this unaffected sense of loving personal connection with and approval of individual creatures which gives the poem its unique spirit and aesthetic and which is one of its greatest original contributions to Christian attitudes toward the environment.[13]

Thus the poem's emphasis shifts subtly in the early lines. While the *Canticle* begins by expressing Francis' appreciation to God *for* creatures, it leads to Francis' expressions of appreciation *of* the creatures themselves in his effort to stimulate gratitude for creation in others. Ideas from Francis' scriptural and spiritual background provided the foundation upon which his appreciation *for* creation could produce a deeper appreciation *of* creation, in its physical beauty and autonomy. The tension between these two motivations produces the complexity of this section of the poem.

However one stresses these new and original elements, though, one should not forget the traditional base and fund of expressions Francis also draws on in the poem. The *Canticle*'s synthesis represents an organic growth from Christian spiritual aesthetic to a physical and poetic one. To ignore the former and see only the latter is to attempt to understand and appreciate a child without knowing its mother.

INTERDEPENDENCE IN THE *CANTICLE*

While Francis unquestionably praised the physical beauty and affirmed the autonomous worth of creatures in his *Canticle*, one should not interpret this in isolation. For just as Francis' appreciation of creatures had many levels, so his understanding of the creatures' position in the universe exceeded his observation of their autonomous existence and value, however significant this was. For in speaking of autonomy one must ask: "in relation to what?" In the *Canticle*, Francis assumed that there was a complex, multifaceted relationship implying much interdependence among creation, humanity, and God. While creation and humankind each had a certain autonomous character, creation at times served people and humankind depended on the aid of creation. Both depended on and served God. In other places, Francis envisioned people subordinating themselves to creation in obedience,[14] and creatures depending on human consideration and respect for their well-being.[15]

Many of these relationships are illustrated succinctly by what Francis says of Brother Sun. By invoking God the Maker of all (*Laudato sie . . . cun tutte le tue creature*), Francis reminds all creatures (including people) that their origin and continued existence depends on divine will. The allusion to Genesis in the case of Sister Moon and the Stars (*in cielo l'hai formate*) makes this more concrete. The sun functions according to divine plan, bringing in the day (*lo quale è iorno*). As the sun relies on God for its origin and continuing function, people rely on the sun to do its duty (*e allumini noi per lui*). The sun serves in another way: it points humans to God in that it functions as a natural symbol of God (*de te, Altissimo, porta significazione*). Amid all this occurs Francis' ecstatic praise of the sun's physical beauty (*Ed ello è bello e radiante cun grande splendore*).

Francis does not elaborate specifically on any relationships between God, people, and Sister Moon and the Stars. But his allusion to Genesis in the verses pertaining to them call to mind their functions established at creation: to rule the night, to be signs and markings for dates, and to light the earth.[16] The wind and weather help God give sustenance to other creatures (*Per lo quale a le tue creature dai sustentamento*). Francis may not only allude to rain and snow, but also to the famous fertilizing spring wind of the troubadour poets.[17] With Sister Water Francis actually employs the adjective "useful" (*utile*), which appears amid other terms clearly intended to be laudatory (*utile e umile e preziosa . . .*). His choice of description shows that he not only regards water as useful in drinking, but associates it with its function in baptism.[18]

Similarly with Brother Fire, utility and interdependence return as themes. By lighting up the night, Fire fulfills its function and aids people.[19] With both Water and Fire, descriptive terms linking them emotionally to people (*umile*, *casta*, *jocondo*) subtly emphasize the close relationship between each element and humankind.

There can be no doubt, either, that with Mother (and Sister) Earth, Francis primarily thinks in terms of usefulness, this time in the particular sense of productiveness (*la quale ne sostenta e governa,/ e produce diversa fructi con coloriti flori ed erba*).[20] The conception of Mother Earth as "governing" in some way is an unusual one for Francis, and its meaning is not immediately apparent from the other expressions in his thought. Possibly it represents an attempt, working through popular expressions rather than philosophy, to struggle toward an idea of Nature as presiding over the order of creation and sustaining it through its fertility.[21] As such it would be unique in Francis' compositions. Its character as a philosophical statement should not be exaggerated, however, as it arises not from philosophy but from poetic expression and the closeness of the early Franciscans to the outlook of hermits and laborers in the fields. Probably all Francis wishes to say in the phrase *la quale ne sostenta e governa* is that people should thank the Earth for sustaining them through the bountiful crops she produces, in the amount she determines, and in the seasons she allots.

In a few other instances, as we have seen, Francis considers humans to be in some ways subordinate to specific creatures. According to Francis, humans should not only submit themselves to other people, "but to all the beasts as well/ and to the wild animals,/ So that they can do what they like with him,/ as far as God allows them."[22] The anecdote which tells of Francis' regret at not giving Brother Fire his cloak when the fire wanted it may illustrate what Francis means here (*LP* 50). Francis and his brothers depended on the fire at night; perhaps because of this intimacy and dependence he considered that the fire should be respected and allowed its wishes in return. Elsewhere, as we have seen, when Francis is disturbed by mice, he seems to make no effort to stop this annoyance, but submits to them, considering they represent a temptation by the Devil which (implicitly) God must wish Francis to endure.[23]

In these instances, Francis' submission to creatures reaches a questionable extreme. Francis' ideas of interdependence, respect, and obedience might well lead to the conclusion that people should submit to creatures animate or inanimate, even when they threaten property, health, or sanitation. While moderns would shy away from such remarkable leniency toward creatures and demanding requirements of people as another of Francis' idealistic yet very impractical views, the saint undoubtedly would reply that this reaction shows not only a disrespect for creatures' wishes, but a lack of trust in God, who governs all creatures for their benefit. As Francis says, a person should obey creatures' wishes "so that they can do what they like with him,/ as far as God allows them." Francis seems to imply that God would restrain his creatures in cases where their desires or demands were inordinate or unfitting. In fact, just this sort of restraint appears to occur in two anecdotes. In one of them, a greedy baby robin receives his due.

> For when the bigger one had had his fill as he wished, he drove the rest away from the food. "See," said the father, "see what this greedy one is doing. Even though he is full and satisfied, he envies his hungry brothers. He will come to a bad end yet." The revenge followed quickly upon the words of the saint. The disturber of his brothers got up on a vessel of water to drink and immediately fell into the water and, suffocating, died. No cat was found nor any beast that would touch the bird that had been cursed by the saint. (*VS* 47)

Divine vengeance, working through the saint's curse, descended upon the unjust creature. Similarly, a greedy sow was disciplined for killing a newborn lamb.

> Upon rising the next morning, the men found the lamb dead and they knew that the sow was guilty of the evil deed. When the kind father heard this, he was moved to wonderful compassion, and, remembering another lamb, he grieved over the dead lamb, saying before all: "Alas, brother lamb, innocent animal, you represent what is useful to all mankind! Cursed be that evil beast that killed you; let no man eat of it, or any beast either." (*VS* 111)

Francis reacted against the needless destruction of an *innocent* and *useful* creature—ideas which hark back to some of the *Canticle*'s conceptions of worth in terms of creatures' purity and usefulness. Even the symbolic value of the lamb is mentioned to highlight its worth, and to justify the saint's outrage at such disrespect shown to the lamb.

The Wolf of Gubbio incident contains similar expressions of Francis' beliefs. The saint, relying on God's power, refuses to fear the wolf. He confronts it with its crimes: It has devoured innocent creatures without mercy, and even devours men who are created in the image of God. For these things, it should be punished. But the saint, God's agent, rectifies the situation by making a peace pact with the wolf.[24]

In the above incidents the saint acted as God's representative in disciplining creatures' immoderate desires. At other times creatures themselves must rely on the bonds of interdependence and respect between humankind and creatures to save them from misfortune. Francis releases a fish, a pheasant, and a waterbird which had been captured and given to him (*VP* 61; *VS* 167, 170). When given a rabbit,

> he held it affectionately and seemed to pity it like a mother. Then, warning it gently not to let itself be caught again, he allowed it to go free. But every time he put it on the ground to let it off, the hare immediately jumped into his arms, as if in some mysterious way it realized the love he had for it. Eventually Francis had the friars bring it off to a safer place in the woods. (*ML* 8:8)

Here human respect and pity save a fellow creature and show a rational concern for its well-being, and the creature responds with affection.

We have extended our discussion a bit in these anecdotes to demonstrate how the *Canticle*'s ideals of creation's worth and the relationships of interlinkage or interdependence among creation, God, and humans formed part of Francis' consistent set of attitudes toward the natural environment.[25] In Francis' view, all creatures, separate in functions, worth, desires, and beauty, are bound together in a harmonious interdependence ensured and presided over by the just and benevolent eye of God. Francis' ideas, while certainly relating to typical medieval views of humankind and creatures in the chain of being,[26] actually represent something profoundly new for the ascetic tradition of the High Middle Ages in their emphasis on autonomy coupled with mutual service, respect, and affection. The *Canticle*'s simple language and unaffected emotion should not hide the fact that its assumptions involve a complex synthesis: a vision of harmony and interdependence between creatures that is lofty, yet intimate and specific;

original, while clearly based on Christian tradition; utilitarian, but also a vehicle for appreciation and respect.

Francis' vision here might well remind us of Doyle's remarks that creation has a "meaning-in-itself"[27]—a comment which resembles also some views of the feminist theologian Rosemary Reuther. In *Sexism and God-Talk*[28] she maintains:

> . . . [W]e must respond to a "thou-ness" in all beings. This is not a romanticism or an anthropomorphic animism that sees "dryads in trees". . . . We respond not just as "I to it," but as "I to thou". . . . The "brotherhood of man" needs to be widened to embrace not only women but also the whole community of life.[29]

Francis similarly envisioned a harmonious and interdependent community of creation. His concern for creatures and his desire that people respect and appreciate them demonstrate his conception of autonomy and reciprocality. His use of familial and chivalric addresses to creatures was not pantheistic, romantic, or oppressive (in a sexist manner). Rather, it was a step toward balancing a perceived "I-it" objectifying relationship with an "I-thou" relationship of respect and affection between humans and creatures. It is in articulating this that Francis comes closest to Reuther's vision of "a new creation in which human nature and nonhuman nature become friends,"[30] whereas in affirming also the hierarchical character of creation under God and its proper use by humanity as a gift from God, Francis remains clearly in touch with traditional medieval conceptions.

Harmony and Reconciliation in the *Canticle*

The remainder of the *Canticle* carries the themes of harmony and reconciliation to their greatest height. Lines 5–22 address harmony and mutual respect between humans and physical creation. Soon after Francis composed these, according to the *Legend of Perugia*, he added lines 23–26, which deal with harmony and ideal relationships between people. Especially apropos to the political situation described by the *Legend*—the feud between the bishop and the *podestà* in Assisi—is line 23, "Be praised, my Lord, for those who grant pardon for love of you." This bridge passage, since it is the same used elsewhere in the *Canticle*, should be seen as similar in function also, in that it acts as a positive injunction to reconciliation in a situation of estrangement Francis considered shameful (*LP* 44). At the time it would have been seen as tantamount to a divine mandate for reconciliation, just as Francis' curses in other places were viewed as inevitable divine judgements (*VS* 47; 111).

Lines 24–26 appear to continue the thought, but in fact change the frame of reference to Francis and the friars. If the *Legend* is correct, the reference to those who endure sickness and trial in peace probably alludes to Francis and his closest followers immediately after the *certificatio*, which may also be mentioned in the unusual beatitude form: "Blessed are those who endure in peace,/ For by You, Most High, they will be crowned."[31] The whole passage very much fits the time of grave illness yet dedication and promise the *Legend* recounts, and thus substantiates its claim that this section was inserted immediately after the *Canticle*'s first section was composed. The emphasis subtly changes from harmony among people to harmony between humankind and God, with the "Most High" calling to mind the opening verses in which the address first appeared.

Some think lines 27–31 to be the most original of the poem.[32] They do have parallels in some of Francis' earlier writings, notably in the fiery sermon at the end of the *Letter to the Faithful*.[33] The theme is quite medieval, however, except for its radically positive elements. Written by Francis immediately before his death (*LP* 100), the lines show the saint reaching out at his end in mystical reconciliation with Sister Death—inexorable for all, terrifying for the wicked, but a friend to the holy, whom she leads to eternal bliss.[34] This section of the poem expresses how the saint made his peace with death—one remembers how Francis made peace with "Brother Body" at the same time (*VS* 210–11)—and transforms the poem into an example of what one might consider the literature of unification and reconciliation often produced when great people are at the point of death.[35] In this context, the last stanza provides a sort of culmination to Francis' ideals of harmony and unity throughout the poem, as Francis enjoins all the universe to unite in a grand chorus of thanksgiving, praise, and pledge of humble service to the Most High God.

HUMANISM IN THE *CANTICLE*

Many authors, including (of all people) the Italian dictator Mussolini, have praised Francis for his "humanism."[36] It is not within the scope of this work to seek out all the different meanings of the word, or even to speculate whether, or to what extent, a Christian humanism is possible.[37] Yet certain elements in the *Canticle* could be interpreted as humanistic in some sense, and this might relate to one's perception of the innovation in Francis' thought.

Although one must of course distinguish early Franciscan humanism from the sophisticated literary and philosophical achievements of the

School of Chartres,[38] one still may draw intriguing parallels between the twelfth-century intellectuals and some aspects of Francis' outlook. For instance, one might look at Francis' *Canticle* in the light of attempts by R.W. Southern and Dom David Knowles to define the humanism of the twelfth century. Southern envisions the threefold foundations of humanistic values as "a strong sense of the dignity of human nature, a recognition of the dignity of nature itself," and finally, a universe appearing "intelligible and accessible to human reason."[39] The scientific sense of the last remark is not very applicable to Francis' *Canticle*, which springs from simpler and more popular attitudes and thus resembles more the outlook of the ninth-century Celtic poem discussed earlier than the Anticlaudianus of the twelfth century. Yet the *Canticle* could be seen to emphasize the accessibility of creation to human appreciation and understanding, and thus to parallel the outlook of the Chartrians on a more popular level. In regard to Southern's other statements, some of the *Canticle*'s best moments are those which hold forth the possibility of human goodness and perfectibility against the background of the saint's tragic illness and decline. Likewise, some of the *Canticle*'s most original and rapturous utterances are those which consider the dignity and honorable station of the natural world, with chivalric titles accentuating the nobility of creatures.

For Knowles, twelfth-century humanism consisted essentially in revealing "a wide literary culture; . . . a personal devotion to certain figures of the ancient world; and, finally, a high value set upon the individual, personal emotions, and upon the sharing of experiences and opinions within a small circle of friends."[40] Certainly Francis' nonintellectual, spontaneous expression has little in common with the first two of these requirements. But the circumstances of the *Canticle*'s composition, discussed above, and its subjective lyrical emotion, link it securely with Knowles' last criterion: The *Canticle* was (among other things) a gift to Francis' faithful intimates, expressing his deepest feelings and beliefs (*LP* 43–44). In fact, the greatest sign of Francis' humanism in the *Canticle* is his revealing statement of his delicate inner emotions[41]—his delight, affection, and sympathy for such homely and overlooked creatures as water and fire. This simple and spontaneous outburst could inspire others to respect, aesthetic appreciation, or even a scientific interest in creation. Francis' fervent expressions held all these possibilities in embryo.

Conclusions

To the casual observer, the *Canticle*, with its rustic language and apparent naiveté and simplicity, might seem to lack a certain depth and sophistication. However, when it is seen in terms of Francis' other works and the motivation behind its composition, the poem in fact acquires indisputable claim to originality and complexity of thought. Although not the product of an intellectual, the *Canticle* is the highest poetic expression of an original Christian thinker. In it Francis built upon Latin models but obviously went beyond them in his choice of the vernacular, his poetic facility, and his intimate and subtly varying emotional expressions. All these make the *Canticle* a work as truly charming as it is innovative. Here Francis' assumptions about the worth of creation, and the complex relationships of interdependence and mutual service among creatures, reach their clearest expression. It is in this area of assumed interrelationships that Francis' poem attains its greatest significance and complexity. The saint expresses his own vision of the archetypal relationships underlying the cosmos, as Eliade would say.[42] Creatures, each having autonomous worth and beauty, are yet brothers and sisters to each other, aiding each other, gladly performing their divinely allotted functions. Humans, as beings aided by other creatures, honor creation's devoted service and beauty by giving thanks to God for it. This complex, balanced synthesis is one of Francis' most original conceptions. By giving creatures their due praise, people overcome their customary callous ingratitude to creatures and to God—another step toward the reconciliation and redemption of humanity envisioned by the end of the poem. This humanism characteristic of Francis—non-intellectual, but encompassing an ideal of the good of creation and the potential of human perfectability—was a triumphant Christian expression of the positive in creation and humanity. It flies in the face of popularized Cathar suspicion of the character of humanity and the physical world, and even of harsh Christian ascetic views of temptations stemming from the material world and the body.[43] Francis had shown there was a way to resolve the ambivalence in ascetic attitudes to creation, and he left his *Canticle* as the ultimate statement of his ideal.

8

Francis: Reality and Legacy

Although it is common and moving to see an era remake great figures of the past in its own image in an effort to draw spiritual sustenance from them, this is not the role of the historian, but of the propagandist. Some modern studies have given the impression that the early Franciscan Order was a sort of countermovement representing a subordinate and radical view advocating respect for creation and opposing the usual Christian exploitation of the environment. This is a projection of modern problems on the past. As we have seen, many Franciscan ideals and practices show clear derivation from the medieval eremetic tradition that had enormous influence, through example and widely read hagiography, on many levels of medieval society. Much of Francis' outlook in this area closely reflects earlier ascetic thought and is easily explicable in terms of the common experiences and ideals of the eremetic life. There are a great number of unoriginal or traditional elements in Francis' reactions to or relations with the natural world: for example, his keeping of pets (well-established within saintly tradition); his authority over and direction of natural objects or living things (again well-established); his cursing of a living thing (this has parallels in both Scripture and saintly tradition); his seeming endowment of the nonhuman with rational comprehension (quite typical in poetry and hagiography); his moral instruction of nonhuman things (again Biblical and well-established in hagiographical tradition); his respect for the individual in creation (unoriginal, as it appears in earlier Christian sources); his love of the inanimate (unoriginal, although unusual in earlier Christian sources)[1]; his conception that creation should and does praise

God (Biblical); his praise of creation (unoriginal); his appreciation of a particular environment (well-established before him); his appreciation of creatures through symbolic associations (completely traditional in origin); his wish to eschew monasteries for huts, caves, and tombs (traditional eremetic); and his special provision for wild animals in winter (unusual but not original).[2]

The listing is of course incomplete. But although the list of unoriginal or typically medieval elements is long, so also is the list of original elements (i.e., original to Western Christianity) in Francis' expressions: his nature mysticism; his specific connection of familial relationships with the things of creation; his application of chivalric terms of address and other chivalric conceptions to natural things; his extraordinarily sustained emphasis on things in the environment as beneficent instead of ambivalent; his direct (as opposed to literary) exhortation even of inanimate objects to serve and praise God; his proposed extension of Christian almsgiving to creatures (*MP* 114); and the celebration of Christmas at Greccio with the inclusion of animals, for whom he provided afterward (*VP* 84ff; *MP* 114).

Many of Francis' expressions which seem original or to have parallels in modern ideals must be understood within their thirteenth-century context, however, so as not to be misinterpreted. For even if they are original, the motivations behind them may be not at all modern. Those concerned with attitudes toward the environment might rejoice to hear that Francis spared flowers and set aside plots for them (*VS* 165; *VP* 81; *MP* 118); cut trees carefully in hopes of their resprouting (*MP* 114, 118), and asked for laws providing food for some wild birds in winter (*MP* 114). Yet a deeper reading of the texts will reveal that Francis protected flowers "out of love for Him Who is called The Rose in the plain and the Lily on the mountain slopes," and spared the vital parts of trees "out of love for Christ, Who willed to accomplish our salvation on the wood of the cross" (*MP* 118). Likewise he wished the larks fed in winter because of their edifying symbolic value (*MP* 113–114). Of course there is no doubt Francis appreciated the individual things of creation in their own right, and that he had concerns that might be labeled "ecological" in the popular definition of "concern for the environment." But although the effect of the above ideals may lean toward modern ideas, the motivation behind them stems from a mind that is, even though original, profoundly medieval.

Certain characteristic (but not systematic) patterns of thought underly Francis' original expressions. One of these is a tendency toward literalism. The same literalistic attitude which led Francis to a conception of the apostolic life also led him to apply the rhetorical liturgical exhortations to creatures and the Biblical injunction to preach the gospel "to all creatures" in a new and literal manner. The conjunction of these two literally interpreted aims produced Francis' first major innovation in his relationship with natural things—his Sermon to the Birds. Francis' fully formed and newly literal ideal of the apostolic life was the crucial new element which enabled an original encounter with the natural world, in contrast with earlier saints who, harboring perhaps implicit conceptions of lost harmony between humankind and creatures, had encountered friendly animals and merely tamed them or ordered them about. Francis and Celano see the Sermon as representing the extension of the restored apostolic life and ideal from humankind to a new plane, that of ancient harmony between humanity and the cosmos. Thus in this respect Francis' expressions may be seen to be the apotheosis of the ascetic tradition's positive yearnings for such harmony.

We have noticed how Celano and Bonaventure perceived Francis' nature mysticism as an essentially literal and conservative interpretation of the mystical journey. Though this interpretation is more theirs than ours, there is some reflection of a sort of literalism in Francis' perception of divinity in an unusually direct manner even in the beauty and worth of individual earthly representatives of divine creation. Francis' elation at this direct vision was so great that it led to his ecstatic experiences while contemplating creation.

The same literalistic mind approached troubadour poetry, the only vital factor outside Christian tradition which influenced, indeed fertilized and deepened, Francis' views. He probably drew on the stylized *Natureingang* of the troubadour poems to voice his spontaneous joy in the midst of natural surroundings, thus applying these rhetorical expressions in a new literal manner.

Yet there was much more to Francis than a literalistic bent. In adapting the secular chivalric ideals to his spiritual purposes, he demonstrated a truly medieval talent: an intuitive genius at passing quickly, subtly, and adeptly from one "level of consciousness" (in modern terms) to another. That he was considered a superb allegorical interpreter of Biblical texts[3] should not surprise us, except for the fact that he was formally untrained in scholastic methods. His mental ability would have developed instead from hearing the allegorical technique used *ad infinitum* in sermons; after his pattern of life gained stability, his constant exposure to the refined metaphorical technique and richly allegorical settings of the liturgical Psalms (some of which we know he interpreted as referring to the Friars Minor), would have exercised and strengthened his talent.[4]

Often, therefore, Francis' mind darted with an almost sportive ease from one spiritual level to another in its delight in observing new spiritual meanings or in bringing together many different levels of meaning in either a written text or the "book of nature." Thus some of his interpretations of things in the natural world can even be examined in the light of the formalized medieval "senses" of allegory (as the mystical symbolism in the *Canticle*), though it is impossible to restrict Francis' ability here to thought only on these levels, or to imagine that he interpreted what he saw with any rigid system explicitly in mind.[5] His ability to interpret the different levels of spiritual meaning in the natural world—a practice as edifying to him as it is horrifying to some modern scholars—was a constant and spontaneous source of spiritual enrichment and perhaps even of ecstasy to him. In this he again translated tradition into innovation by a new depth and directness of involvement.

Considering Francis' literalistic ideals and conservative modes of thought, it is not surprising that his biographers understood many of his most significant original expressions as a return to Christian conservatism and simplicity, rather than exploring their dramatic originality and unique background. Francis' admirers could interpret his expressions as supremely orthodox—and indeed, this conclusion was not an error, even though Francis' actions and motivations were not always explicable in, or limited to, the ways they believed. Such good fortune furthered acceptance of otherwise suspect innovation.

Francis' attitudes in general, shown in the *Canticle* specifically, reveal one of the most positive developments of that potential visible in the whole range of medieval reactions to the natural world. Francis demonstrated concretely, through both word and action, the tremendous and almost total extent to which the medieval ascetic ambivalence to the natural world—the core of any more generalized medieval negativism and ambivalence to it—could be resolved, and in its resolution, explode into a burst of original positive reactions to creation. Francis' deep acceptance of the natural world led him to concentrate intuitively on positive doctrinal support for his beliefs and to extend Christian teaching on his own in that direction. We can see this process occurring in the most famous examples of Francis' demonstrations of love and concern for creatures—the Sermon to the Birds and the *Canticle*. By his Sermon Francis demonstrated graphically that humanity should concern itself with the welfare of creatures as a part of the Christian mission. With his words, which proved through Scripture that there was divine notice of and provision for animals, he proclaimed the indissoluble kinship and community between humans and their fellow creatures under God.

The *Canticle* unquestionably represents Francis' most profound and complex legacy in this area. This unique document, which at first appears to be the simple lyrical statement of a simple man, proves instead to possess a great complexity—a complexity one should respect even more considering its author's lack of intellectual training. It summarizes the assumptions Francis had voiced and acted upon all his life. Its vision of the worth of creation in many different senses, from the aesthetic to the utilitarian, and its vision of the complicated interlinkages and interdependences between humankind and creatures, along with its sense of the relative autonomy of creatures at the various levels in the divine hierarchy, make it a *tour de force* in medieval thought, one worthy of comparison with any other contemporary or earlier medieval Christian expression. Its proclamation of the harmony and reconciliation between humans and creatures—the "I-thou" relationship—is unparalleled in its vividness, and overflows with potential. The motivation behind it—to exhort people to appreciate creation, respect it, and recognize human kinship to other creatures—is unique in its directness, clarity, and dedication.

Francis' Legacy: Immediate and Long-Term

The impact of Francis' expressions concerning creation varied during the centuries immediately following his life. The record reveals striking losses of some elements of his vision that were not widely accepted into Western Christian tradition, yet others had a dramatic and profound effect. While I must leave extensive discussion of Francis' influence on these and later eras to other authors,[6] I wish to note in conclusion one area of temporary loss and one instance of strikingly successful transmission of his legacy to generations immediately after him.

Francis' openness to animals and interest in the physical environment continued to influence his Order, as can be seen in anecdotes of St. Giles and St. Anthony of Padua, and in the poetry of Jacopone da Todi.[7] But Francis' nature mystical experiences, which interested Celano and Bonaventure to the extent that they endeavored to assimilate them into Christian tradition, found few imitators—none in the early Order.[8] One other saint in the thirteenth century, Douceline (died c. 1274), who admired Francis deeply, does appear to have had nature-mystical experiences similar to his.[9] Possibly with the clericalization and sophistication of the Order, Francis' legacy lost its primary context and relevance. It was too eremetic in origin, too delicately individual, too easily intellectualized away by those removed (mentally and physically) from creation's sublimity to which Francis was so close, and with which he so intimately sympathized. A full appreciation of his importance and the rich potential in his thought in this regard had to wait until much later.[10]

Francis' concern for creatures and intense connection with the physical environment, however, had a tremendous impact in an area he would not have expected: art. As Vincent Moleta remarks in *From St. Francis to Giotto: The Influence of St. Francis on Early Italian Art and Literature*,

> the life of the Umbrian saint and wonder-worker was a gift to the high creative talent that proliferated in central Italy during the several generations that followed his death. Not only did the rise of a superb lay culture in Italy during the thirteenth and early fourteenth century coincide with the Franciscan rebirth of religious life in Italy. The ideal and example of St. Francis was present to the men of genius who founded that national culture, and St. Francis himself is the subject of some of their most important and moving artistic works.[11]

As the research of many modern authors has discovered, following the lead of Thöde's work in the last century,[12] Francis' legend stimulated the imagination of pre-Renaissance and Renaissance artists. Gurney-Salter[13] believes Francis was the most frequently represented saint in Italian art. The large and spacious Franciscan churches, well suited to a more popular art of immediate impact on their large congregations, provided building projects and wide expanses for dramatic and influential frescoes such as those in the Assisi basilica. These and other new artistic works,

> reflecting a new, naturalistic style, provided visual accompaniment to a popular preaching not in Latin but in the spoken language. . . . [W]e can also discern his [Francis'] profound humanity and his joyful response to nature behind the rediscovery of the natural world and frankly human vision of the sacred story that mark the best Italian art of the period.[14]

Although the dating and attribution of some major early paintings showing the Franciscan legend are still in doubt (including the attribution and date of the Assisi basilica frescoes),[15] it seems that artists (especially Giotto) by the mid-fourteenth century had seized upon the Franciscan legend as a challenge to their new values of artistic realism and interest in the physical world. Their creations would astound Renaissance artists as late as Vasari (died 1574), who gave the Assisi chapel the "grandest encomium" he had to offer, particularly praising it for the "variety of the compositions, for the costumes of the period, for the arrangement, proportion, vivacity, and naturalness of the figures." He saw the "verisimilitude" of the events portrayed, and took them as a "celebration of life."[16]

More than in literature or any other form, it is perhaps through art that Francis' vision of creation was most powerfully transmitted immediately after his death. As Stubblebine's excellent study notes,

> Clearly, it was the obligation of the artists at work on the St. Francis cycle in the upper chapel at Assisi to instruct, explain, delight, and even amuse or do whatever else was necessary to inspire the common people. It is extraordinary that still today groups of people cluster in front of certain frescoes at Assisi, for example, the miracle of the Spring, or the Sermon to the Birds, their faces filled with comprehension, and therefore with pleasure and wonderment.[17]

The example Francis set—the striking, key incidents reported by his early biographers—inspired art of such direct beauty and new, intense realism, that it may well have conveyed his message far more widely than his biographers could with words. This fortunate conjunction of Franciscan vision and art may have dramatically influenced the course of Western art toward increased appreciation and representation of the natural world in the Renaissance, and moved uncounted numbers of observers toward interest in the physical universe.

Francis' Legacy for the Present Day

This study has questioned or rejected many of the more extravagant recent interpretations of Francis' importance. To some readers, this examination of the traditional elements in Francis' beliefs and expressions, along with its attempt to understand this great man within the context of his medieval milieu, may seem to have struck a blow at their image of him. Yet when one can see Francis in terms of the Western traditions from which he arose, the way is open not only for a better appreciation of his actual tremendous originality, but for the perception that the Western Christian tradition of thought about the relationship between humankind and other creatures is not static and rigid, but contains abundant potential, a constant ability to grow and to absorb profound innovation while remaining true to its fundamental values. Surely this is not irrelevant to those involved in the modern struggle to transform, in a way fitting to Western tradition, contemporary attitudes about human ecological responsibilities. A glimmer of hope for this modern effort shines through the evidence that Western tradition has indeed undergone such dramatic changes in the past. And at the center of this hope is the humble, gentle man of Assisi. Francis looked beyond others of his time to envision a world in which humankind shared a concern for the whole community of creatures, and he expressed his concern and love in such original and moving ways that they may still give us inspiration today. For who can afford to ignore the example of one who spent whole days praising in public the creatures of the world (*VP* 80), who had such concern and compassion for creatures "that if anyone did not treat them properly he was upset" (*LP* 49); and whose responsiveness to the beauty of the environment was so great, his joyful openness to it so boundless, that he experienced mystical ecstasy while contemplating a flower?

APPENDIX I

Francis and Catharism

No other modern researcher in the area seems to have read "Franziskus von Assisi und die Katharer seiner Zeit," the definitive article on the subject, by a distinguished Franciscan historian, Catejan Esser.[1] In it the author studies the relationship between Francis' views and Catharism,* and concludes that there was no heretical influence on Francis, who demonstrated a sophisticated undersanding of the peril here both in his *Rules* and in his reactions to Cathar beliefs when confronted with them directly. Francis' beliefs should be seen, at least implicitly, as an orthodox manifesto against extreme Cathar asceticism and its suspicion of the natural world.[2]

Modern critics have come to some quite mistaken conclusions about the origin of Francis' ideas because they did not read Esser's work. For example, Lynn White maintains,

> . . . [W]hat Sir Steven Runciman calls "the Franciscan doctrine of the animal soul" was quickly stamped out. Quite possibly it was inspired, consciously or unconsciously, by the belief in reincarnation held by the Cathar heretics who at the time teemed in Italy and southern France, and who presumably had got it originally from India. . . . But Francis held neither to transmigration of souls nor to pantheism. His view of nature and man rested on a unique

*The best recent research in this area includes W. Wakefield's *Heresy, Crusade and Inquisition in Southern France*, 1100–1250 (Berkeley, 1974)—an excellent historical overview. E. Ladurie's *Montaillou, The Promised Land of Error*, trans. B. Bray (New York, 1979) attempts to recreate Cathar society and its cultural setting. See the Bibliography following these appendices for further sources.

> sort of pan-psychism of all things animate and inanimate, designed for the glorification of their transcendent Creator. . . .[3] [T]he prime miracle of St. Francis is the fact that he did not end at the stake, as many of his left-wing followers did. He was so clearly heretical that a General of the Franciscan order, St. Bonaventura, a great and perceptive Christian, tried to suppress the early accounts of Franciscanism.[4]

Here White distorts historical evidence to suit his interpretation. Francis' early biographers, including Bonaventure, did not suppress Francis' views on creation, but rather celebrated and praised them as revealing something fundamentally orthodox and Christian, as we have seen. Surely if they suspected heresy here they would have suppressed all his views immediately, as they attempted to do with other matters, such as Francis' unusually cordial relationships with women.[5] When Bonaventure suppressed the other early lives of Francis, his concern was not to suppress Francis' views of creation, which lived on freely in his *Canticle* and Bonaventure's own writings about Francis, but to ensure that certain ideas about the correct observance of Franciscan poverty and the right to learning would not be challenged by the more rigorous early writings.[6]

Lynn White's claim that Francis was a pan-psychist heretic runs into many problems even without Esser's arguments. No Catholic biographer, whether early or late, has seen Francis' interpretation of the natural environment as unorthodox. More important, in all the thirteenth-century discussions on Franciscan issues with papal advisors or with popes themselves, the subject never arises. Church officials were hardly uncritical of the new Order. It faced opposition on many fronts from its very inception.[7] Further, all the officials involved would have been well aware of possible danger here, as the Cathars provided an explosive contemporary example of a popular movement erring precisely in the crucial area of its interpretation of the material world. Given the situation, it is simply unthinkable that officials would have neglected to point out the danger if they believed that any existed. And they are silent.

APPENDIX II

Analysis of the Early Franciscan Sources

One should approach the many early Franciscan texts only with a clear understanding of their complex origins and transmission (see Figure 1).[1] With this understanding, a hierarchy of the authentic and most reliable sources can be erected.

Any of Francis' own statements must take priority over secondary accounts. Brown maintains correctly that

> It is in his writings that the personality of the Poverello finds its best expression. Nothing gives us a more intimate knowledge of it, and the best guarantee of the authenticity of the early documents is their agreement with Francis' own testimony about himself.[2]

The early secondary accounts have a complicated relationship to each other. The present study draws on four of the texts that have the greatest claims to importance in terms of their date of composition, closeness to Francis' inner circle, and atmosphere. Celano's *Vita Prima* was composed within two years after the saint's death (1226) by the well-trained hagiographer who had actually met Francis.[3] It is the most respected early source for many anecdotes. The *Legend of Perugia* must come next in consideration, since the technical research of Fortini,[4] Bigaroni,[5] and Brooke,[6] has shown that the early basis for chapters of the *Legend* goes back to the now-missing writings of Brother Leo—an invaluable source, as he was for many years the intimate and articulate companion of Francis. The

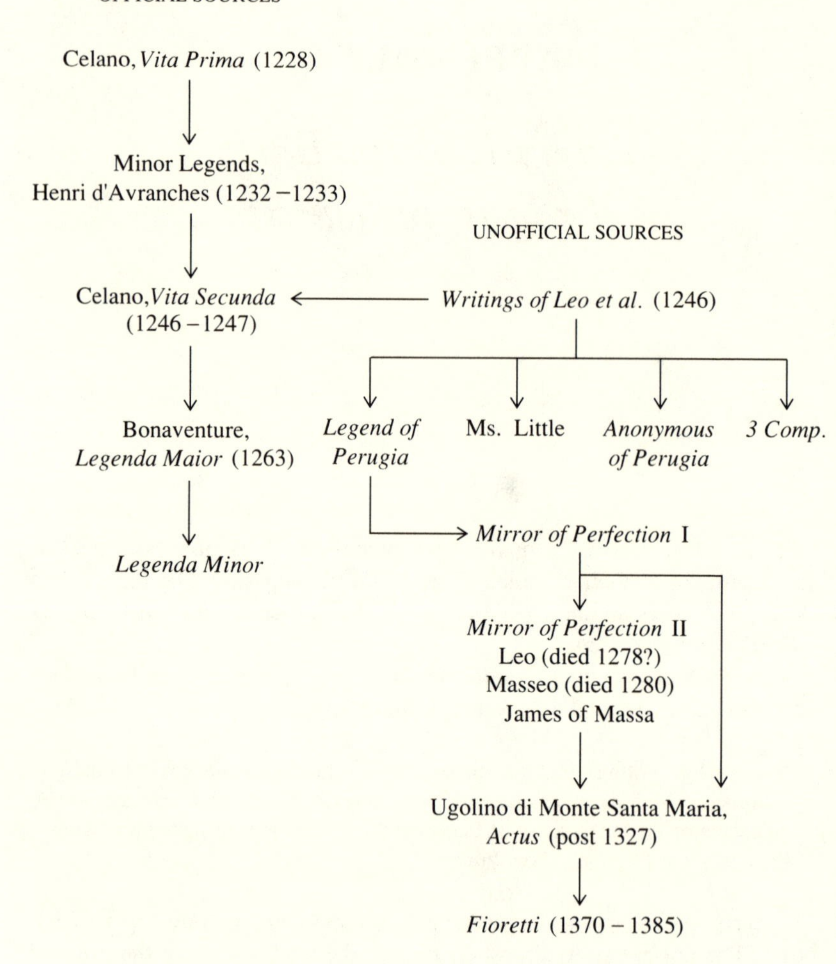

FIGURE 1. The Origin and Transmission of Franciscan Sources

Legend thus arguably reflects the views of Francis and his inner circle of followers. Celano's *Vita Secunda* uses this (or its basis) and other early material.

The *Actus-Fioretti* represent the culmination of an oral tradition that diverges from the official sources of Celano and Bonaventure. Indeed, the author of the *Actus* seems never to have read Celano,[7] perhaps because of the Order's effective 1266 ban on early *vitae*.[8] Thus in spite of its late date (post 1327), its elaborations of miraculous elements, and occasional confusions, the *Actus* account is still very valuable to modern historians.

> The substance of their [the historians'] verdict is that the *Actus* represents, not folklore, but a direct oral tradition transmitted by several of the Saint's closest friends—Leo, Masseo, and Giles—through a few intermediaries to the author, and that this oral tradition, although occasionally inaccurate in chronology and topography, is in the main reliable, unless disproved by earlier evidence.[9]

> Contemporary critics are much less disdainful of the Fioretti than were their predecessors. Granted that the author has added his own contribution to it, that the painter has stylized his picture, that the masterpiece, containing so much that is historic, contains some more than is legendary. Yet [in the chapters dealing with St. Francis] there are no false notes; the tone rings true; the themes are those that only the Poverello could invent; the atmosphere wherein the Franciscan adventure develops is incomparable; the portrait of St. Francis has never been painted in so lifelike a manner.[10]

Occasionally the *Legend* and *Actus-Fioretti* preserve accounts that seem both fresher and longer than Celano's.[11] Celano places his material in an extremely interpretive and compressed structure. This sometimes results in many similar incidents from different times being lumped together, or anecdotes being abbreviated even to the point of becoming cryptic.[12] In these cases, the more rambling account of the *Legend* and *Actus* can furnish crucial details and allow more certain chronological placement.[13] Armstrong's study provides many other comparative analyses of different versions of incidents.

APPENDIX III

The Sermon to the Birds in the Early Sources

No less than six early accounts of the Sermon to the Birds exist, all composed at different dates, with different degrees of probable authenticity and usefulness (see Figure 2). Of these six, however, only those in Celano's *Vita Prima* and the *Actus-Fioretti* are really important for our present purpose.[1]

The most important is clearly that found in *VP* 58. Its grounds for authority are obvious: It is the first account, composed less than twenty years after the event. It appears to be self-authenticating in that it explicitly states that it rests on the authority of Francis himself and the followers who were present at the incident ("as he himself used to say and the brothers who were with him")—which we know from *Actus-Fioretti* were Angelo and Masseo.[2] Celano, who knew Francis personally, gives an account which is moderately rich in details concerning the setting, speech, and the effects of the encounter with the birds upon Francis' outlook. The account fails to give adequate chronological reference, for it appears at a point where the author steps out of chronological order and inserts some edifying miraculous incidents. Thus the account merely begins, "Meanwhile, while many were joining the Order, as was said . . ."[3] and allows only the vaguest of placement—from roughly 1212–1217. Further, Celano's account of the Sermon itself, while not as ornate as many of his other passages, is still presented in Latin—not in the original Old Italian in which it surely was given—and is couched in rhythmic and rhymed *cursus*.[4] In spite of these factors, the account in Celano has an unrivalled authority because of its internal self-authentication and early date of composition.

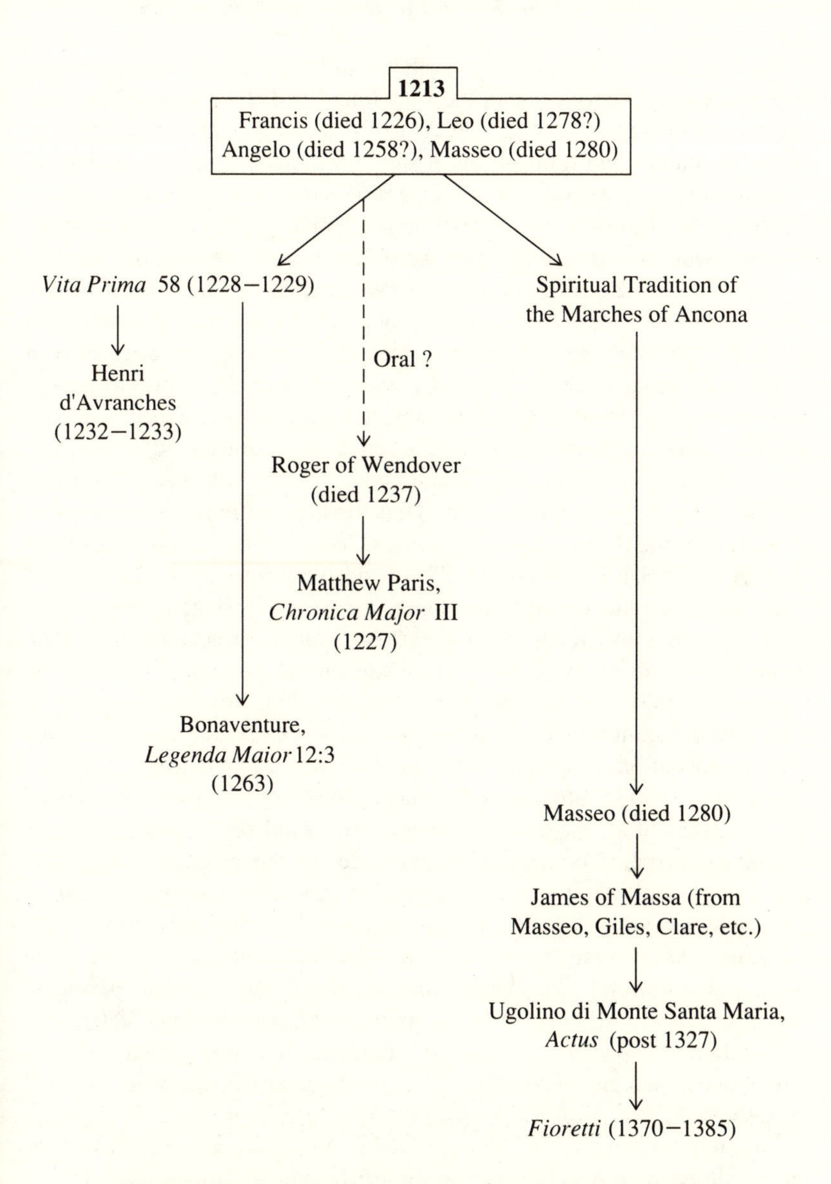

FIGURE 2. Tradition of the Account of the Sermon to the Birds

The other, unofficial, branch of the tradition evidently long remained in oral form, and derives from the very long-lived Br. Masseo.[5] He later became a contemplative in the Marches of Ancona, preserving his memory of the encounter and transmitting it through a disciple, James of Massa, to Ugolino di Monte Santa Maria. Ugolino then used it in compiling his *Actus* account (taken over without major alteration by the translator of the *Fioretti*) well over a century after the original encounter had occurred.[6]

Although the late date of the *Actus* (which seems to have been written down sometime after 1327)[7] and its propensity toward mythic elaboration make it a difficult source for the researcher, its account does have a distinct advantage over the shorter Celano version in that it provides more historical setting for dating the incident. Its introduction, which discusses Francis' crisis of heart at the time when he last considered renouncing the evangelical ideal, tells of Francis' consultation with Sister Clare and Brother Silvester, as we have seen. Thus the incident must have occurred, if we accept the *Actus*' statements, after Clare and her companions were established at San Damiano (1212), yet not very long after, for Francis' doubt and his reliance on Clare signal a very early stage in his career. Upon receiving his friends' encouragement, Francis launched himself with great fervor into Umbria, and it is while on his preaching tour that he encountered the birds. Raphael Brown connects this missionary campaign with that including Francis' meeting with Count Orlando, resulting in the saint's acquisition of Mount La Verna. This was arranged May 8, 1213.[8] The *Vita Prima* (35–36) seems to confirm this early sequence of events,[9] but it leaves out all the details—a pattern we shall see repeated.

Another piece of corroborating evidence for the postulated date may exist from a different source. Francis' *Exhortation to Praise God*, a document recently studied at length by Esser,[10] is attributed to the year 1213, the date in which the tiny chapel it dedicated was founded. The work consists of selected verses from the liturgy and Biblical passages, one of which is, "All birds of the air, praise the Lord!" (Daniel 3:80). This exhortation is especially fitting and significant if it was selected shortly after Francis had encountered the birds with the emotional results related by Celano.

The *Actus* account is probably garbled at times. It places the Stilling of the Swallows before the Sermon to the Birds, and at Cannara, as opposed to Celano's placement at Alviano, after the Sermon.[11] In this case, the earlier account should be accepted. Further, it mentions Francis' intention to begin the Third Order (a lay order)—but if this is the case, the Order was not organized until some years after Francis thought of it.[12]

The long Sermon text in the *Actus* abounds with Latinate rhetorical devices (especially anaphora) and *cursus* rhythms.[13] Cellucci deems it "a piece of bravura," developed with "copious fantasy," based on Celano's "sober exposition." Armstrong also maintains that "the writer, Bible in hand, has extended Celano's account."[14] The *Actus* itself, however, asserts that its account rests on named oral sources: James of Massa, from Br. Masseo.[15] Is the compiler obscuring his reliance on Celano, or is his source completely independent? Armstrong evidently did not compare the two accounts in the original. If he had done so, he would have discovered that there are no verbal parallels between the Sermon texts in the *Vita Prima* and in the *Actus*. In fact, there are no textual parallels anywhere in the chapters recounting the incident in Celano and the *Actus*. As medieval authors were notoriously "sticky-fingered" with regard to the sources they used, this must be considered very significant.

From textual study, it seems that the *Actus* stories have a consistent and peculiar relationship to the several stories in Celano they parallel.[16] None of them have any verbal similarities sufficiently noteworthy to suggest any influence from the *Vita Prima*. Not only do they differ consistently in phrasing, but they quite often differ in details,[17] emphasis, introductions and conclusions, and length. Celano, by comparison, is often too concise, leaving out details and at times becoming cryptic. In fact, Celano even hints in his Sermon account that he has cut down his material, for he says, "Among the many things he [Francis] spoke to them [the birds] were these words he added. . . ."[18] For almost every incident common to both Celano and the *Actus*, the *Actus* preserves a fuller, more detailed account, even though, of course, some of the details and chronology are confused. One could maintain that the length of the *Actus*' accounts is due to mythic elaboration. This is clearly true in a few cases, such as the invention of the spectacular symbolic cross-figure which the birds create upon flying away after Francis' Sermon. This appears only in the *Actus-Fioretti*. But other details of the setting—Francis' inner crisis and his consultation with his comrades—receive some confirmation elsewhere in Celano, even though his passages are cryptic.[19] His narrative structure would have made it difficult for him to include many of the *Actus*' details when he related the Sermon, for his main concern at that point is not with Francis' inner doubts, or with a long Sermon, but with examples of edifying miracle stories.[20]

All these factors seem to indicate that the *Vita Prima* and the *Actus* are two completely independent accounts based on similar oral sources. Celano's account may have been lost to the *Actus* compiler due to the

Order's 1266 ban on earlier lives.[21] The *Actus*' length and detail would make more sense if no other account were available; this would have encouraged a more thorough preservation. Nevertheless, the *Actus* reports from such a great chronological distance, and is so oratorical, that no historian could accept its elaborated version as anything more than a sincere attempt to fill in what Francis said as remembered and transmitted through three generations of dedicated followers.

If the *Actus* does represent a tradition completely independent of Celano, it confirms Celano's accuracy to some extent, as his account, for all its greater conciseness, strongly resembles the *Actus* version. The whole atmosphere is very similar, and some common Biblical sources are used.[22] Because of these strong similarities, it seems possible that Francis actually did say something quite near that reported in Celano, since that is the earliest and less ornate account. The suggestions by Tamassia[23] that Celano manufactured the story using earlier events in hagiography have been amply refuted by Bihl's research.

Bihl argues that, in every instance cited by Tamassia, the earlier parallels to the Sermon account either are essentially different from Celano's intent, or cannot be made to cast doubt on the fact that Francis himself composed the Sermon. There are three parallels analyzed by Bihl that are of special value to us. The first comes from Gregory the Great (*Dialogues*, 3:15). Florentius, a simple monk, called a pet bear *frater*. But Bihl points out justly that in the *Dialogue*'s context, this term means (fellow-)monk, not brother. Then Bihl discusses the parallel between Martin's meeting with a flock of birds (Severus, *Letter* 3:7–9), and Francis' encounter. The emphases of the two accounts differ radically. In the first, Martin sees waterfowl as a "picture of demons," and "exorcizes" them from the area with the same authority he has to govern demons. Martin's sermon is not *to* the birds, but *about* the birds, as symbols of the demonic; Francis addresses the birds directly, as birds. Celano's account stresses, in contrast to Severus', the willing obedience of the birds, along with Francis' loving acceptance of things in creation. Finally, there is the incident, discussed earlier, from Caesarius' *Dialogue*, in which a Cistercian prior gives a circling flock of storks permission to migrate. Though the setting is somewhat similar, the incidents differ in ideas, exposition, and even the species of birds (mentioned by chance in each account). No sermon is involved in Caesarius. None of the parallels above is sufficient to make one doubt the originality of Francis' Sermon.[24]

Armstrong, who is often unfair in his judgments of Celano because of his desire to contrast Francis' "progressivism" with his biographer's "conservatism,"[25] criticizes Celano in ways which could be taken to undermine the authenticity of his early account. First, he considers the moralizing purpose of the account in the particular place it occurs.

> It cannot be accidental that he [Celano] placed the chapter "of his preaching to the birds and of the obedience of the creatures" as an auspicious prelude to the saint's evangelistic tour through Umbria and the Marches and immediately after his chronicle of the failure of his mission to the Saracens. Thus he shows that if Moslems rejected the saint's preaching, birds, although many thought them of little account, did not.[26]

Yet one could maintain that Celano's exposition has a more normal logic: After recounting the history of Francis' missions, quickly spanning the years 1212–1219, Celano then returns, in chapters 58–70, to insert stories of miracles which happened during that same time, but which would have impeded his narrative sequence if given in chapters 55–57. The implicit (if existent) connection with the Saracen mission cannot challenge the evident historical occurrence of the Sermon to the Birds at the commencement of Francis' Italian mission effort—an occurrence which, as we have already noted, the *Actus* account also relates and in more useful detail. Moralistic purposes, if evident, do not threaten the evidence of the historical setting.

Armstrong presents a bizarre argument when he accuses Celano of expansion and adornment in specifying the types of birds Francis saw beside the road before his Sermon.

> He alone particularizes some of the species constituting the congregation—doves, rooks, and jackdaws—a selection of conspicuous and well-known species, strangely omitting passerine songsters. If his feeling for nature had been intense, he would surely have mentioned birds with pleasanter associations than the Corvidae.[27]

He accuses Celano of embroidery, and then berates him for not doing it well enough! It would have been much simpler if Armstrong had taken these details as one more of the many internal signs that the account is authentic. Crows and the like did have unpleasant associations for medieval people[28]—their mention in this account of the Sermon works for, not against, authenticity. It serves to show how Francis' new love for creation stepped even in a small way beyond tradition, and preserves the realism of a chance encounter.

Notes

INTRODUCTION

1. Edward Gibbon, *The History of the Decline and Fall of the Roman Empire*, with notes by the Rev. H. Milman (London, n.d.), vol. 2, pp. 985–97.
2. P.F. Anson, *The Call of the Desert: The Solitary Life in the Christian Church* (London, 1964), p. 14. Gibbon's *Decline and Fall*, chapter 37, shows his emotional prejudice and resulting lack of insight in treating the early ascetic movement.
3. C. Glacken, *Traces on the Rhodian Shore: Nature and Culture in Western Thought from Ancient Times to the End of the Eighteenth Century* (Berkeley, 1967), p. 349.
4. The Count de Montalembert, in his *The Monks of the West, from St. Benedict to St. Bernard* (London, 1861), attempted to refute earlier claims, but his own religious biases obscured the validity of the points he made, e.g., in vol. 1, pp. 71ff.
5. G.C. Coulton, *Five Centuries of Religion* (Cambridge, 1923).
6. Ibid., vol. 1, p. 179.
7. Originally printed in the *International Journal of Environmental Studies* 3 (1972): 141–46, as "The Religious Background of the Present Environmental Crisis"; quoted here from D. and E. Spring, eds., *Ecology and Religion in History* (New York, 1974), p. 145.
8. L. White, Jr., "The Historical Roots of our Ecologic Crisis," first printed in *Science Magazine* 19 Mar 1967; quoted here from Spring, *Ecology and Religion*, p. 25.
9. White, in Spring, pp. 26–31.
10. See H. Adams, *Mont-Saint-Michel and Chartres* (New York, 1961), pp. 25, 336.
11. P. Sabatier, in his *Life of Saint Francis of Assisi*, trans. L. Houghton (New York, 1894), saw Francis as an early sort of Protestant stifled by the Catholic hierarchy.
12. G.K. Chesterton's *Saint Francis of Assisi* (New York, 1924) presents a strong argument for Francis' basic orthodoxy.

13. L. Boff, in his *Saint Francis: A Model for Human Liberation*, trans. J.W. Dierckmeier (New York, 1982) interprets Francis' life in this mode. However, the writer's bizarre style, with its dense terminology, is a disservice to a perspective worthy of serious consideration. Two excellent recent biographies are: J. Green, *God's Fool: The Life and Times of Francis of Assisi*, trans. P. Heinigg (San Francisco, 1985); and O. Englebert, *Saint Francis of Assisi: A Biography*, trans. E. Cooper, 2nd ed. (Chicago, 1972). The hardbound 1972 edition of Englebert's work contains superb scholarly appendices to which I will refer, while the much more accessible paperback 1979 edition (Servant Books, Ann Arbor, Michigan)—on which I rely for some insights in the biography itself—lacks the appendices.
14. White, in Spring, p. 29.
15. F.P. Longford, *Francis of Assisi: A Life for All Seasons* (London, 1978).
16. One can find this even in E.A. Armstrong's otherwise valuable book, *St. Francis: Nature Mystic* (Berkeley, 1973), where he expresses revulsion and disbelief at incidents "unworthy" of Francis, or attempts to blame Francis' early biographers for presenting "unprogressive" attitudes Francis held, instead of seeing them as a part of the whole Franciscan synthesis. See his pp. 113–15.
17. L. Cunningham, ed., *Brother Francis: An Anthology of Writings by and about Saint Francis of Assisi* (New York, 1972), pp. x–xi; xvii. See also *L'immagine di San Francesco nella storiografia dall'umanesimo all' ottocento* (Assisi, 1983).
18. White, in Spring, pp. 29–30. This mistaken opinion, however, in no way lessens White's great contributions to the history of science and technology.
19. M. Bishop, *Saint Francis of Assisi* (Boston, 1974), p. 187.
20. Ibid., p. 73.
21. See ahead, p. 144.
22. See *VS* 102–4.
23. The *Major Life* was composed 1261–1263.
24. See Appendix II.
25. Translated in M. Habig, ed., *St. Francis of Assisi, Writings and Early Biographies: English Omnibus of Sources*, 3rd ed., rev. (Chicago, 1973); new edition in C. Esser, *Die Opuscula des Hl. Franziskus von Assisi, neue textkritische edition* (Rome, 1976). Scholars owe the Habig edition a great debt; most of the translations in this current work are from his collection. For another new edition of Francis' writings, see R. Armstrong and I. Brady, trans., *Francis and Clare: The Complete Works* (Ramsey, New Jersey, 1982).
26. See Habig, pp. 179ff.
27. Ibid., pp. 186ff, 959–71.
28. See R. Brooke, Introduction to *Scripta Leonis, Rufini, et Angeli* (Oxford, 1970); and Habig, pp. 959–71.
29. See Francis' *Office of the Passion* (Vespers); *Admonition* 15; *Admonition* 5.

30. See especially Psalm 148, Daniel 3:23ff. (The Hymn of the Three Young Men, in the *Vulgate*). For the influence of these texts in Francis' *Canticle*, see V. Branca, "Il Cantico di Frate Sole," *Archivum Franciscanum Historicum* 41 (1948): 62–78.
31. Francis' *Canticle*, as we will see, is based on Genesis 1 and 2, Psalm 148, and Daniel 3, as far as Biblical sources are concerned. His most fundamental ideas about humankind's relationship to creation thus stem from these well-known Biblical passages.

CHAPTER 1

1. H. Waddell, *Medieval Latin Lyrics* (New York, 1929), p. 69.
2. Ibid., p. 71.
3. F.J.E. Raby, *A History of Secular Latin Poetry in the Middle Ages* (Oxford, 1934).
4. Waddell, p. 27.
5. Ibid., p. 31.
6. Ausonius, *Poems*, trans. H. White (London, 1963), p. 279.
7. Waddell, p. 39.
8. Ibid., p. 63.
9. See Waddell, pp. 79–100; F.J.E. Raby, *A History of Christian Latin Poetry*, 2nd ed. (Oxford, 1953), pp. 154–96; C.W. Previté-Orton, *The Shorter Cambridge Medieval History* (Cambridge, 1971), p. 339.
10. See Raby's analysis in *Secular Latin Poetry*, pp. 154–96.
11. See e.g., Waddell, p. 115.
12. T.H. White, *The Bestiary: A Book of Beasts* (New York, 1960), pp. 14ff.
13. See Isidore of Seville, *Traité de la Nature*, ed. J. Fontaine (Bordeaux, 1960), pp. 272–77, 304–6; Bede, *De natura rerum*, in *Patrologia Latina, cursus completus*, vol. 90, ed. J.-P. Migne (Paris, 1904); Rauban Maur, *De universo*, in *Patrologia Latina, cursus completus*, vol. 111(5), ed. J.-P. Migne (Paris, 1864).
14. Macrobius, *Commentary on the Dream of Scipio*, trans. W.H. Stahl (New York, 1952), pp. 189–91.
15. Augustine, *Concerning the City of God against the Pagans*, trans. H. Bettenson (Harmondsworth, 1972), book 22, chapter 24 (p. 1075).
16. For analysis of this, see A. Armstrong, *The Cambridge History of Later Greek and Early Medieval Philosophy* (Cambridge, 1970), pp. 518–31; J. O'Meara, *Eriugena* (Cork, 1969); J. O'Meara, ed., *The Mind of Eriugena* (Dublin, 1970).
17. *Periphyseon: On the Division of Nature, by John the Scot*, trans. M. Uhlfelder (Indianapolis, 1976), p. 203.
18. Ibid., p. 295.
19. Ibid., p. 307.

20. A good introduction to these works may be found in D. Knowles, *The Evolution of Medieval Thought* (New York, 1962); M.D. Chenu, *Nature, Man, and Society in the Twelfth Century*, trans. J. Taylor and L. Little (Chicago, 1968).
21. Alan of Lille, *Anticlaudianus, or, The Good and Perfect Man*, trans. J. Sheridan (Toronto, 1973), book I, 181ff, 277ff.
22. For vernacular lyrics, see, e.g., C. Kennedy, *An Anthology of Old English Poetry* (New York, 1960).
23. Ibid., p. 71.
24. For Italian collections, see R. Busk, *Folk-Songs of Italy* (London, 1887); C. Muscetta and P. Rivalta, *Poesia del duecento e del trecento* (Turin, 1956). As these songs are very obscure and cannot be dated, it is impossible to postulate any exact relationship between any of them and Francis' work.
25. Count de Montalembert, *The Monks of the West, from St. Benedict to St. Bernard* (London, 1861).
26. Ibid., vol. 1, p. 71.
27. A. Biese, *The Development of the Feeling for Nature in the Middle Ages and Modern Times* (London, 1905).
28. Biese skips over the early Dark Ages and post-Carolingian eras in the West.
29. E.g., G. Stockmayer, *Über Naturgefühl in Deutschland im 10 und 11 Jahrhundert* (Leipzig, 1910).
30. H.B. Workman, *The Evolution of the Monastic Ideal* (London, 1913), pp. 23, 221, 287ff.
31. A. Zimei, *La concezione della natura in San Francesco d'Assisi: studio psicologico e letterario* (Rome, 1929), pp. 83–84. This is in some ways an excellent work neglected by modern scholars.
32. C. Glacken, *Traces on the Rhodian Shore: Nature and Culture in Western Thought from Ancient Times to the End of the Eighteenth Century* (Berkeley, 1967).
33. G. Williams, *Wilderness and Paradise in Christian Thought* (New York, 1962).
34. Expertly studied by D.J. Chitty, *The Desert a City* (Oxford, 1966); and P. Brown, *The Making of Late Antiquity* (Cambridge, Mass., 1978).
35. P. Brown, pp. 82ff; Sulpicius Severus, *Postumianus*, chapter 3, in *The Western Fathers*, ed. and trans. F.R. Hoare (New York, 1965), p. 72.
36. Athanasius, *Life of Antony*, chapter 50, in *Select Writings and Letters of Athanasius, Bishop of Alexandria*, ed. A. Robertson, in The Nicene and Post-Nicene Fathers of the Christian Church, second series, vol. 4 (New York, 1892), p. 209.
37. Socrates, *Ecclesiastical History*, book 4, chapter 23, in *The Ecclesiastical History of Socrates Scholasticus*, trans. A.C. Zenos, in The Nicene and Post-Nicene Fathers of the Christian Church, second series, vol. 2 (Oxford, 1890), p. 107.

38. Chitty, p. 6.
39. See Chitty, passim; P. Brown, pp. 82ff; Williams, pp. 30ff.
40. Williams, p. 38.
41. Ibid.
42. Ibid., p. 41.
43. W. Short, *Saints in the World of Nature: The Animal Story as Spiritual Parable in Medieval Hagiography* 900–1200 (Rome, 1983).
44. E.g., in *VP* 58. This present research will accept the major Franciscan stories it analyzes as stemming from authentic early Franciscan sources of varying reliability, and very useful in revealing early Franciscan attitudes. Embroidery, although possible, is more unlikely here than in other hagiography because of the closeness of the sources and writers to the relevant incidents.
45. Severus, *Postumianus*, chapter 16, in Hoare, p. 87.
46. Athanasius, *Life of Antony*, chapter 9 (Robertson, pp. 198–99); chapters 22–23 (Robertson, p. 202).
47. With La Verna, as we shall see later.
48. Biese, pp. 32–33. I have compared with the Loeb, *St. Basil, The Letters*, trans. R. Deferrari (Cambridge, Mass., 1926), where the passage appears, pp. 107–11, in Letter 14 to Gregory Nazianzus.
49. Gibbon, chapter 37 (pp. 985–97 in edition above). For the originality of Basil's view, see D.S. Wallace-Hadrill, *The Greek Patristic View of Nature* (Manchester, 1968), pp. 89–91.
50. Wallace-Hadrill, p. 33. See also Basil's Letter 8 (end), in Deferrari.
51. Workman, p. 31 (Jerome's *Letter* 58).
52. For discussion of this see Fontaine's edition of the *Life of Martin* (Sulpice Sévère, *Vie de Saint Martin* [Paris, 1967], Introduction).
53. Even if the stories from Egypt are concocted, they are highly representative. The inclusion of the Origenist controversy (chapters 6–8, Hoare, pp. 74–77) adds weight to their authenticity.
54. *Life of Martin*, chapter 13 (Hoare, pp. 26–28). It is only fair to say, though, that the pagans showed no aesthetic interest in the tree, either.
55. Severus, *Postumianus*, chapters 10, 13, 14, 15 (Hoare, pp. 80; 84; 84–85; 86–87; 87).
56. Glacken, p. 310, quoting Montalembert.
57. Severus, *Postumianus*, chapter 14 (Hoare, pp. 84–85).
58. John Moschus, *Pratum Spiritale* (early sixth century), chapter 107, in *Le Pré Spirituel*, trans. M.R. de Journel (Paris, 1946).
59. Severus, *Postumianus*, chapter 25 (Hoare, p. 97).
60. Ibid., section 2, 2–3 (Hoare, pp. 103–6); Severus, *Gallus*, chapters 3 and 9 (Hoare, pp. 125–26, 131–32).
61. Severus, *Postumianus*, section 2, 9–10 (Hoare, pp. 114–16). Some of these gain authority from Jesus' remarks on birds and lilies, and Romans 1:20.

62. Gregory the Great, *The Dialogues*, book 2, chapter 2, trans. O. Zimmerman, in Fathers of the Church, vol. 39 (New York, 1959).
63. See Severus, *Letter* 3 (Hoare, p. 57—water fowl as demons).
64. See Gregory the Great, *Dialogues*, book 3, chapter 15; M. Bihl, "De praedicatione a S. Francesco avibus facta," *Archivum Franciscanum Historicum* 20 (1927): 202–6.
65. *Dialogues*, book 2, chapter 33.
66. E.A. Armstrong, pp. 31, 34–37.
67. Bede's *Life of Cuthbert*, chapters 10, 12, 17, and 19–21; found in *Two Lives of St. Cuthbert*, ed. and trans. B. Colgrave (Cambridge, 1940), pp. 189–91, 195–97, 215–17, 221–27.
68. See Introduction to *Felix's Life of Guthlac* ed. and trans. B. Colgrave, (Cambridge, 1956).
69. Ibid., chapter 19 (p. 83).
70. *Aeneid*, book 2, line 268, in *Virgil, with an English translation by H.R. Fairclough* (Cambridge, Mass., 1960).
71. Colgrave, *Life of Guthlac*, chapters 24–25 (pp. 87–89).
72. See the discussion in E.M. Palumbo, *The Literary Use of Formulas in Guthlac II and their Relation to Felix's Vita Sancti Guthlaci* (The Hague, 1977), p. 17. On Felix's use of Vergil, see Palumbo, p. 30.
73. Colgrave, *Life of Guthlac*, chapter 25 (p. 89). "Deeply loved" is *adamato*.
74. Here one sees a hagiographer transmitting the ascetic ideals of his saint, yet "intellectualizing" at the same time, with Felix and Guthlac. Guthlac of course had never read Vergil, and to see his ascetic ideals as in any conscious way Vergilian would be absurd. Yet the hagiographer may well have been faithful to the barbaric warrior ideals Guthlac would have transferred to his new saintly combats and outlook. We shall have to make similar careful distinctions between Francis and his hagiographers.
75. See E.A. Armstrong, pp. 31, 34–37.
76. See L. Kervran, *Brandan, le grand navigateur celte du Vle siècle* (Paris, 1977), pp. 121–22 for dating. Also see C. Selmer, Introduction to "Navigatio Sancti Brendani Abbatis" from *Early Latin Manuscripts* (Notre Dame, 1959).
77. Kervran, p. 121, my translation.
78. E.A. Armstrong, pp. 34–41, 182–83.
79. A. Tommasini, *Irish Saints in Italy*, trans. J. Scanlan (London, 1937), pp. 445ff.
80. For the story, see, e.g., M. Lambert, *Medieval Heresy: Popular Movements from Bogomil to Hus* (New York, 1976), pp. 67ff.
81. E.A. Armstrong, p. 183.
82. *Voyage of Brendan*, chapter 15.
83. Ibid.
84. The complete text of the Hymn is found in the Vulgate, Daniel 3:51–90, where the verses quoted here are 57, 76, and 80. In the *New Oxford Annotated*

Bible with the Apocrypha, the Hymn is in the Apocrypha and entered as Daniel 3:28–68, with the verses I quote being 35, 54, and 58.

85. *Voyage of Brendan*, chapter 17.
86. E.A. Armstrong, pp. 66–67.
87. E.g., chapter 11 of the *Voyage*; and Short, pp. 127–47.
88. See Zimei, p. 83.
89. Jonas, *Life of Columban*, chapter 60, in *Jonas, Life of Columban*, ed. D.C. Munro, Translations and Reprints from the Original Sources of European History, vol. 2, no. 7, rev. ed. (New York, 1908), p. 35.
90. See Workman, pp. 236ff; Gerald of Wales, *Journey Through Wales*, book 1, section 3, in Giraldus Cambrensis, *The Journey Through Wales, and The Description of Wales*, trans. L. Thorpe (Harmondsworth, 1978).
91. From L. Bieler, *Ireland, Harbinger of the Middle Ages* (London, 1963), pp. 59–61.
92. Ibid. The "you" (last line) refers to a fictitious Irish king to whom the poem is supposedly addressed. Compare White's comment: "Legends of saints, especially the Irish saints, had long told of their dealings with animals but always, I believe, to show their dominance over creatures" (Spring, p. 29).
93. See e.g., Biese, pp. 59ff; Glacken, pp. 307ff.
94. Biese, p. 59.
95. Glacken, p. 308.
96. Stockmayer, pp. 9, 11, 38, et passim.
97. Ibid., pp. 9, 42.
98. Glacken, pp. 330ff; Coulton, vol. 2, pp. 16ff.
99. Stockmayer, pp. 38–39.
100. Ibid., p. 41.
101. Ibid., p. 11.
102. See especially H. Grundmann's "Neue Beiträge zur Geschichte der religiösen Bewegungen im Mittelalter," in *Ausgewählte Aufsätze*, Teil 1, Schriften der Monumenta Germaniae Historica, Band 25, 1 (Stuttgart, 1976), pp. 38–91.
103. Ibid., pp. 46ff.
104. Ibid.; see also J.R. Russell, *Dissent and Reform in the Early Middle Ages* (Berkeley, 1965); Lambert, pp. 29ff.
105. See Lambert and Grundmann as above.
106. See Russell; Grundmann; and Lambert, pp. 29ff.
107. For many detailed studies of this see, e.g., M. Pennington, ed., *The Cistercian Spirit* (Spencer, Mass., 1970), especially J. Leclercq, "The Intentions of the Founders of the Cistercian Order," pp. 95ff.
108. See Grundmann, pp. 61ff.
109. For a comparison of attitudes to the environment (less extensive and more popular than ours), see R. Dubos, "Franciscan Conservation versus Benedictine Stewardship," in Spring, pp. 113–36. He attributes the *Description of Clairvaux* to Bernard, however, rather than to a slightly later Cistercian.

110. J. Leclercq, in Pennington, p. 120.
111. J. Leclercq, "Le thème de la jonglerie chez S. Bernard et ses contemporains," *Rev. d'Hist. de la Spiritualité* 48 (1972): 385–400. Francis would wish it literally, seeing his followers as fools and singers for Christ; Bernard sees it metaphorically, in that monks stand the world's values on their heads and thus appear to the secular world as jesters standing on their heads.
112. For the decline of this practice, see, e.g., Workman, pp. 236ff; Gerald of Wales, book 1, 3.
113. Benedict, *Rule*, chapter 48, in *The Rule of St. Benedict in Latin and English with Notes*, ed. and trans. T. Fry (Collegeville, Minn., 1981), pp. 249–53.
114. Glacken, p. 308.
115. Bernard, *Letter* 107, in *The Letters of St. Bernard of Clairvaux*, trans. B.S. James (Chicago, 1953), pp. 155–56.
116. É. Gilson, "Sub umbris arborum," *Medieval Studies* 14 (1952): 149.
117. J. Leclercq, *The Love of Learning and the Desire for God*, trans. C. Misrahi (New York, 1961), p. 164.
118. Walter Daniel, *Life of Aelred*, chapter 5, M. Powicke, ed. and trans., *The Life of Ailred of Rievaulx by Walter Daniel* (Oxford, 1978), pp. 12–13.
119. É. Gilson, "Sub umbris," p. 154.
120. The letter reads: "aliquid . . . sub umbris arborum senseris" versus "didicisses in scholis." See Gilson, "Sub umbris."
121. Also see Glacken, p. 308.
122. See J. Leclercq, *Love of Learning*, pp. 164–65; Glacken, pp. 308ff; Gerald of Wales, book 1, 3.
123. Considering also J. Leclercq's comments on Bernard's appreciation of the natural environment, in *Bernard of Clairvaux and the Cistercian Spirit* (trans. C. Lavoie [Kalamazoo, Mich., 1976], p. 18), one may relegate the story of Bernard's obliviousness to the beauty of Lake Leman (see A. Luddy, *A Life of St. Bernard* [Dublin, 1927], p. 36), to the footnote it deserves. Francis himself ignored whole towns when he was in mystic trance. For more on Cistercian paradisal imagery and conception of the ancient roots of their way of life, see the letter of William of St. Thierry (in J. Morison, *The Life and Times of St. Bernard* [London, 1884], p. 33): "I tarried with him (Bernard) a few days, unworthy though I was, and whichever way I turned my eyes I marvelled, and thought I saw a new heaven and a new earth, and the old pathways of the Egyptian monks our fathers, with recent footsteps of the men of our time left in them. The golden age seemed to have revisited the world then at Clairvaux. There you could see men, who had been rich in the world, glorying in the poverty of Christ."
124. See Idung of Prüfening, *A Dialogue between Two Monks*, in *Cistercians and Cluniacs: the Case for Cîteaux,* Cistercian Fathers Series 33 (Kalamazoo, Mich., 1977), book 2, 54, p. 94.
125. Ibid. He even harks back to the early Eastern fathers in defense of customs—see book 2, 21ff.

126. Ibid., 2, 54.
127. Translated by H. Scott and C. Bland (London, 1929).
128. English in *Life and Works of St. Bernard, Abbot of Clairvaux*, trans. S. Eales, 2nd ed. (London, 1912), vol. 2, pp. 460–66; Latin in *Selectae Sancti Bernardi Epistolae*, ed. J. Gaume (Paris, 1855), pp. 1–8.
129. See Caesarius (Scott), Introduction.
130. Ibid., book 10, 48 (Scott, pp. 218–19).
131. Ibid.
132. E.g., Francis' preaching to the birds, *VP* 58 (c. 1213); or his praising God with marsh birds, *ML* 8, 9 (c. 1219).
133. Habig, p. 211.
134. Caesarius, book 1, 15 (Scott, p. 22).
135. Ibid., book 5, 2 (Scott, pp. 315–18); book 9, 8ff.
136. English text in Eales, vol. 2, pp. 460–66. Latin in Gaume, pp. 1–8.
137. See Glacken, pp. 213–14; for the correct dating see Montalembert, vol. 1, p. 72; A. de Joubainville, *Études sur l'état interieur des abbayes Cisterciènnes, et principalement de Clairvaux, au XIIe et au XIIIe siècle* (Paris, 1858), pp. 329ff; Louis Lekai, O.S.C., placed it in the mid-thirteenth century (personal communication).
138. J. Leclercq, *Love of Learning*, p. 165.
139. In Eales, p. 460.
140. Ibid.
141. R. Dubos, "Franciscan Conservation and Benedictine Stewardship," in Spring, pp. 114–37. However, the article treats Franciscan views in a simplistic manner, and looks at only those elements in medieval views relevant to modern times.
142. Eales, p. 466.
143. Ibid.
144. Ibid., p. 461.
145. Ibid., p. 464.
146. Ibid., p. 466.
147. Ibid., p. 461.
148. Ibid., p. 464; *VP* 58.
149. See e.g., *F* 11, 1–2, where Francis enjoys wilderness.
150. Eales, p. 467—the river charms and works for the monks alone; for Francis and affectionate robins, see *VS* 47; *LP* 108; *MP* 107.
151. Eales, p. 466.
152. Ibid., p. 462.
153. See his "The Religious Background of the Present Environmental Crisis," in Spring, pp. 137–51.
154. Eales, p. 463.
155. Glacken, pp. 302ff.
156. K. Haines, "The Death of St. Francis of Assisi," *Franziskanische Studien* (1976): 27–46, details his unusual stamina under austere conditions—a com-

mon characteristic of saints (though in Francis' case, this held even through ill-health until the end).

Chapter 2

1. A. Mockler, *Francis of Assisi: The Wandering Years* (Oxford, 1978), p. 131.
2. Englebert (1972), p. 12.
3. For an interesting psychological analysis of this period in Francis' life, see É. Leclerc, *The Canticle of Creatures, Symbols of Union*, trans. M. O'Connell (Chicago, 1977), pp. 137ff.
4. Even though, as Mockler says, a few central ideas were not new, their cultural context and personal interpretation in Francis' case made for tremendous original ramifications, as we shall see.
5. *3 Comp* 55.
6. *VP* 34. Francis excepted only places that housed the Eucharist from the rule of austerity. For this, see his *Testament*, in Habig, pp. 67–70.
7. Compare the descriptions of early ascetic life in D.J. Chitty with the early Franciscans' mode of life.
8. E.g., P.F. Anson, *The Pilgrim's Guide to Franciscan Italy* (London, 1926); H.E. Goad, *Franciscan Italy* (London, 1926).
9. This may be deduced from the last sentence of *VP* 60.
10. *LP* 49. Francis' gentle and non-threatening personality would certainly not have repulsed the curious animals.
11. Short, pp. 39–101.
12. For the complete text, see Goad, p. 113.
13. Englebert (1972), p. 358.
14. J. Leclercq, *Love of Learning*, pp. 164–65.
15. Socrates, *Ecclesiastical History*, book 4, chapter 23 (Zenos, p. 107).
16. Luke 12:27.
17. Severus, *Letter* 3 (in Hoare, p. 57).
18. Severus, *Postumianus*, section 2, 10 (Hoare, pp. 115–16).
19. Short, pp. 39ff.
20. E.A. Armstrong, p. 154.
21. Short, pp. 101–2.
22. Severus, *Gallus*, chapter 9 (Hoare, pp. 131–32).
23. *Admonition* 5.
24. White, in Spring, p. 29.
25. See, e.g., Caesarius, *Dialogue*, book 10, 48.
26. E.g., *VP* 60; *VP* 77–79; *VS* 168; *VS* 170; *VS* 47.
27. See, e.g., T.H. White.
28. For Godric, see E.A. Armstrong, p. 196. For examples of Francis' concern, see *VP* 60; *VP* 61; *VP* 77–80; *VP* 87; *VS* 165; *VS* 167; *VS* 200; *LP* 51; *LP* 110; *LP* 49–50; *MP* 118; *MP* 114. See also Short, pp. 79ff.

29. E.A. Armstrong, pp. 65–70. Yet (pace Armstrong) none of these incidents in the Franciscan legend seem derivative. They have a convincing freshness and are packed with detail. Some of the earlier parallels involve a confusion between birds and angels. This was not present in the Franciscan anecdotes.
30. See, e.g., *RB*, chapter 1: "The Rule and life of the Friars Minor is this, namely, to observe the Holy Gospel of our Lord Jesus Christ by living in obedience, without property. . . ."
31. E.g., lambs, in *VP* 77–80.
32. Chapter 15. The prohibition is general, and probably included pets as well as animals kept for food or travel.
33. In 1260. See E.A. Armstrong, p. 7.
34. See Habig, pp. 186ff; Brooke, Introduction to *Scripta Leonis*.
35. See the discussion in Habig, pp. 1534ff.
36. Ibid., pp. 1566ff (chapters 25, 31, and 64).
37. E.A. Armstrong, pp. 160–62; 197–98.
38. From his *Sentences*, trans. in Habig, p. 849.
39. For earlier medieval parallels to these conceptions, see Short, pp. 9–11, 195ff.
40. For the passages, see A.O. Lovejoy and G. Boas, *A Documentary History of Primitivism and Related Ideas: Primitivism and Related Ideas in Antiquity* (Baltimore, 1935), e.g., pp. 43–102, 230–39; Glacken, pp. 133–36. The Celano passage seems to reveal a belief not entirely Christian in basis, but which was perhaps pagan and even archetypal in its conception of cosmic renewal and decline. See M. Eliade, *The Myth of the Eternal Return*, trans. W. Trask (New York, 1954).
41. See e.g., Severus, *Letter* 2 (Hoare, pp. 51–55), mourning the loss of St. Martin of Tours.
42. On this large topic, see especially M. Bloomfield, ed., "Joachim of Fiore: A Critical Survey," *Traditio* 13 (1957): 249–311; M. Reeves, *Joachim of Fiore and the Prophetic Future* (New York, 1976), pp. 30–40; C. Lyttle, "The Stigmata of St. Francis, Considered in the Light of Possible Joachimite Influence upon Thomas of Celano," *American Society of Church History Papers*, 2nd series, 4 (1914): 77–88; Stanislao da Campagnola, *L'Angelo del sesto sigillo e l'alter christus* (Rome, 1971).
43. *ML*, preface; Reeves.
44. *VS* 52. See also Brooke's *LP* (in *Scripta Leonis*) 34.
45. *VS* 35–36; 37. See also Brooke's *LP* 34.
46. An idea which has parallels going back even to the Hebrew prophets. See Brooke's *LP* 34.
47. The Wolf of Gubbio incident, recorded only in *Actus-Fioretti* 21, also illustrates this complex of assumptions, clearly linking the saint's action in taming the wolf to divine power and to the restoration of human piety from prior discord and sin. See Habig, pp. 1502–4 for discussion of the incident. While the anecdote possibly could have arisen from a natural occurrence, the story must have been elaborated and magnified by *Actus-Fioretti*. Its specific authenticity

is shaky; however, much of its ideals are congruent with what we know of Francis.

CHAPTER 3

1. As told in Englebert (1979), pp. 23ff. Some material in this present chapter on the Sermon to the Birds also appears in my "Tradition and Innovation in Saint Francis of Assisi's Sermon to the Birds," *Franciscan Studies* 43 (1983):396–407.
2. Englebert (1979), pp. 20–22.
3. I.G. Barbour, ed., *Western Man and Environmental Ethics* (Reading, Mass., 1973), pp. 93–113.
4. See Williams.
5. See *VP* 60, last sentence, and *F* 7.
6. *3 Comp*. 55.
7. On the difficulty of this combination and the medieval background of the issue, see D. Nicholson, *The Mysticism of Saint Francis of Assisi* (London, 1923), pp. 300–303; J. Leclercq, *Love of Learning*.
8. *3 Comp*. 49.
9. See Englebert (1972), pp. 432–35.
10. See Haines.
11. Francis' attempt was much more systematic and demanding than those of his twelfth century predecessors such as Bruno, Stephen of Muret, and William of Vercelli, who also, to some extent, attempted to combine introverted eremetic isolation with periods of evangelical wanderlust. See Anson, pp. 87–104.
12. *F* 16. *VP* 35 alludes to this incident.
13. Ibid.
14. Ibid.
15. For the best texts, see *VP* 58 and *F* 16.
16. I.e., the one belonging to Francis, not necessarily to all his Order.
17. E.g., Psalm 148; the Canticle of the Three Young Men (Dan. 3:23ff in the *Vulgate*).
18. This synthesis of ideas from disparate areas of experience is one of the most common processes of intuitive creativity. See A. Koestler, *The Act of Creation* (New York, 1964); I.G. Barbour, *Issues in Science and Religion* (New York, 1966), pp. 142ff.
19. L. Cellucci, "Varie redazione della predica di San Francesco agli uccelli," *Archivum Romanicum* 24 (1940): 301–8; see also E.A. Armstrong, p. 58.
20. For analysis of Celano's style, see Cellucci.
21. E.A. Armstrong, p. 58.
22. See Appendix III.
23. *VP* 58: "*ut ipse dicebat et qui cum eo fuerant fratres*."
24. *VP* 58, beginning.
25. Acts 2:41.

26. Luke 4:30.
27. Mark 16:15, "*omni creaturae*" (Vulgate).
28. To the modern observer the incident hardly seems miraculous. Those who have occasionally walked through fields in which flocks of birds are eating will recognize most of the birds' reactions—flapping wings, turning towards the observer—as responses to a threat. Even the *Fioretti*'s symbolic ending, which has the birds forming a cross in the sky, could have arisen from the observers remarking the particular manner in which the flock swirled away. A rational analysis makes clear just how much mythic ideology was actually present in the minds of the people at the event. They were projecting powerful ideas upon a situation only slightly unusual.
29. The *Legend of Perugia* uses *curialis*. We will study this later.
30. E.A. Armstrong, p. 60.
31. See pp. 25, 46; and C.G. Loomis, *White Magic: An Introduction to the Folklore of Christian Legend* (Cambridge, Mass., 1948), pp. 66–69.
32. *VP* 80; *ML* 9:1. Lawrence Cunningham, *Saint Francis of Assisi* (Boston, 1976), pp. 54–57; Lynn White, Jr., and Doyle.
33. S.J.P. van Dijk, "The Breviary of St Francis," *Franciscan Studies* 9 (1949): 13–40. This issue is discussed more fully in our Chapter 7.
34. Ibid., p. 180; *VS* 102.
35. Esser, *Die Opuscula*, pp. 282–83.
36. Daniel 3:35, 58.
37. Psalm 148:3–5.
38. See also the flattery of the elements in Francis' *Canticle*.
39. Matthew 7:29.
40. *F* 16 tells of the birds forming a cross, which predicts the Order's future successes. Yet even the elation reported in the *Vita Prima* would have stimulated Francis on his journey.
41. *ML* 12:4.

CHAPTER 4

1. See Englebert (1979), pp. 10ff.
2. See, e.g., ibid., p. 13; E.A. Armstrong, p. 21; Mockler; *VS* 21; and P. Rajna, "S. Francesco d'Assisi e gli spiriti cavallereschi," *Nuovo Antologia* (October 1926): 385–95.
3. Nicholson, p. 329.
4. *3 Comp.* 3.
5. Englebert (1979), p. 28.
6. See *LP* 71, which appears to allude to an obscure incident in Arthurian romance.
7. E.g., *F* II:1; *F* 37.
8. E.A. Armstrong, p. 21.
9. See Englebert (1972), p. 437.

10. Bonaventure (*ML* 4:9) shared his view, according to the original Latin.
11. Englebert (1979), p. 131; *F* II:1.
12. *VP* 6.
13. Englebert (1979), p. 132.
14. The birds "neither sow nor reap" (*VP* 58).
15. Chesterton, in *Saint Francis*, considers much of Francis' action in deference to creation a "sort of symbolic joke," intended to stress Francis' reverence to God in all creation (p. 139).
16. E.A. Armstrong (p. 21) also notes a link between chivalry and Francis' reactions to creation, but does not pursue his discovery. The lack of recognition for Francis' uniqueness in this area is not surprising, since here, for all his originality, he proved himself a man of his time. No one today would think of appreciating the environment through medieval conceptions of chivalry.
17. It appears only in the *Actus-Fioretti*, and in the part of the Latin text only discovered at the beginning of this century. See R.P. Josė de Elizondo, "Boletin Franciscano," *Estudis Francanos* 11 (1913): 43–44. But it is lengthy and detailed. One cannot dismiss an anecdote simply because it has no parallels in the earliest documents. To do so would be to dismiss Francis' crisis and consultation with Clare (*F* 16), "How St. Francis made Brother Juniper Twirl Around" (*F* 11), and the settlement of La Verna and reception of the Stigmata (*F* 11:1–2). The incident possesses a spirit of authenticity.
18. I avoid using "courtesy" since moderns might take it for granted and not realize its close link with chivalric culture and other values at this period.
19. See S. Painter, *French Chivalry* (Ithaca, New York, 1940), pp. 32–33; and of course, C.S. Lewis, *The Allegory of Love, A Study in Medieval Tradition* (Oxford, 1938).
20. On this, see B. Tierney, *Medieval Poor Law: A Sketch of Canonical Theory and its Application in England* (Berkeley, 1959).
21. *VS* 166; *LP* 48. E. Pax, in his "Bruder Feuer: Religionsgeschichtliche und volkskundliche Hintergrunde" (*Franziskanische Studien* [1951]: 238–50), argues that the word *curialis* means being on intimate terms. This is too narrow a definition.
22. Francis prayed to God for aid and blessed the fire with the sign of the cross (*VS* 166; *LP* 48).
23. Francis' conception of chivalrous deference to and consideration for creatures as a form of charity, or as something resembling it theologically, includes his giving "alms" to creatures (*VP* 80–87), and relates to a view of Aquinas' that charity should be extended to all creation. See E.A. Armstrong, p. 236, note 17.
24. Nicholson, p. 86, quoting from J. Jorgenson, *Der Heilige Franz von Assisi* (New York, 1924).
25. In Habig, pp. 133–34. Francis' last statements here are based on John 19:11; thus his attitude here has an obvious Biblical base in Christ's submission to

all worldly power. The word "nature" is from the *Omnibus* translation and is not in the Latin original.

26. More on the Cathars later. They were noteworthy and powerful in Francis' time, and were divided into many sects. They were gradually eradicated by the Albigensian crusade (1209 and after) and the Inquisition. For more information, see Appendix I.
27. On Francis the epicure, see *LP* 29; *MP* 111.
28. Habig, p. 34.
29. In H.S. Canby, ed., *The Selected Works of Thoreau* (Boston, 1975), p. 50.
30. See L. Lekai, *The Cistercians* (Kent, Ohio, 1977), pp. 368–69.
31. See C. Esser, *Origins of the Franciscan Order* (Chicago, 1970), p. 95.
32. See, e.g., *VP* 51–52; *VS* 131; *LP* 40; *MP* 61.
33. For treatment of the Cathars, see R. Moore, ed., *The Birth of Popular Heresy* (New York, 1975), and M. Loos, *Dualist Heresy in the Middle Ages* (Prague, 1974). There were some variations in the Cathar sects.
34. See Loos, p.251; Moore, pp. 91, 152.
35. C. Esser, "Franziskus von Assisi und die Katharer seiner Zeit," *Archivum Franciscanum Historicum* 51 (1958): 241.
36. *Letter to the Faithful*, 6, in Habig, p. 95.
37. See Moore, p. 152.
38. See Caesarius, *Dialogue*, book 5, chapters 20–24.
39. See Moore, pp. 75–76.
40. Loos, p. 251; Moore, pp. 91, 152.
41. E. Ladurie, *Montaillou: The Promised Land of Error*, trans. B. Bray (New York, 1979), p. 344.
42. R. Zaehner, *Mysticism, Sacred and Profane* (Oxford, 1957), p. 28.
43. Ibid., p. 29. Also see M. Knowles, *The Nature of Mysticism* (New York, 1966), p. 127.
44. E.A. Armstrong, p. 16.
45. Zaehner, pp. 84ff.
46. E.A. Armstrong, pp. 16–17.
47. Ibid., pp. 9–17.
48. S. Katz, "Language, Epistemology, and Mysticism," in his *Mysticism and Philosophical Analysis* (New York, 1978), p. 59.
49. Ibid., p. 46.
50. Katz, *Mysticism and Religious Tradition*, pp. 3–51.
51. E.A. Armstrong, p. 17.
52. G. Sabatelli, "Studi recenti sul Cantico di Frate Sole," *Archivum Franciscanum Historicum* 51 (1958): 4–5.
53. D. Knowles, *Evolution*, p. 243.
54. Psalm 50:1–2.
55. Psalm 65:12–13.
56. Psalm 146:7ff.

57. For an elaboration of this, see W. Eichrodt, *Theology of the Old Testament*, vol. 1, trans. J. Baker (Philadelphia, 1961), pp. 140, 318.
58. Ibid., pp. 140, 176, 410. Also see H.W. Robinson, *Inspiration and Revelation in the Old Testament* (Oxford, 1946), pp. 1–33; Glacken, pp. 165–66.
59. Glacken, pp. 27ff.
60. See the discussion of Basil's remarks, above, pp. 19–20.
61. See E.R. Dodds, *The Greeks and the Irrational* (Berkeley, 1973), pp. 64ff; Apuleius, *The Golden Ass*, chapter 12, 35ff (in *The Transformations of Lucius, otherwise known as The Golden Ass, by Lucius Apuleius*, trans. R. Graves [Harmondsworth, 1976], p. 170); Lucian, *Lucius*, 35ff (in *Selected Satires of Lucian*, ed. and trans. by L. Casson [New York, 1968], pp. 80–81); Lucius, *Alexander the Quack Prophet*, in Casson, pp. 267ff; Porphyry, *Letter to Anebo* (in A.R. Sodano, ed., *Porphyrio, Lettera ad Anebo* [Naples, 1958]). Poetic creations of Bacchic frenzies, as in Euripides' *Bacchae*, 135ff, 725ff (in *Ten Greek Plays in Contemporary Translations*, ed. L.R. Lind [Boston, 1957], pp. 333–34; 347), are associated with the natural environment, but some classical figures even evince discomfort at these expressions. (Pseudo-) Longinus, who criticizes the passages in the *Bacchae* in his *On the Sublime* 15 (ed. and trans. W.R. Roberts, Cambridge, 1935, pp. 83–91), says they show exaggeration and exceed the bounds of credibility.
62. *Phaedrus*, 238d, trans. R. Hackforth, in *The Complete Dialogues of Plato*, ed. E. Hamilton and R. Cairns (Princeton, 1973), p. 486.
63. Ibid., 242, 244ff (pp. 489–91).
64. See e.g., F. Grant, *Ancient Roman Religion* (New York, 1957); L. Farnell, *The Cults of the Greek States* (New York, 1906); W. Fowler, *The Religious Experience of the Roman People* (London, 1911).
65. *Symposium*, 210e–211c, trans. M. Joyce, in Hamilton, pp. 562–63.
66. *Enneads*, book 2, 9:16, in *Plotinus, The Enneads*, trans. S. MacKenna, 4th ed. rev., London, 1969, p. 149.
67. Ibid., book 6, 7:21–22 (in MacKenna, pp. 578–79).
68. See Glacken, pp. 183–204; Wallace-Hadrill.
69. Glacken, p. 200 (Augustine's *Sermon* 241).
70. Glacken, p. 199 (*Contra Epist. Manich., liber unus*, 41; 48).
71. Augustine, *Confessions*, 10:34 (ed. and trans. R.S. Pine-Coffin [Baltimore, 1961], pp. 239–40).
72. Cousins, in Katz, *Mysticism and Religious Traditions*, p. 179.
73. Augustine, *Confessions*, 9:10 (Pine-Coffin, pp. 196–99).
74. Ibid.
75. E.A. Armstrong, p. 16.
76. Gregory the Great, *Dialogues*, book 3, chapter 15.
77. Ibid., book 2, chapter 2.
78. *Voyage of Brendan*, chapters 7, 15, 23.
79. Ibid., chapter 22.

80. *Soliloquy*, chapter 2, 11, in *The Works of Bonaventure*, vol. 3, *St. Bonaventure: Opuscula*, Second Series, trans. J. de Vinck (Paterson, New Jersey, 1966), pp. 86–87.
81. Ibid., chapter 1, 7, in de Vinck, pp. 46–47.
82. Bonaventure's *Mind's Road to God* presents a more positive approach, but its whole point is the ascent from the mere traces of the divine to the divine essence itself. This is basically the same argument found in the *Soliloquy*, where the message is couched in monitory tones.
83. S. Katz, *Mysticism and Religious Traditions* (Oxford, 1983), p. 165.
84. Ibid., p. 166.
85. Ibid., pp. 167–68.
86. Ibid.
87. Ibid., p. 168. Cousins refers only to Bonaventure and Francis' historical mysticism in his actual arguments. Yet the parallels here are very clear and one may safely extrapolate to Celano and Francis' nature mysticism, as Cousins in other places compares Francis' two types of mystical experiences and would undoubtedly see Celano and Bonaventure as performing similar functions here.
88. Acts 12:11.
89. Prayer in this instance might signify noncontemplative prayer. But considering how similarly Celano discussed the comparable episode, which definitely was mystical, it seems reasonable to suggest that in this instance a mystical experience also occurred. Celano himself, however, may not have been as fully aware that this was the case.
90. Katz, *Mysticism and Religious Traditions*, pp. 166ff.
91. In Latin, *exhilarationem*—a word commonly used in the mystical tradition to signify the occurrence of a mystical experience.

CHAPTER 5

1. Cunningham, *Saint Francis*, p. 54.
2. For notes on these areas see White, in Spring; Doyle; and Glacken, pp. 214–16.
3. Cunningham, *Saint Francis*, p. 56.
4. Ibid., p. 55.
5. See Englebert (1972), Appendix VIII. Major opponents of the view accepted here are G. Abate and L. Benedetto. Their arguments are discussed in A. Fortini, "Altre ipotesi sul luogo dove fu composto Il Cantico del Sole" (Assisi, 1956), and in Englebert (1972), Appendix VIII.
6. Englebert (1972), p. 453.
7. Ibid., and *LP* 43–44; *MP* 100–101.
8. *LP* 100.
9. See, e.g., E.A. Armstrong, pp. 223–25; Doyle, pp. 399–400; Cunningham, *Saint Francis*, pp. 52–57.

10. For research on this, see van Dijk, pp. 13–40; G. Abate, "Il primitivo Breviario francescano (1224–27)," *Miscellanea Francescana* 60 (1960): 47–240.
11. See van Dijk, pp. 17ff; R.D. Sorrell, *Tradition and Innovation in Saint Francis of Assisi's Interpretation of Nature* (Diss., Cornell University, 1983), pp. 216–19.
12. Esser, *Die Opuscula*, pp. 122–34, 277–85, 313–22.
13. Text from Englebert (1972), p. 458. Also see Branca, pp. 83–87, for original text with critical annotations.
14. My translation, compared with that of P. Hermann (Habig, p. 130).
15. G. Getto, *Francesco d'Assisi e il Cantico di Frate Sole* (Università di Torino, Pubblicazione della Facoltà di Lettere e Filosofia, Vol. 8, No. 2, 1966), p. 68.
16. Branca, pp. 62–79.
17. L. Benedetto, *Il Cantico di Frate Sole* (Florence, 1941), pp. 14–17.
18. Esser, *Die Opuscula*, p. 130; Branca, pp. 78–79.
19. *VP* 58–60; *VS* 165.
20. Notably in the *Exhortation to Praise God* and the *Praises before the Office*.
21. The *Legend of Perugia* account explains both these problems, and is examined later.
22. See, e.g., R. Brown, in Englebert (1972), p. 441.
23. G. Sabatelli, p. 7.
24. Found in P. Gueranger, *The Liturgical Year*, trans. L. Shepherd, vol. 1: Advent (Westminster, Maryland, 1948), pp. 225–26.
25. See *F* II:1; *VP* 16.
26. By Bernard de Ventadorn, from F. Goldin, *Lyrics of the Troubadours and Trouvères* (New York, 1973), pp. 137–38.
27. Goldin, p. 279.
28. Consider Francis' marriage to Lady Poverty, *VP* 7.
29. By the merchant turned bishop, Folquet de Marseilles, in Goldin, p. 277.
30. *VP* 16.
31. The *Mirror of Perfection* is a source that, although compiled later than the *Legend of Perugia*, often includes valuable early material. See Habig, pp. 1105ff.
32. *MP* 100.
33. Brooke's translation of *LP* 43, in *Scripta Leonis*.
34. A. Vicinelli, *Gli Scritti di San Francesco d'Assisi e I Fioretti* (Milan, 1955), pp. 88ff.
35. Ibid., p. 189.
36. Ibid., p. 194.
37. See Esser, *Die Opuscula*, p. 131.
38. Ibid., pp. 277–83, for analysis.
39. Based on Esser's Latin text, *Die Opuscula*, pp. 282–83.
40. Roman Psalter (as noted in Esser, ibid.).
41. The *Vulgate* reads *filii hominum*.

42. Roman Psalter.
43. Ibid.
44. From the Antiphon of the Introit from the Mass of the Holy Trinity. See Esser, *Die Opuscula*, p. 282, "Satz 16."
45. From the Mass of St. Michael. See Esser, *Die Opuscula*, p. 282, "Satz 17."
46. See *VP* 35–36, 58; *F* 16.
47. Line 12.
48. Psalm 139:19; 141:7.
49. Also it cannot be denied that in its place upon the altar the *Exhortation* would have been seen in the light of a Eucharistic hymn and prayer. One can easily imagine the depth of emotion felt, for example, at the consecration of the host upon such an altar, emblazoned as it was with such a vision of all creation joining in cosmic unity to praise God's miraculous presence in the sacramental bread and wine. (For Francis' deep devotion to the Eucharist, see his *Letter to the clerics; VS* 201.) This linkage of creatures with Francis' mystical devotions is reminiscent of Francis' nature mysticism. Some of his gravest and most portentious lines in the *Exhortation* are explained by this deep Eucharistic reverence: "Fear the Lord and give him honor/ Worthy is the Lord to receive praise and honor/ . . . Worthy is the lamb which was slain."
50. Vicinelli, pp. 202–205.
51. Ibid., p. 204, *RNB* 23.
52. Vicinelli, p. 207.
53. Ibid., p. 212.
54. *LH* lines 2, 3, 7, 8; compare these with *EX* lines 2, 15, 5, and 15 again.
55. Esser, *Die Opuscula*, p. 320; Habig, pp. 138–39.
56. Esser, *Die Opuscula*, p. 320; Habig, pp. 138–39.
57. From Habig, pp. 132–34.
58. Ibid., pp. 138–39.
59. Revelation 4:8.
60. Revelation 4:11.
61. Revelation 5:12.
62. Daniel 3:57.
63. Revelation 19:5.
64. Revelation 5:13.
65. E. Benz, *Die Vision: Erfahrungsformen und Bilderwelt* (Stuttgart, 1969), p. 474.
66. Bede, *Ecclesiastical History of the English People*, ed. B. Colgrave and R. Mynors (Oxford, 1969), book 4, 24 (pp. 415–21).
67. See Branca, pp. 62–79.
68. See Vicinelli, pp. 226ff. It is important to note also that the melody Francis composed for the *Canticle* probably was in the style of ecclesiastical chant. This contributed even more to the wide dissemination of the *Canticle*. See Branca, p. 63.
69. Branca, p. 79.

CHAPTER 6

1. Two others may be dealt with briefly. M. Casella has proposed *per* as *propter quod*, with a philosophical interpretation ("Il Cantico," *Studi Medievali* 16 [1950]: 102–34. But no early sources see the *Canticle* in this way—a fatal lack of support, considering the strength of the other explanations. P. Hermann (Habig, p. 130) proposes *per* as "through," and Doyle (p. 397) agrees. Hermann cites Matthew Arnold ("Pagan and Mediaeval Religious Sentiment", in *Matthew Arnold, Complete Prose Works*, vol. 3, *Lectures and Essays in Criticism*, ed. R.H. Super [Ann Arbor, 1962], pp. 212–58) and E. Platzeck (*Das Sonnenlied des Heiligen Franziskus von Assisi* [Munich, 1956]), in support. But Arnold's essay translates *per* as "for." Platzeck's arguments are weak, as he does not consult the early sources. In support of Hermann one could cite the passive "*Laudato si*" of the *Canticle* and *VP* 80, which says Francis praised God "in all elements and creatures" (*in omnibus elementis et creaturis*). *VP* 81 and *VS* 217, however, definitely intend *per* as "by," and both the *Legend* and the *Mirror* understand it as "for," as we shall see later. It is my argument that most passages in the authoritative early sources interpret *per* as "for" or "by," and that the best sources, the *Legend* and the *Mirror*, justify the translation as "for," which gives a more consistently acceptable and unforced reading of the poem as a whole.
2. R. Brown, in Englebert (1972), p. 442.
3. *St. Francis*, p. 53; also see Sabatelli, p. 4.
4. *VP* 58; 81. Also, *per* in the sense of the French *par* was an early Italian usage, as Englebert (1972) shows (p. 442). Possibly Francis, who knew some Old French (or more likely, Old Provençal) could have been influenced by this usage.
5. *VS* 217. Bonaventure may allude to the *Canticle* in his *ML* 9:1, but his reference is too vague. In final support of this interpretation, a manuscript of the *Actus in Valle Reatina* (c. 1416) substitutes Italian *da* (from, by) for *per* in the critical *Canticle* lines. See Brown, in Englebert (1972), p. 443.
6. See the arguments in H. Adams, pp. 25, 336; White, in Spring; and Cunningham, *St. Francis*, pp. 54, 109ff.
7. See White, in Spring; and Doyle.
8. Doyle devotes some time to this view, but does not establish its validity.
9. Englebert (1972), Appendix VIII, p. 443; P. Bigaroni, *Il Cantico di Frate Sole: Genesi del Cantico* (Assisi, 1956), p. 42–43; Fortini, pp. 11ff.
10. See Englebert (1972), Appendix VIII; Bigaroni; Fortini as above; and Brooke, Introduction to *Scripta Leonis*.
11. Fortini, p. 23.
12. Not in a scientific, but in an attitudinal sense—that is, oriented toward a responsible vision of humanity's relationship to the environment. This is the popular sense in which we will quote Doyle later, and is the only sense in which this book will use the term.

13. Doyle, p. 399.
14. Ibid.
15. Ibid., pp. 397–98.

CHAPTER 7

1. For instance, Francis' personal experience with campfires probably stimulated his love for fire expressed in the *Canticle*. See *LP* 48–50; *MP* 115–19.
2. See Genesis 1:26–30; 1 Timothy 4:1–5.
3. *VP* 80 (worms and Christ); *VP* 77 (lambs).
4. See, e.g., T.H. White.
5. *MP* 118; É. Leclerc, pp. 76, 98; Getto, p. 53.
6. Goad, p. 71.
7. Vicinelli, p. 250.
8. Ibid., p. 246, note 70.
9. See other examples in *VP* 58; *LP* 48.
10. Doyle, p. 397.
11. Though Francis held the ancient conception of the four elements, he chose a poetic and original grouping—wind, water, fire, earth—rather than the classical earth-water-air-fire arrangement. His grouping is more Biblical and hierarchical. See E. Platzeck, pp. 26ff.
12. *VP* 80.
13. If the *Canticle* is a rhetorical argument to propagate feelings of appreciation for creation, then it is very effective. As Vicinelli maintains (p. 230), the *Canticle*'s most vivid and lyrical moments are exactly those least Biblically based; those containing the ecstatic praise of creatures and the expressions of their familial relationship with humanity.
14. See the end of the *Praises of the Virtues*.
15. See the anecdotes about lambs, such as *VP* 77–79.
16. Genesis 11:13–15.
17. The Famous Zephyr—see Goldin, p. 97.
18. See É. Leclerc, p. 98.
19. Line 18.
20. The enthusiasm and focus on beauty here are Franciscan, though the passage may have arisen from the model of Genesis 1:11 and 29.
21. Vicinelli, p. 246, note 20, mentions that this is a possibility, but I doubt that a comparison with the ideals of the School of Chartres is required.
22. Habig, p. 134.
23. *LP* 43. Also, people must submit to another creature: death (see line 28 of the *Canticle*).
24. See our Chapter 2, note 47, for further discussion and questions about the authenticity of this incident.
25. Doyle and White oversimplify and do not realize all the implications here. E.A. Armstrong does not notice the many different levels of Francis' appreciation of creatures, or the consistent ideas of interdependence present.

26. See A.O. Lovejoy, *The Great Chain of Being* (Cambridge, 1948).
27. See p. 123, above.
28. R. Reuther, *Sexism and God-Talk* (Boston, Mass., 1983).
29. Ibid., p. 87.
30. Ibid., p. 92.
31. This sentiment is echoed in the recently discovered consolation Francis composed in Italian for the Poor Ladies at San Damiano—a text which also helps to substantiate the timing of the *Canticle* supported above (see V. Moleta, *From St. Francis to Giotto: The Influence of St. Francis on Early Italian Art and Literature* [Chicago, 1983] for text). The two compositions share other poetic devices, e.g., alternation between grand phrases and simple lilting alliterative phrases.
32. Vicinelli, p. 246. The allegorization of death in such a way is unusual, but see 1 Corinthians 15:54–55.
33. Habig, pp. 97–99.
34. Vicinelli, p. 246, note on this verse.
35. Another example is Boethius' *Consolation of Philosophy*.
36. See Zimei, p. 168. For others, see e.g., Vicinelli, p. 250.
37. For background, see D. Knowles, *The Evolution of Medieval Thought*; J. Pelikan, *The Christian Tradition*, vol. 3: *The Growth of Medieval Theology* (Chicago, 1978).
38. For this, see e.g., W. Wetherbee, *Platonism and Poetry in the Twelfth Century* (Princeton, 1972).
39. R.W. Southern, *Medieval Humanism* (New York, 1970), pp. 29ff; for Knowles, see his "The Humanism of the Twelfth Century," in *Studies* 30 (1941): 43–58.
40. Found in B. Tierney, *The Middle Ages*, vol. 2: *Readings in Medieval History* (New York, 1974), pp. 189ff.
41. Here his ideals link with the Chartrians, who gave "human feeling" an "intrinsic significance" in their poetry—see Wetherbee, p. 143.
42. Eliade, p. 9 et passim.
43. For the harsher Christian attitude, see *F* 18, where Francis prohibits friars from wearing breastplates and iron rings.

CHAPTER 8

1. See Biese, p. 59; Bieler, pp. 59–61.
2. E.G., for bees, see *VS* 165; *MP* 114. See Stockmayer, p. 41 (Ansfried, squire of Otto I).
3. *VS* 102–4; and see Francis' *Admonitions* for other examples.
4. For new literalism, see *LP* 51 (Francis and the rock). See also *MP* 26; for Psalms referring to friars, see Francis' *Office*, in Habig, p. 153, Psalm 68:33. Celano perceives this allegorical interpretation, *VS* 170.

5. For Francis' specific reference to interpretations, see *VS* 103, and his *Testament*, which he wished to be followed "*simpliciter et sine glossa*."
6. See Cunningham, *Saint Francis*, pp. 109ff; Moleta; E. Gurney-Salter, *Franciscan Legends in Italian Art* (London, 1905); G. Kaftal, *St. Francis in Italian Painting* (London, 1950); J.H. Stubblebine, *Assisi and the Rise of Vernacular Art* (New York, 1985); *San Francesco e il franciscanesimo nella letteratura italiana del Novecento*, Convegno nazionale su San Francesco e il francescanisimo nella letteratura italiano del Novecento (Assisi, 1983); *L'immagine di San Francesco nella controriforma*, Comitato nazionale per la manifestazioni culturali per l'viii centenario della nascita di San Francesco di Assisi (Rome, 1982); *L'immagine di San Francesco nella storiografia dall' umanesimo all' ottocento* (Assisi, 1983).
7. For Giles, see E.A. Armstrong, pp. 55–56; for Anthony of Padua, see *F* 40; in poetry of Jacopone, see Moleta, p. 34.
8. The anecdotes of Giles come the closest.
9. See J.H. Albanès, *La Vie de Saint Douceline* (Marseilles, 1879), chapters 7–9.
10. See Cunningham and other references in the notes above.
11. Moleta, p. 1.
12. H. Thöde, *Franz von Assisi und die Anfänge der Kunst der Renaissance in Italien* (Berlin, 1904).
13. *Franciscan Legends*, p. 46.
14. Moleta, p. 2.
15. See, e.g., Moleta and Stubblebine for a range of disagreements.
16. Stubblebine, pp. 88–89.
17. Ibid., p. 91.

Appendix I

1. *Archivum Franciscanum Historicum* 51 (1958): 223–55.
2. For this, see Esser, "Franziskus von Assisi," and also the discussion in his *Origins of the Franciscan Order* (Chicago, 1970), especially p. 95. An extensive explanation of *VS* 78, in which Francis is confronted by a Cathar, is given above, pp. 77–78.
3. White, in Spring, pp. 29-30.
4. Ibid., p. 31.
5. See Sabatier, p. 149; E.A. Armstrong, p. 236.
6. For the history of this dispute, see J.H.R. Moorman, *A History of the Franciscan Order from its Origin to the Year 1517* (Oxford, 1968), pp. 246–47 et passim.
7. See Englebert (1979), pp. 56–70; and Moorman, *A History of the Franciscan Order*.

APPENDIX II

1. Mostly derived from P. Bigaroni, p. 51.
2. Englebert (1972), p. 342.
3. See Habig, pp. 179ff.
4. In "Altre ipotesi."
5. *Il Cantico*, pp. 58ff.
6. *Scripta Leonis*, especially the Introduction; and Brooke's "Recent Work on St. Francis of Assisi," *Analecta Bollandiana* 100 (1982): 653–76.
7. For parallel stories in Celano and *Actus*, see *F* 2 and *VP* 24; *F* 3 and *VP* 53; *F* 16 and *VP* 58; *F* 18 and *VP* 100, *VS* 191; *F* 27 and *VP* 49. None of these in the *Actus-Fioretti* have any verbal parallels noteworthy enough to suggest Celano's influence.
8. For details, see Moorman, pp. 246–47 et passim.
9. R. Brown, in Habig, p. 1283.
10. Brown, in Englebert (1972), p. 358.
11. Compare *LP* 43–44 to *VP* 80–81; *LP* 48 to *VS* 166 in the original. Also see the parallels between Celano and *Fioretti* passages listed in note 7. Brooke's "Recent Work," p. 661, discusses *LP* accounts that are more detailed than Celano and gives them some support.
12. E.g., *VS* 165; *VS* 166 as compared to *LP* 48.
13. As in the comparison of the Sermon to the Birds accounts in *VP* 58 and *F* 16.

APPENDIX III

1. Of the others, Henri d'Avranches' *Legenda versificata* (text in *Analecta Franciscana* vol. 10 [Quaracchi, 1941], pp. 405–91) is merely a poetic restatement of Celano. Matthew Paris *Chronica Maior* account (F. Klingender, "St. Francis and the Birds of the Apocalypse," *Journal of the Warburg and Courtauld Institutes* 16 [1953]: 13–23), is very corrupt, either from Roger of Wendover's invention, myth-making oral tradition, or a conflation of Francis' Sermon with St. Anthony of Padua's Sermon to the Fishes. Matthew Paris also knew a version more similar to Celano's (Klingender). Bonaventure's account (*ML* 12:3) seems totally derivative from Celano, with no evidence he consulted any new sources.
2. *VP* 58: "*ut ipse dicebat et qui cum eo fuerant fratres*." See also *F* 16.
3. "*Interea dum, sicut dictum est, multi appositi sunt ad fratres*."
4. For an analysis, see Cellucci, p. 302.
5. Englebert (1979), p. 133; *F* 16.
6. For a comparison of the two accounts, see Cellucci, who rather flatters the *Fioretti* too much. He also forgets that Celano's account must have the greatest historical authenticity, as opposed to literary beauty.
7. Habig, p. 1281.

8. See Englebert (1979) pp. 132–33.
9. *VP* 35 ("They all conferred together . . .") to *VP* 36 ("Francis . . . went around the towns and villages").
10. Esser, *Die Opuscula*, pp. 282–83.
11. *VP* 58–59.
12. Celano, however, also hints that Francis conceived the idea of a lay order very early. See *VP* 34–35, and the discussion by P. Hermann in Habig, pp. 165–67. This lends more credibility to the *Actus* account.
13. Cellucci.
14. E.A. Armstrong, p. 58.
15. ". . . *sicut recitavit frater Jacobus de Massa, sanctus homo, qui omnia supradicta habuit ab ore fratris Massei, qui fuit unus de iis qui tunc erant socii sancti patris*" (*Actus* 16:21).
16. For parallel stories in the *Vita Prima* and the *Fioretti*, see *F* 2 and *VP* 24; *F* 3 and *VP* 53; *F* 16 and *VP* 58; *VP* 35; *F* 18 and *VP* 100 or *VS* 191; *F* 27 and *VP* 49.
17. In the *Actus* Sermon account, the birds are "sisters," not brothers, as in Celano. While it is difficult to tell which author is correct in this case, as Francis sometimes addressed birds either way, it is even more difficult to believe the *Actus* compiler would have made such a change with Celano directly in front of him.
18. *VP* 58.
19. *VP* 35–36.
20. This was his conscious practice at certain points—see his statement on inserting miracle stories, in the prologue of *VP*, 2.
21. Habig, pp. 1277.
22. E.g., Luke 12:24.
23. N. Tamassia, *Saint Francis of Assisi and His Legend*, trans. L. Ragg (London, 1910), pp. 108–9.
24. It is likely that Celano knew some of these sources, especially Severus' writing on Martin, which the Franciscan refers to in the famous case of Francis and the cloak (*VS* 1:5). For echoes of Gregory the Great in Celano, see J.H.R. Moorman, *The Sources for the Life of St. Francis of Assisi* (Manchester, 1940), p. 63; and Tamassia, pp. 114–20. Celano's competence within the hagiographical tradition has never been questioned. Yet expertise does not have to imply fabrication, especially when an account is claimed to have come from the very mouths of Francis and his followers, some of whom were still alive to contradict it if necessary.
25. See E.A. Armstrong, pp. 160–62; 197–98.
26. Ibid., p. 59.
27. Ibid., p. 58.
28. See Caesarius, book 1, chapter 15; and E.A. Armstrong, p. 96, note 90, among many examples.

Bibliography

Abate, G. "Il primitivo Breviario francescano (1224–27)." *Miscellenea Francescana* 60 (1960): 47–240.

Adams, H. *Mont-Saint-Michel and Chartres*. New York, 1961.

Adamnan. *Life of Columba*. Ed. and trans. A. and M. Anderson. London, 1961.

Alan of Lille. *Anticlaudianus, or, The Good and Perfect Man*. Trans. J. Sheridan. Toronto, 1973.

Allers, R. "Microcosmos from Anaximandros to Paracelsus." *Traditio* 2 (1944): 320–62.

Anson, P.F. *The Call of the Desert: The Solitary Life in the Christian Church*. London, 1964.

———. *The Pilgrim's Guide to Franciscan Italy*. London, 1926.

Apuleius. *The Golden Ass*. In *The Transformations of Lucius, otherwise known as The Golden Ass, by Lucius Apuleius*. Trans. R. Graves. Harmondsworth, 1976.

Aquinas, T. *Summa Contra Gentiles* III: *Providence*, Part 2. Trans. V. Brouke. Notre Dame, 1975.

Armstrong, A. *The Cambridge History of Later Greek and Early Medieval Philosophy*. Cambridge, 1970.

Armstrong, E.A. *Saint Francis: Nature Mystic. The Derivation and Significance of the Nature Stories in the Franciscan Legend*. Berkeley, 1973.

Arnold, M. "Pagan and Mediaeval Religious Sentiment." In *Matthew Arnold, Complete Prose Works*. Vol. 3: *Lectures and Essays in Criticism*. Ed. R.H. Super. Ann Arbor, 1962.

Athanasius. *Life of Antony*, in *Select Writings and Letters of Athanasius, Bishop of Alexandria*. Ed. A. Robertson. In The Nicene and Post-Nicene Fathers, second series, vol. 4. New York, 1892.

Augustine. *Concerning the city of God against the pagans*. Trans. H. Bettenson. Harmonsworth, 1972.

———. *Confessions*. Ed. and trans. R.S. Pine-Coffin. Baltimore, 1961.

Ausonius. *Poems*. Trans. H. White. London, 1963.

d'Avranches, H. *Legenda versificata*. In *Analecta Franciscana* 10 Quaracchi (1941): 405–91.

Barbour, I.G. *Issues in Science and Religion*. New York, 1966.

———, ed. *Western Man and Environmental Ethics*. Reading, Mass., 1973.

Basil. *Letters*. In *Saint Basil, The Letters*. Ed. and trans. R.J. Deferrari. New York, 1926.

Bede. *De natura rerum*. In Patrologia Latina, cursus completus, vol. 90. Ed. J.-P. Migne. Paris, 1904.

———. *Ecclesiastical History*. In *Bede's Ecclesiastical History of the English People*. Ed. B. Colgrave and R. Mynors. Oxford, 1969.

———. *Life of Cuthbert*. In *Two Lives of Saint Cuthbert*. Ed. and trans. B. Colgrave. Cambridge, 1940.

Benedetto, L. *Il Cantico di Frate Sole*. Florence, 1941.

Benedict. *Rule*. In *The Rule of St. Benedict in Latin and English with Notes*. Ed. T. Fry. Collegeville, Minn., 1981.

Benz, E. *Die vision: Erfahrungsformen und Bilderwelt*. Stuttgart, 1969.

Bernard. *Letters*. In *The Letters of St. Bernard of Clairvaux*. Trans. B.S. James. Chicago, 1953.

Biblia Sacra, iuxta Vulgatam Clementinam, nova edition. Ed. A. Colunga, O.P. and L. Turrado. 4th ed. Biblioteca de Autores Cristianos. Madrid, 1965.

Bieler, L. *Ireland, Harbinger of the Middle Ages*. London, 1963.

Biese, A. *The Development of the Feeling for Nature in the Middle Ages and Modern Times*. London, 1905.

Bigaroni, P. *Il Cantico di Frate Sole: Genesi del Cantico*. Assisi, 1956.

Bihl, M. "De praedicatione a S. Francesco avibus facta." *Archivum Franciscanum Historicum* 20 (1927): 202–6.

Bishop, M. *Saint Francis of Assisi*. Boston, 1974.

Bloomfield, M. "Joachim of Fiore: A Critical Survey." *Traditio* 13 (1957): 249–311.

Boase, T. *Saint Francis of Assisi*. Bloomington, Indiana, 1968.

Boff, L. *Saint Francis: A Model for Human Liberation*. Trans. J.W. Diercksmeier. New York, 1982.

Bonaventure, *Legenda Maior*. In *Analecta Francescana* 10 (1941): 557–652.

———. *Legenda Minor*. In *Analecta Francescana* 10 (1941): 655–78.

———. *The Major Life of Saint Francis*. Trans. P. Oligny. In *Omnibus*, ed. Habig. Chicago, 1973.

———. *The Minor Life of Saint Francis*. Trans. P. Oligny. In *Omnibus*, ed. Habig. Chicago, 1973.

———. *Soliloquy*. In *The Works of Bonaventure*. Vol. 3, *St. Bonaventure: Opuscula*, Second Series. Trans. J. de Vinck. Paterson, New Jersey.

Borst, A. *Die Katharer*. Stuttgart, 1953.

Branca, V. "Il Cantico di Frate Sole." *Archivum Franciscanum Historicum* 41 (1948): 62–79.
Brooke, R. "Recent Work on St. Francis of Assisi." *Analecta Bollandiana* 100 (1982): 653–76.
———. Ed. and trans. *Scripta Leonis, Rufini, et Angeli*. Oxford, 1970.
Brown, P. *The Making of Late Antiquity*. Cambridge, Mass., 1978.
Brown, R. *Fifty Animal Stories of Saint Francis as Told by his Companions*. Chicago, 1958.
———. *Franciscan Mystic: The Life of Blessed Brother Giles of Assisi, Companion of Saint Francis*. New York, 1962.
Busk, R. *Folk-Songs of Italy*. London, 1887.
Butler, C. *Western Mysticism*. 3rd ed. London, 1967.
Caesarius of Heisterbach. *Dialogue on Miracles*. Trans. H. Scott and C. Bland. London, 1929.
Campagnola, S. da. *L'Angelo del sesto sigillo e l'alter christus*. Rome, 1971.
Casella, M. "Il Cantico delle Creature." *Studi Medievali* 16 (1950): 102–34.
Celano, Thomas of. *Vita Prima*. In *Analecta Francescana* 10 (1941): 4–115.
———. *Vita Secunda*. In *Analecta Francescana* 10 (1941): 129–268.
———. *First Life of St. Francis*. Trans. P. Hermann. In *Omnibus*. Ed. Habig. Chicago, 1973.
———. *Second Life of St. Francis*. Trans. P. Hermann. In *Omnibus*. Ed. Habig. Chicago, 1973.
———. *Treatise on the Miracles of St. Francis*. Trans. P. Hermann. In *Omnibus*. Ed. Habig. Chicago, 1973.
Cellucci, L. "Varie redazione della predica di San Francescò agli uccelli." *Archivum Romanicum* 24 (1940): 301–8.
Chenu, M.D. *Nature, Man, and Society in the Twelfth Century*. Trans. J. Taylor and L. Little. Chicago, 1968.
Chesterton, G.K. *Saint Francis of Assisi*. New York, 1924.
Chitty, D.J. *The Desert a City*. Oxford, 1966.
Colgrave, B., ed. *Felix's Life of Saint Guthlac*. Cambridge, 1956.
Collingwood, R. *The Idea of Nature*. Oxford, 1945.
Comito, T. *The Idea of the Garden in the Renaissance*. New Jersey, 1978.
Coulton, G.C. *Five Centuries of Religion*. Cambridge, 1923.
———. *From St. Francis to Dante*. London, 1906.
Cousins, E., trans. *Bonaventure*. Classics in Western Spirituality 20. New York, 1978.
———. "Francis of Assisi: Christian Mysticism at the Crossroads." In *Mysticism and Religious Traditions*. Ed. S. Katz. Oxford, 1983.
Culler, J. *Structuralist Poetics*. Ithaca, New York, 1975.
Cunningham, L., ed. *Brother Francis: An Anthology of Writings by and about Saint Francis of Assisi*. New York, 1972.
———. *Saint Francis of Assisi*. Boston, 1976.

Cuthbert, Fr. *Life of Saint Francis of Assisi*. 3rd ed. London, 1921.

Daniel, W. *Life of Aelred*. In *The Life of Ailred of Rievaulx by Walter Daniel*. Trans. M. Powicke. Oxford, 1978.

Dijk, S.J.P. van. "The Breviary of Saint Francis." *Franciscan Studies* 9 (1949): 13–40.

Dodds, E.R. *The Greeks and the Irrational*. Berkeley, 1973.

Doyle, E. "The Canticle of Brother Sun." *New Blackfriars* 55 (1974): 392–402.

Dubos, R. "Franciscan Conservation versus Benedictine Stewardship." In *Ecology and Religion in History*. Ed. D. and E. Spring. New York, 1974.

Eales, S. *Life and Works of St. Bernard, Abbot of Clairvaux*. 2nd ed. London, 1912.

Eichrodt, W. *Theology of the Old Testament*. Vol. 1. Trans. J. Baker. Philadelphia, 1961.

Eliade, M. *The Myth of the Eternal Return*. Trans. W. Trask. New York, 1954.

Elizondo, R.P.J. de. "Boletin Franciscano." *Estudis Francanos* 11 (1913): 43–44.

Englebert, O. *Saint Francis of Assisi: A Biography*. Trans. E. Cooper. 2nd ed. Chicago, 1972.

———. *Saint Francis of Assisi: A Biography*. Trans. E.M. Cooper. 2nd ed. (paperback). Ann Arbor, 1979.

Esser, C. *Die Opuscula des Hl. Franziskus von Assisi, neue text kritische edition*. Rome, 1976.

———. "Franziskus von Assisi und die Katharer seiner Zeit." *Archivum Franciscanum Historicum* 51 (1958): 223–55.

———. *Origins of the Franciscan Order*. Chicago, 1970.

———. *Studien zur den Opuscula des Hl. Franziskus von Assisi*. Rome, 1973.

Euripides, *Bacchae*, In *Ten Greek Plays in Contemporary Translations*. Ed. L.R. Lind. Boston, 1957.

Fairclough, H. *Love of Nature among the Greeks and Romans*. New York, 1963.

Farnell, L. *The Cults of the Greek States*. New York, 1906.

I Fioretti di San Francesco. Ed. P.A. Cesari. Milan, 1857.

The Fioretti. Trans. R. Brown. In *Omnibus*. Ed. Habig. Chicago, 1973.

Fortini, A. *Altre ipotesi sul luogo dove fu composto Il Cantico del Sole*. Assisi, 1956.

———. *Nuova Vita di San Francesco*. Florence, 1959.

———. *Francis of Assisi*. Trans. H. Moak. New York, 1981.

Fowler, W. *The Religious Experience of the Roman People*. London, 1911.

Francis of Assisi. *Opuscula. Die Opuscula des Hl. Franziskus von Assisi, neue textkritische edition*. Ed. C. Esser. Spicilegium Bonaventurianum 13. Rome, 1976.

———. *Works*. Trans. B. Fahy. In *Omnibus*. Ed. Habig. Chicago, 1973.

Gaume, J., ed. *Selectae Sancti Bernardi Epistolae*. Paris, 1855.

Getto, G. *Francesco d'Assisi e il Cantico di Frate Sole*. Vol. 8, no. 2. Università di Torino, Pubblicazione della Facoltà di Lettere e Filosofia, 1966.

Gibbon, E. *The History of the Decline and Fall of the Roman Empire*. Vol. 2, with notes by the Rev. H. Milman. London, n.d.

Gilson, É. *The Philosophy of Bonaventure*. New Jersey, 1965.

———. "Sub umbris arborum." *Medieval Studies* 14 (1952): 148–52.

Giraldus Cambrensis. *The Journey through Wales, and the Description of Wales*. Trans. L. Thorpe. Harmondsworth, 1978.

Glacken, C. *Traces on the Rhodian Shore: Nature and Culture in Western Thought from Ancient Times to the End of the Eighteenth Century*. Berkeley, 1967.

Goad, H.E. *Franciscan Italy*. London, 1926.

Goldin, F. *Lyrics of the Troubadours and Trouvères*. New York, 1973.

Grant, F. *Ancient Roman Religion*. New York, 1957.

Greeley, A. *Ecstasy: A Way of Knowing*. New Jersey, 1974.

Green, J. *God's Fool: The Life and Times of Francis of Assisi*. Trans. P. Heinegg. San Francisco, 1985.

Gregory, T. *Anima Mundi: La filosofia di Guglielmo di Conches e la Schola di Chartres*. Florence, 1955.

Gregory the Great. *The Dialogues*. Trans. O. Zimmerman. Fathers of the Church 39, New York, 1959.

Grundmann, H. "Neue Beitrage zur Geschichte der religiosen Bewegungen im Mittelalter." *Schriften der Monumenta Germaniae Historica*, Band 25,1. *Ausgewählte Aufsätze*, Teil 1. Stuttgart, 1976.

Gueranger, P. *The Liturgical Year*. Trans. L. Shepherd. Vol. 1, *Advent*. Westminster, Maryland, 1948.

Gurney-Salter, E. *Franciscan Legends in Italian Art*. London, 1905.

Habig, M.A., ed. *Saint Francis of Assisi, Writings and Early Biographies: English Omnibus of the Sources for the Life of Saint Francis*. 3rd ed., rev. Chicago, 1973.

Haines, K. "The Death of Saint Francis of Assisi." *Franziskanische Studien* (1976): 27–46.

Hansen, W. *Saint Francis of Assisi: Patron of the Environment*. Chicago, 1971.

Henry, P. *La Vision d'Ostie*. Paris, 1938.

Hermann, P. *Via Seraphica*. Chicago, 1959.

Huxley, A. *The Doors of Perception*. London, 1954.

Idung of Prüfening. *A Dialogue between Two Monks*. In *Cistercians and Cluniacs, The Case for Cîteaux*. Cistercian Fathers Series 33. Kalamazoo, Mich., 1977.

L'immagine di San Francesco nella controriforma, Comitato nazionale per la manifestazioni culturali per l'VIII centenario della nascita di San Francesco di Assisi. Rome, 1962.

L'immagine di San Francesco nella storiografia dall' umanesimo all' ottocento. Assisi, 1983.

Isidore of Seville. *Traité de la Nature*. Ed. J. Fontaine. Bordeaux, 1960.

James, W. *Varieties of Religious Experience*. New York, 1929.

John the Scot. *Periphyseon: On the Division of Nature*. Trans. M. Uhlfelder. Indianapolis, 1976.

Jonas. *Life of Columban*. Ed. D.C. Munroe. In Translations and reprints from the original sources of European history, Vol. 2, no. 7. Rev. ed. New York, 1908.

Jorgensen, J. *Der Heilige Franz von Assisi*. New York, 1924.

Joubainville, A. de, *Études sur l'état interieur des abbayes Cisterciennes, et principalement de Clairvaux, au XIIe et au XIIIe siècle*. Paris, 1858.

Jowett, S. *God's Troubadour: The Story of Saint Francis of Assisi*. New York, 1940.

Kaftal, G. *St. Francis in Italian Painting*. London, 1950.

Katz, S., ed. *Mysticism and Philosophical Analysis*. New York, 1978.

———, ed. *Mysticism and Religious Traditions*. Oxford, 1983.

Kennedy, C. *An Anthology of Old English Poetry*. New York, 1960.

Kervran, L. *Brandan, le grand navigateur celte du VIe siècle*. Paris, 1977.

Klingender, F. "Saint Francis and the Birds of the Apocalypse." *Journal of the Warburg and Courtauld Institutes* 16 (1953): 13–23.

Knowles, D. *The Evolution of Medieval Thought*. New York, 1962.

———. "The Humanism of the Twelfth Century." in *Studies* 30 (1941): 43–58.

———. *The Monastic Order in England*. Cambridge, 1950.

Knowles, M. *The Nature of Mysticism*. New York, 1966.

Koestler, A. *The Act of Creation*. New York, 1964.

Ladurie, E. *Montaillou: The Promised Land of Error*. Trans. B. Bray. New York, 1979.

Lambert, L.M. *Franciscan Poverty: The Doctrine of the Absolute Poverty of Christ and the Apostles in the Franciscan Order*, 1210–1323. London, 1961.

———. *Medieval Heresy: Popular Movements from Bogomil to Hus*. New York, 1976.

Leclerc, É. *The Canticle of Creatures: Symbols of Union*. Trans. M. O'Connell. Chicago, 1977.

Leclercq, J. *Bernard of Clairvaux and the Cistercian Spirit*. Trans. C. Lavoie. Kalamazoo, 1976.

———. "Le thème de la jonglerie chez S. Bernard et ses contemporains." *Revue d'Historie de la Spiritualité* 48 (1972): 385–400.

———. *The Love of Learning and the Desire for God*. Trans. C. Misrahi. New York, 1961.

Leff, G. *Heresy in the Late Middle Ages*. New York, 1967.

The Legend of Perugia. In *Scripta Leonis, Rufini, et Angeli Sociorum S. Francisci*. Ed. and trans. Brooke. Oxford, 1970.

"The Legend of the Three Companions." *Archivum Franciscanum Historicum* 67 (1974): 89–144.

Lekai, L. *The Cistercians*. Kent, Oh., 1977.

Leuba, J. *The Psychology of Religious Mysticism*. London, 1925.

Lewis, C.S. *The Allegory of Love: A Study in Medieval Tradition*. Oxford, 1938.

Lind, L. *Lyric Poetry of the Italian Renaissance*. New Haven, 1954.

Longford, F.P. *Francis of Assisi: A Life for All Seasons*. London, 1978.

Loomis, C.G. *White Magic: An Introduction to the Folklore of Christian Legend*. Cambridge, Mass., 1948.

Loos, M. *Dualist Heresy in the Middle Ages*. Prague, 1974.

Lovejoy, A.O. *The Great Chain of Being*. Cambridge, Mass., 1948.

Lovejoy, A.O., and Boas, G. *A Documentary History of Primitivism and Related Ideas: Primitivism and Related Ideas in Antiquity*. Baltimore, 1935.

Lucian. *Alexander the Quack Prophet*. In *Selected Satires of Lucian*. Ed. and trans. L. Casson. New York, 1968.

———. *Lucius*. In *Selected Satires of Lucian*. Ed. and trans. L. Casson. New York, 1968.

Luddy, A. *A Life of St. Bernard*. Dublin, 1927.

Lyttle, C. "The Stigmata of St. Francis, Considered in the Light of Possible Joachite Influence upon Thomas of Celano." *American Society of Church History Papers*, 2nd series, 4 (1914): 77–88.

Macrobius, *Commentary on the Dream of Scipio*. Trans. W.H. Stahl. New York, 1952.

Marling, J. *The Order of Nature in the Philosophy of Aquinas*. Washington, D.C., 1934.

Martianus Capella, *The Marriage of Mercury and Philology*. In *Martianus and the Seven Liberal Arts*. Vol. 2. Trans. W.H. Stahl and R. Johnson. New York, 1977.

Marx, L. "Pastoral Ideals and City Troubles." In *Western Man and Environmental Ethics*. Ed. Barbour. Reading, Mass., 1973.

Maur, Rauban. *De universo*. In *Patrologia Latina, cursus completus*. Vol. 111(5). Ed. J.-P. Migne. Paris, 1864.

Mockler, A. *Francis of Assisi: The Wandering Years*. Oxford, 1978.

Moleta, V. *From St. Francis to Giotto: The Influence of St. Francis on Early Italian Art and Literature*. Chicago, 1983.

Montalembert, Count de. *The Monks of the West, from St. Benedict to St. Bernard*. London, 1861.

Moore, R.I., ed. *The Birth of Popular Heresy*. New York, 1975.

Moorman, J.H.R. *A History of the Franciscan Order from Its Origin to the Year 1517*. Oxford, 1968.

———. *The Sources for the Life of Saint Francis of Assisi*. Manchester, 1940.

Morison, J. *The Life and Times of St. Bernard*. London, 1884.

Moschus, John. *Pratum Spiritale*. In *Le Pré Spirituel*. Trans. M.R. de Journel. Paris, 1946.

Muscetta, C., and Rivalta, P. *Poesia del Duecento e del Trecento*. Turin, 1956.

Nelli, R. *La Philosophie du catharisme*. Paris, 1975.
The New Oxford Annotated Bible with the Apocrypha. Expanded Edition. Revised Standard Version. Ed. H.G. May and B.M. Metzger. New York, 1977.
Nicholson, D. *The Mysticism of Saint Francis of Assisi*. London, 1923.
Nykl, A. *Hispano-Arabic Poetry and Its Relations with the Old Provençal Troubadours*. Baltimore, 1946.
O'Leary, J., trans. *The Most Ancient Lives of St. Patrick*. New York, 1875.
O'Meara, J. *Eriugena*. Cork, 1969.
———. *The Mind of Eriugena*. Dublin, 1970.
Painter, S. *French Chivalry*. Ithaca, New York, 1940.
Painter, S., and Tierney, B. *Western Europe in the Middle Ages*, 300–1450. 3rd ed. New York, 1978.
Palumbo, E.M. *The Literary Use of Formulas in Guthlac II and their Relation to Felix's Vita Sancti Guthlaci*. The Hague, 1977.
Passmore, J. *Man's Responsibility for Nature*. New York, 1974.
Pax, E., " 'Bruder Feuer': Religionsgeschichtliche und volkskundliche Hintergrunde." *Franziskanische Studien* (1951): 238–50.
Pelikan, J. *The Christian Tradition*. Vol. 3: *The Growth of Medieval Theology* (600–1300). Chicago, 1978.
Pennington, M. ed. *The Cistercian Spirit*. Spencer, Mass., 1970.
Plato. *Phaedrus*. Trans. R. Hackforth. In *The Complete Dialogues of Plato*. Ed. E. Hamilton and R. Cairns. Princeton, 1973.
———. *Symposium*. Trans. M. Joyce. In *The Complete Dialogues of Plato*. Ed. E. Hamilton and R. Cairns. Princeton, 1973, pp. 526–75.
Platzeck, E. *Das Sonnenlied des Heiligen Franziskus von Assisi*. Munich, 1956.
Plotinus. *The Enneads*. Trans. S. MacKenna. 4th ed. London, 1969.
Porphyry. *Letter to Anebo*. In *Porphyrio, Lettera ad Anebo*. Ed. R. Sodano. Naples, 1958.
Previté-Orton, C.W. *The Shorter Cambridge Medieval History*. Cambridge, 1971.
Pseudo-Longinus. *On The Sublime*. Ed. and trans. W.R. Roberts. Cambridge, 1935.
Raby, F.J.E. *A History of Christian Latin Poetry*. 2nd ed. Oxford, 1953.
———. *A History of Secular Latin Poetry in the Middle Ages*. Oxford, 1934.
Rajna, P. "S. Francesco d'Assisi e gli spiriti cavallereschi." *Nuovo Antologia* (October, 1926): 385–95.
Reeves, M. *Joachim of Fiore and the Prophetic Future*. New York, 1976.
Reuther, R.R. *Sexism and God-Talk*. Boston, 1983.
Robinson, H.W. *Inspiration and Revelation in the Old Testament*. Oxford, 1946.
Roger of Wendover. *Flowers of History*. Trans. J. Giles. Vol. 1. London, 1849.
Rougement, D. de. *Love in the Western World*. Trans. M. Belgion. New York, 1956.
Runciman, S. *The Medieval Manichee: A Study of the Christian Dualist Heresy*. Cambridge, 1960.
Russell, J.R. *Dissent and Reform in the Early Middle Ages*. Berkeley, 1965.

Sabatelli, G. "Studi recenti sul Cantico di Frate Sole." *Archivum Franciscanum Historicum* 51 (1958): 3–24.

Sabatier, P. *Life of Saint Francis of Assisi*. Trans. L. Houghton. New York, 1894.

The Sacrum Commercium. Trans. P. Hermann. In *Omnibus*. Ed. Habig. Chicago, 1973.

San Francesco e il franciscanesimo nella letteratura italiana del Novecento, Covegno nazionale su San Francesco e il francesanesimo nella letteratura italiano del Novecento. Assisi, 1983.

Schaeffer, F. *Pollution and the Death of Man*. London, 1972.

Selmer, C. *"Navigatio Sancti Brendani Abbatis" from Early Latin Manuscripts*. Notre Dame, 1959.

Severus, Sulpicius. *Life of Martin*. In *Sulpice Sévère, Vie de Saint Martin*. Ed. and trans. J. Fontaine. Paris, 1967.

———. *Works*. In *The Western Fathers*. Ed. and trans. H.R. Hoare. New York, 1965.

Shannon, A. *The Popes and Heresy in the Thirteenth Century*. Villanova, 1949.

Short, W. *Saints in the World of Nature: The Animal Story as Spiritual Parable in Medieval Hagiography*, 900–1200. Rome, 1983.

Socrates, *Ecclesiastical History*. In *The Ecclesiastical History of Socrates Scholasticus*. Rev. A.C. Zenos. The Nicene and Post-Nicene Fathers of the Christian Church. Second series. Vol. 2. Oxford, 1890.

Sorrell, R.D. *Tradition and Innovation in Saint Francis of Assisi's Interpretation of Nature*. Diss. Cornell University, 1983.

———. "Tradition and Innovation in Saint Francis of Assisi's Sermon to the Birds." *Franciscan Studies* 43 (1983):396–407.

Southern, R.W. *Medieval Humanism*. New York, 1970.

———. *The Making of the Middle Ages*. London, 1953.

Spitzer, L. "Classical and Christian Ideas of World Harmony." *Traditio* 2 (1944): 415–63.

Spring, D. and E., eds. *Ecology and Religion in History*. New York, 1974.

Stace, W. *Mysticism and Philosophy*. London, 1960.

Stockmayer, G. *Über Naturgefühl in Deutschland im 10 und 11 jahrhundert*. Leipzig, 1910.

Stubblebline, J.H. *Assisi and the Rise of Vernacular Art*. New York, 1985.

Sullivan, J. "Fast and Abstinence in the First Order of Saint Francis," *Catholic University of America Canon Law Studies* 374. Washington, D.C., 1957.

Tamassia, N. *Saint Francis of Assisi and His Legend*. Trans. L. Ragg. London, 1910.

Tart, C. *Altered States of Consciousness*. New York, 1969.

Thèry, G. "Autour du Decret de 1210: David de Dinant, Étude sur son pantheisme materialiste," *Bibliotèque Thomiste* 16 (1925).

Thöde, H. *Franz von Assisi und die Anfänge der Kunst der Renaissance in Italien*. Berlin, 1904.

Thompson, J.W. *The Literacy of the Laity in the Middle Ages*. New York, 1963.

Thoreau, H.D. *The Selected Works*. Ed. H. S. Canby. Boston, 1975.

Thouzellier, C., ed. *Livre des deux principes*. Sources Chrétiennes 198. Paris, 1973.

Tierney, B. *Medieval Poor Law: A Sketch of Canonical Theory and Its Application in England*. Berkeley, 1959.

———. " 'Natura Id Est Deus': A Case of Judicial Pantheism?" *Journal of the History of Ideas* 24(1963):307-22.

———. *The Middle Ages*. Vol. 2: *Readings in Medieval History*. New York, 1974.

Tommasini, A. *Irish Saints in Italy*. Trans. J. Scanlan. London, 1937.

Ugolino di Monte Santa Maria. *Actus beati Francisci et Sociorum Ejus*. Ed. Paul Sabatier. (*Collection d'Études et de Documents IV*). Paris, 1902.

Underhill, E. *Jacopone da Todi: Poet and Mystic*, 1228–1306. New York, 1919.

Vergil. *The Aeneid*. In *Virgil, with an English Translation*, by H.R. Fairclough. Cambridge, Mass., 1960.

Vicinelli, A. *Gli Scritti di San Francesco d'Assisi e I Fioretti*. Milan, 1955.

La Vie de Saint Douceline. Trans. J. Albanès. Marseilles, 1879.

Waddell, H. *Medieval Latin Lyrics*. New York, 1929.

———. *The Wandering Scholars*. London, 1927.

Wadding, L., ed., *Annales Minorum, seu trium ordinem a S. Francisco institutorum*. Rome, 1731.

Wakefield, W. *Heresy, Crusade, and Inquisition in Southern France*, 1100–1250. Berkeley, 1974.

Wallace-Hadrill, D.S. *The Greek Patristic View of Nature*. Manchester, 1968.

Wetherbee, W. *Platonism and Poetry in the Twelfth Century*, Princeton, 1972.

White, Lynn, Jr. *Medieval Religion and Technology*. Berkeley, 1978.

———. "Natural Science and Naturalistic Art," *American Historical Review* (52) 1947, 425–33.

White, T.H. *The Bestiary: A Book of Beasts*. New York, 1960.

Whitehead, A.N. *Science and the Modern World*. Cambridge, 1926.

Williams, G. *Wilderness and Paradise in Christian Thought*. New York, 1962.

Willibrord de Paris, R. "Rapports de Saint Francois d'Assise avec le mouvement spirituel du XIIe siècle," Études Franciscanes, new series, 27. Tome 12 (1962): 129–43.

Workman, H.B. *The Evolution of the Monastic Ideal*. London, 1913.

Zaehner, R. *Mysticism, Sacred and Profane*. Oxford, 1957.

Zimei, A. *La concezione della natura in San Francesco d'Assisi, studio psicologico e letterario*. Rome, 1929.

Index

Acts of the Apostles, Celano's quotation of, 62
Actus Beati Francisci et Sociorum Eius (Actus), 7, 150 (fig.), 153(fig.), 154, 155–56
Actus-Fioretti, 45–46, 60, 65, 67, 151, 152, 154, 155. *See also Fioretti*
Adam and Eve. *See* Eden
Aelred of Rievaulx, 29, 30
Alan of Lille, 13
Alcuin, poem of, 26–27, 99
Allegories
  of Christ, 127
  and Francis' Biblical interpretation, 140
  and Francis' interpretation of creation, 43(tab.), 46–47, 48, 141
Almsgiving and alms begging
  Francis' extension of, 139
  in Francis' views on chivalry, 72–73
Altmann, Bishop, 27
Angelo, Brother, 152, 153(fig.)
Animals, Francis' concern for, 43–44(tab.), 53. *See also specific animals*
  and asceticism, 49
  Bonaventure on, 52–53
  and *Canticle*, 124
  and Cathar refusal to eat meat, 78
  and eremetic life, 42–44, 48–49
  and Franciscan Order, 142
  and nature mysticism, 94
  originality and unoriginality of, 139
Anonymous of Perugia, 150(fig.) *See also Legend of Perugia*
Anselm, Saint, 4–5
Ansfried (squire), 27
Anticlaudianus (Alan of Lille), 13
Anthony of Padua, Saint, 142
Antony, Saint
  as ascetic, 19
  and "Book of Nature," 16, 46
  and Francis, 39
  and Guthlac, 23
Ants
  and creation as education, 43(tab.)
  and Francis' allegory, 46
Armstrong, Edward A., 23, 25, 46, 52, 64, 80–81, 87, 151, 155, 156–57
Artistic creation, as Francis' legacy, 143–44
Asceticism. *See also* Eremitic tradition
  and Bonaventure on Francis, 53
  of Catharism, 75, 77–78, 147. *See also* Catharism
  and Cistercians, 28, 30
  and Franciscans, 28
  Francis resolves ambivalence in, 137, 141
  and harmony, 140
  of High Middle Ages, 133
  historians on, 3–5
  and nature mysticism, 87–89
Asceticism of Francis, 39, 57
  and ascetic-monastic view, 19

Asceticism of Francis (*continued*)
and attachment to creatures, 49
and *Canticle*, 124
and demonic presence, 44
and food, 76–77
and Francis' biographers, 54
and originality, 51
and Sermon to the Birds, 59, 62
Ascetic-monastic tradition, 28
Ascetic-monastic view
of creation, 14–19
expressions of in early East and West, 19–27
Athanasius, 16
Augustine, Saint, 12–13
mysticism of, 86–87, 88, 92, 96
Augustinian Platonism, 91
Ausonius, 10–11, 99
Austerity
of Francis' eremetic life, 40–42
in Francis' medieval context, 6
Autonomy
of creatures in *Canticle*, 130, 134
and High Middle Ages, 133

Baptism, and water in *Canticle*, 127, 131
Basil, Saint, 19–20, 29
Bear, and Florentius (monk), 21, 156
Bede, Saint, 12, 21–22, 87, 114
Bees
and creation as education, 43(tab.)
and Francis' concern for animals, 44(tab.)
and mysticism, 43(tab.)
Begging, and Francis' views on chivalry, 72
Benedict of Aniane, 27
Benedict of Nursia, 21, 88
Benedictine Rule, and Cistercians, 28, 28–29
Benz, E., 113
Bernard, Saint
and *Description of Clairvaux*, 32, 34, 35
and manual labor, 29–30
Bernard of Quintavalle, 59
Bestiaries, medieval
and Francis' symbolic associations, 48, 127
in popular tradition, 12
Bible. *See also* Psalms
in *Actus* and Celano, 156
allegory in, 140
and *Canticle*, 102, 126–27, 179n.13
Cistercians and Franciscans link creation to, 35
and creation, 17, 46
and *Exhortation*, 154
and food, 75
and Francis' innovation, 51
and Francis' view of creation, 7–8, 138–39
in Franciscan and Irish expressions, 24
and *Jubilemus omnes*, 105
and mysticism, 84
and *Praises before the Office*, 111
and Sermon to the Birds, 65–66, 126
Biese, A., 15
Bigaroni, P., 149
Bihl, M., 156
Biographers. *See* Bonaventure, Saint; Celano, Thomas of; Sources, early
Birds. *See also* Sermon to the Birds; Waterfowl; *other specific birds*
and St. Brendan, 25
and creation as education, 43(tab.)
Francis' concern for, 44(tab.), 139
Francis' greeting to, 71
Francis sings with, 49, 57(tab.)
and Francis' thaumaturgy, 43(tab.)
and Martin, 46
propitious greeting from, 42
Bishop, Morris, 6
Bishop of Assisi, and *Canticle*, 98, 122, 134
Blackbird, as Tempter (Benedict of Nursia), 21, 88
Boethius, 13
Bonaventure, Saint, 150(fig.), 153(fig.)
abstract interpretation by, 50
on *Canticle*, 116, 117, 118, 120, 123
and Francis as Angel of Sixth Seal, 54
and Francis' chivalry, 69–70
and Francis' concern for animals, 52
and Francis' nature mysticism, 90, 92, 93, 95, 140, 142
Knowles on, 83
Legenda Major by, 7
vs. oral tradition, 151
Soliloquy of, 88

suppression of early sources by, 148
and tradition, 51
Branca, V., 102
Brendan, Saint, 23–25
Breviary, of Francis, 99
Brooke, R., 149
Brother Fire. *See also* Fire
Cauterization by, 50, 63–64, 73–74
Francis' chivalrous deference to, 73
Francis submits to, 52
praise of (*Canticle*), 44, 100, 101, 127, 136
Brown, Raphael, 149, 154
Buddhism, 74

Caesarius of Heisterbach, 31–32, 156
Canticle of Brother Sun, 69, 98–99, 136–37, 142
and Bible, 102, 126–27, 179n.13
chivalric compliment in, 71
Cousins on, 89
creatures as objects of appreciation in ("causal" interpretation), 115, 118–22, 123–24
creatures as praising God in (creation as agent), 115, 116–18, 122–23
and eremetic life, 44
flattery and enfraternization in, 127–28, 129
and folk-barbarian tradition, 14
and Francis' extension of Christian teaching, 141
Francis' intention in, 114, 115
and Francis' mysticism, 92, 97
and Francis' recovery from illness, 45
harmony and reconciliation in, 134–35, 142
humanism in, 135–36, 137
influences on, 99, 102–8, 114
and interdependence of humans and animals, 49, 130–34, 137
and *Legend of Perugia*, 50
levels of appreciation in, 125
mystical symbolism in, 141
as praise for Lord, 96
and progression in Francis' poetry, 108–14
Sabatelli on, 83
and Sermon to the Birds, 66, 68
structure in, 128–30
text and translation of, 100-101
Umbrian as language of, 114, 121–22
Canticles, liturgical
Francis influenced by, 99
and *Praises before the Office*, 111
Canticum of the Three Young Men, 31, 99, 102–4, 108, 116, 117, 118, 121
Carceri hermitage, 42
Carolingian civilization, appreciation of environment in, 26–27
Carolingian monasteries, 11
Catharism, 75, 77–79, 173n.26
and Francis, 77–79, 147–48
and humanism of *Canticle*, 137
Cauterization by Brother Fire, 50, 63–64, 73–74
Celano, Thomas of, 7
abstract interpretation by, 50
on animals's obedience, 46
and Armstrong, 156–57
on Brother Pacifico, 70
on *Canticle*, 116–17, 118, 119, 120, 122–23
on Cauterization by Brother Fire, 64
on eremetic life, 40
on Francis' Biblical symbolism, 126–27
on Francis' chivalry, 69–70
and Francis' concern for animals, 48
and Francis' harmony, 53–54
and Francis' joy in nature, 55–56
and Francis' nature mysticism, 90, 91, 92–93, 94, 95, 96, 97, 140, 142
vs. oral tradition, 151
and problems of credibility, 17
on release of rabbit, 58
on Sermon to the Birds, 61–63, 67–68, 140, 152, 154, 155–56, 157
and situation of *Exhortation*, 110
and Stilling of Swallows, 154
and tradition, 51
and *Vita Prima*, 149, 150(fig.). *See also* *Vita Prima*
and *Vita Secunda*, 150(fig.). *See also* *Vita Secunda*
Cellucci, L., 155
Celtic conception of ascetic life, 23
Certificatio of Francis, 119, 120, 135
Chain of being, 133

Charity. *See* Almsgiving and alms begging
Chitty, D. J., 16
Chivalry in Francis' outlook, 69–75
  and *Canticle*, 108
  Francis' adapting of, 140
  and Francis' attitude toward creatures, 90
  as original, 139
Christ, dedication to things imitating, 48
Chronica Major (Matthew Paris), 153(fig.)
Cicada (cricket)
  and Francis' concern for animals, 44(tab.)
  Francis exhorts, 121
  Francis releases, 49
  Francis sings with, 49
  and Francis' thaumaturgy, 43(tab.), 47
Cistercians, 28
  and ascetic view, 28, 30, 31–32
  and creation, 28–31, 36–37
  and *Description of Clairvaux*, 32–35
  dietary abstinence of, 76
  and Franciscan thought, 35–38
  and Franciscan way of life, 40–41
Clairvaux, *Description* of, 31, 32–35
Clare, Sister, 59, 153(fig.), 154
Classical culture
  on creation, 10–12
  and mysticism, 84, 85
Classical philosophy, and John Scotus Eriugena, 13
Columba, Saint, 9
Columban, Saint, 25
Commentary on the Dream of Scipio (Macrobius), 12
Conservation, of trees by Francis, 127. *See also* Ecological concerns
Contemplative life. *See* Ascetic-monastic tradition
Coulton, G. C., 4
Cousins, E., 89, 90, 92, 96
Creation
  ascetic-monastic view of, 14–19
  ascetic-monastic view of (range of expressions), 19–27
  and *Canticle*, 115, 119, 125. *See also* *Canticle of Brother Sun*
  Cistercian attitude toward, 28–38, 36–37
  Cistercian and Franciscan thought on, 35–38
  classical (poetic) view of, 10–12
  early Christian attitudes toward, 9–10
  folk-barbarian tradition on, 14
  in Francis' criticism of medieval society, 119
  Francis resolves ambivalence toward, 137, 141
  as linked directly to humans (*Canticle*), 108
  scientific tradition on, 12–14
  and Sermon to the Birds, 62
Creation, Francis' view of, 7–8, 138–39
  and animals' serving God, 43(tab.), 46. *See also* Animals, Francis' concern for
  artistic legacy of, 144
  as ascetic, 54
  and *Canticle*, 98, 126, 127. *See also* *Canticle of Brother Sun*
  and chivalry, 71
  as deferent, 74
  and early years of Francis, 55
  and nature mysticism, 90, 97
  and Sermon to the Birds, 59, 67, 68
  and union of evangelical and eremitic, 59
Cricket. *See* Cicada
Cuckoo, and creation as education, 43(tab.)
Cunningham, Lawrence, 98, 115–16
Curses, of Francis, 134, 138
Cuthbert, Saint, 19, 21

Daniel, Walter, 30
Death, as reconciliation for Francis, 135
Decline and Fall of the Roman Empire (Gibbon), 3
Democracy among animals, and Francis' views, 6, 47
Demonic presence, 21
  in ascetic's surroundings, 17, 18, 32
  Francis' perception of, 44–46
  and Francis' thaumaturgy, 43(tab.)
  Martin sees birds as, 156
  in Temptation by Mice, 74
De mundi universitate (Silvester), 13
De natura rerum (Isidore), 12
De philosophia Mundi (Conches), 13
Description of Clairvaux, 31, 32–35, 35, 36, 44, 49
Dialogue on Miracles (Caesarius of Heisterbach), 31, 156
Dialogues (Gregory the Great), 21

Divine vengeance, 132
Dogs, and Martin of Tours, 21
Dominic, Saint, 4
Donkey, Francis annoyed by, 58
Douceline, Saint, 142
Doves, and Francis' allegory, 43(tab.)
Doyle, E., 123, 124, 128, 134

Early sources. *See* Sources, early
Earth, in *Canticle*, 44, 127, 131
Ecological concerns
  and *Canticle*, 123, 124
  Francis' concern for, 139
  and Francis' legacy, 144
  and Francis' precursors, 4
"Ecology," 8
Eden (Adam and Eve)
  and Francis' interactions with animals, 52
  and poverty, 51
  and Severus on Egyptian ascetics, 20
Edmund Rich, St., 4
Education, by creatures, 43(tab.), 46–47
Egyptian ascetics or hermits, 16, 20
Eliade, M., 137
Elias, Brother, 59
Enfraternization, in *Canticle*, 127–28, 129
England, and ascetic interest in nature, 21
Englebert, Omer, 39
Eremetic life of Francis, 39–42
  apostolic evangelism combined with, 58–59, 64
  and dedication to austerity, 37–38
  and Francis' attitude toward creatures, 42–44, 48–49
Eremetic tradition, 15–16. *See also* Asceticism
  Franciscan ideals derived from, 138
Esser, Cajetan, 77, 102, 147, 154
Evangelism, apostolic, of Francis, 58–59, 64
  and *Canticle*, 124
  and Francis' attitude toward creatures, 90
  and Francis' attitude toward food, 75, 76, 79
  Francis considers renouncing, 154
  and Sermon to the Birds, 59, 67
Exhortation to the Praise of God, 57, 64, 99, 108, 109–11, 113–14, 116, 121, 154

Falcon
  and Francis' concern for animals, 44(tab.)
  humans aided by, 49
Famine, Francis' staving off, 54
Felix's Life of Guthlac, 22–23
Fioretti (*Little Flowers of St. Francis*), 44, 61, 66, 67, 70, 100, 150(fig.), 153 (fig.), 154. *See also Actus-Fioretti*
Fire. *See also* Brother Fire
  and Francis' concern for animals, 44(tab.)
  and Francis' thaumaturgy, 43(tab.)
  humans aided by, 49
First Life of Francis (Celano) *See Vita Prima*
Fish
  Francis releases, 44(tab.), 48, 133
  Francis prays with, 95–96
  and Francis' thaumaturgy, 43(tab.), 48
Flame, and Francis' allegory, 43(tab.)
Florentius (monk), 21, 156
Flowers
  and Francis' allegory, 43(tab.)
  Francis' concern for, 139
  and Francis' concern for animals, 44(tab.)
Food, Francis' attitudes toward, 75–79
Fortini, A., 149
Fortunatus, 11, 99
Francis, Saint. *See also specific works and biographers of*
  and animals, 42–44. *See also* Animals, Francis' concern for; *specific animals*
  and asceticism, 39, 57, 137. *See also* Asceticism of Francis
  and Bible, 7–8, 138–39. *See also* Bible
  and Catharism, 147–48. *See also* Catharism
  and chivalry, 69–75, 90, 108, 139, 140
  and combination of evangelism and eremetic life, 58–59, 64
  and creation, 7–8, 54, 74, 138–39. *See also* Creation, Francis' view of
  early sources on, 6–7
  early years of, 55–56, 57(tab.)
  legacy of, 142–45
  modern views of, 5–6
  nature mysticism of, 35, 79, 87, 89–97, 139, 140
  as reformer and innovator, 6. *See also* Originality of Francis

Francis, Saint (*continued*)
  self-perception of, 54, 58
  and tradition, 51, 54, 138–39. *See also* Tradition, and Francis
Franciscan approach
  austerity of, 37–38
  and Cistercians, 35–38
  primitive social grouping of, 37
Franciscan friars
  life of, 58
  as minstrels or jongleurs of God, 28, 107–8, 114, 122
Franciscan Order
  and charity, 73
  and Francis' legacy, 142–43
  and Francis' view of creation, 127
  modern view of, 138
  opposition to, 148
Fraternity, in *Canticle*, 127–28, 129
From St. Francis to Giotto . . . (Moleta), 143

Gall, Saint, 25
Genius loci, 5, 18
Gibbon, Edward, 14, 19
  on ascetic movement, 3–4
Giles, Saint, 59, 142, 151, 153(fig.)
Gilson, E., 30
Giotto, 143
Glacken, C., 20, 27, 32
Godric of Finchale, 48
Golden age, Francis seen as bringing, 54
Gregory the Great, 21, 87–88, 156
Grundmann, H., 28
Gurney-Salter, E., 143
Guthlac, Saint, 22–23

Hagiography. *See also* Bonaventure, Saint; Celano, Thomas of
  and accounts of miracles, 17–18
  and Francis' encounters with creatures, 46, 48
  and nature mysticism, 88
  and rationality for nonhumans, 138
  saints mourned by, 53
Hare, and Martin of Tours, 21
Harmony
  and ascetic tradition, 20, 25, 140
  and *Description of Clairvaux*, 32, 36
  in *Canticle*, 134–35, 142
  Francis' restoration of, 53, 54, 60
Hay, and Francis' concern for animals, 44(tab.)
Henri d'Avranches, 150(fig.), 153(fig.)
Heresy
  of Cathars, 77
  and St. Francis, 5, 6, 54, 148
Hermits, 4. *See also* Asceticism; Eremetic tradition
Hierarchy
  in *Canticle*, 134–35
  and Francis' viewpoint, 8, 47, 66
Honey, and Francis' concern for animals, 44(tab.)
Hugh of Lincoln, 4–5
Humanism, in *Canticle*, 135–36, 137
Humility
  and chivalry, 73
  and eremetic life, 40
Hunting dogs, and Martin of Tours, 21
Hymn of the Three Young Men, 24

Idung of Prüfening, 31
Innocent III (pope), 58
Innovation. *See* Originality of Francis
Interdependence
  in *Canticle*, 49, 130–34, 137
  Francis' vision of, 49
Interpretation
  and early accounts of Francis, 50
  by Francis of self, 54, 58
Irish tradition
  and ascetic interest in nature, 23–26
  as influence of Francis, 23–24
Isidore, Saint, 12
Isola Maggiore of Lake Trasmene, 42, 57
"I-Thou" relationship, 134, 142

Jacopone da Todi, 142
James of Massa, 150(fig.), 153(fig.), 154, 155
Jerome, Saint, 20
Joachim of Fiore, 54
John of Cappella, 59
John Scotus Eriugena, 12–13
Jubilemus omnes, 105, 106

Katz, S., 81–82, 87
Knightly success, Francis' attempt at, 56
Knowles, David, 83, 136
Knowles, M., 80

Ladurie, E., 78
Lamb(s)
  and creation as education, 43(tab.)
  and Francis' allegory, 43(tab.)
  Francis' concern for, 48
  sow's killing of, 132–33
Lamb, Lady Jacoba's
  as example, 46
  and Francis' concern for animals, 44(tab.)
Language used by Francis, 61, 114, 121–22
Largesse, in Francis' views, 72
Larks
  and creation as education, 43(tab.)
  and Francis' allegory, 43(tab.), 46, 139
Leclercq, J., 29–30, 32
Legenda Maior (Bonaventure), 123, 150 (fig.), 153(fig.)
Legenda Minor (Bonaventure), 150(fig.)
Legend of Perugia (*Legenda Perugina*), 7, 149–51
  abstract interpretation lacking in, 50
  on *Canticle*, 98, 107, 114, 119–20, 121, 122, 134
  on Cauterization by Fire, 63
  and Francis' chivalry, 72
  and Francis' concern for creatures, 42
  and Francis' nature mysticism, 94
  origin of, 119
  on Pacifico, 70
  and Sermon to the Birds, 61
  on temptation by mice, 45
Legend of the Three Companions (*3 Comp.*), 150(fig.)
Leo, Brother, 7, 45, 99, 119, 149, 150 (fig.), 151, 153(fig.)
Letters of Francis, and *Canticle*, 108
Life of Antony, 21
Life of Cuthbert (Bede), 21–22
Life of Guthlac (Felix), 22–23
Lights, and Francis' allegory, 43(tab.)
Literalism of Francis, 139–40
Little, Ms., 150(fig.)
Little Flowers of St. Francis, The. See Fioretti
Loci, Franciscan, 41–42
Lucretius, 53

Macrobius, 12
Major Life (*Legenda Maior*) (Bonaventure), 7
Malmesbury, early scholar at (on creation), 9–10
Manicheanism, of Augustine, 86
Marches of Ancona, 153(fig.), 154
Martin of Tours, 20–21, 46–47, 52, 156
Marx, Leo, 56–57
Masseo, Brother, 150(fig.), 151, 152, 153 (fig.), 154
  Letter of, 45
Matthew Paris, 153(fig.)
Maur, Rauban, 12
Mice
  and creation as education, 43(tab.)
  temptation by, 45, 74, 132
Miracles, stories of, 17–18, 47, 48
Mirror of Perfection, 107, 176n.31, 114, 119–20, 121
Mirror of Perfection I, 150(fig.)
Mirror of Perfection II, 150(fig.)
Mockler, A., 39
Moleta, Vincent, 143
Monastic orders, and security over environment, 18. *See also specific orders*
Money, and Francis' thaumaturgy, 43(tab.)
Monks, ascetic, 4
Monotheism, and nature, 5, 36
Montalembert, Count de, 14
Moschus, John, 87
Moslems, Francis' mission to, 157
Murdach, Henry, 29
Mussolini, Benito, Francis praised by, 135
Mystical symbolism
  in *Canticle*, 141
  and Francis' concern for animals, 48
  and Francis' nature mysticism, 93
Mysticism, 81–82. *See also* Nature mysticism
  and bees, 43(tab.)
  and classical world, 85

Mysticism (*continued*)
  of Francis, 35–36, 96
  "of the historical event," 89

Nativity, Francis' attempt to recreate, 128
Nature. *See also* Creation
  and ascetic movement, 4–5
  and Francis' views, 7–8
  medieval views of, 5
  science and mysticism in medieval reactions to, 88
Nature mysticism, 79–86
  of Francis, 35, 79, 87, 89–97, 139, 140
  and Franciscan Order, 142
  possible ascetic examples of, 87–89
Neoplatonism, 13. *See also* Plotinus
Neoplatonism, Christian, 89, 90, 93, 94
Noblesse oblige, in Francis' views, 72, 74

Office of the Passion (Francis'), 108
Origen, 13
Originality of Francis, 50–51, 54, 97, 139
  in *Canticle*, 114, 117, 118, 124, 129, 134, 137
  in *Exhortation*, 110
  interpretation of as orthodox, 141
  in levels of interpretation, 141
  literalism as source of, 139–40
  and Sermon to the Birds, 66, 157
  and vision of interdependence, 49
Orlando, Count, 41, 57(tab.), 71, 154
Otto, Bishop, 27
Ovid, 53

Pacifico, Brother, 70, 107–8
Pan-psychism, and Francis, 128, 147–48
Pantheism
  and *Canticle*, 117, 128, 134
  and Francis, 5, 147
Paul, Saint, 62
Paulinus, 11, 99
"Pastoral Ideals and City Troubles" (Marx), 56–57
Peace, Francis' interceding for, 54
Pets, and Francis, 44(tab.), 49–50, 138
Phaedrus (Plato), 84–85
Pheasant
  and Francis' concern for animals, 44(tab.), 133
  and Francis' thaumaturgy, 43(tab.)
Plato, *Phaedrus*, 84–85
Platonism, Augustinian, 91
Plotinus, 85, 86
Podestà of Assisi, and *Canticle*, 98, 122, 134
Poetic (classical) tradition, on creation, 10–12
Poetry of Francis, progression in, 108–14. *See also specific works*
Postumianus (Severus), 20
Poverty. *See also* Asceticism; Eremitic tradition
  and Francis' early writings, 148
  Francis' ordering of, 37
  and *Sacrum Commercium*, 51
Praise of God, 108
Praises before the Hours, 99
Praises before the Office, 108, 111, 113, 113–14, 121
Prosperity, Francis' interceding for, 54
Psalms
  Canticle allusion to, 126
  as *Canticle* influence (Psalm 148), 99, 102, 103, 103(tab.), 104, 104(tab.), 108, 116, 117, 118, 121
  and Cistercians, 31
  Francis influenced by, 99, 140
  on God's impact, 83–84
  and *Praises before the Office*, 111
  and Sermon to the Birds, 60, 64
Pseudo-Dionysius, 13

Rabbit
  and Francis' concern for animals, 44(tab.), 58
  Francis releases, 42, 57(tab.), 58, 133
Raby, F. J. E., 10, 11
Rauban Maur, 12
Reconciliation, in *Canticle*, 134–35, 142
Renaissance art, as Francis' legacy, 143–44
Reuther, Rosemary, 134
Rievaulx, description of, 30
Robbers, Francis accosted by, 56, 57(tab.)
Robin(s)
  anecodote of greed of, 46, 132
  and Francis' concern for animals, 44(tab.)
  Francis sees as friars, 49
Roger of Wendover, 153(fig.)

Romanticism, and *Canticle*, 117, 128
Rule of 1221, 49, 75, 77
Rule of 1223, 49–50
Rules of Francis, and *Canticle*, 108
Runciman, Steven, 147

Sabatelli, G., 83
Sacraments (baptism), and water in *Canticle*, 127, 131
Sacrum Commercium, 51
Saints in the World of Nature (Short), 42
Salute to the Virgin Mary, 108
Salute to the Virtues, 108, 111, 112
San Gemini Lauds, 109. *See also* *Exhortation to the Praise of God*
Saracens, Francis' mission to, 157
Scholastica (Benedict's sister), 21
School of Chartres, 13, 135–36
Scientific interest, and Francis' humanism, 136
Scientific tradition, on creation, 12–14
Second Life of Francis (Celano). *See Vita Secunda*
Sermon to the Birds, 57(tab.), 59–60
  Biblical allusion in, 65–66, 126
  Celano on, 61–63, 67–68, 140, 152, 154, 155–56, 157
  and chivalry, 72
  and creatures as praising Creator, 116
  and democracy of animals, 47
  direct exhortations in, 121
  divine intervention in, 63, 171n.28
  in early sources, 152–57
  effect of on Francis, 47, 67–68
  and *Exhortation*, 110
  and Francis' extension of Christian teaching, 141
  and Francis' literalism, 140
  Francis' probable interpretation of, 62
  in fresco, 144
  new conceptions in, 64–66
  and "Paradise of Birds," 25
  texts of, 60–61
Serpent, and Francis' thaumaturgy, 43(tab.)
Severus, Sulpicius, 20–21
  and Martin's meeting birds, 156
  and mysticism, 87
  and thaumaturgical control, 52
Sexism and God-Talk (Reuther), 134
Sheep
  and Martin, 46
  and Francis' concern for animals, 44(tab.)
Shelley, Percy Bysshe
  and poetic description, 126
  as quotable, 35
Shepherd, L., 105
Short, William, 17, 42, 46
Silvester, Bernard, 13
Silvester, Brother, 59, 154
Soliloquy (Bonaventure), 88
Song of Songs, 35
Sources, early, 6–7, 50–54, 163n.44. *See also* Bonaventure, Saint; Celano, Thomas of
  and abstract interpretation, 50
  analysis of, 149–51
  Sermon to the Birds in, 152–57
  suppression of, 148, 155–56
Sources for Sermon to the Birds, 61
Southern, R. W., 136
Sow
  and creation as education, 43(tab.)
  and Francis' thaumaturgy, 43(tab.), 47
  lamb killed by, 132–33
Stilling of the Swallows, 57(tab.), 68, 154
Stockmayer, G., 27
Stones, and Francis' allegory, 43(tab.)
Storks, Caesarius on, 31–32, 156
Stubblebine, J. H., 144
Sulpicius Severus. *See* Severus, Sulpicius
Sun, and Francis' allegory, 43(tab.)
Swallows
  and creation as education, 43(tab.)
  as example, 46
  and Francis' thaumaturgy, 43(tab.), 47
  stilling of, 57(tab.), 68, 154

Tamassia, N., 156
Temptation, in ascetic view of nature, 15, 21, 24. *See also* Demonic presence
Temptation by Mice, 45, 74, 132
Thaumaturgy
  of ascetics, 21, 32
  and Francis' interpretation of creation, 43(tab.), 47, 48
  and interpretation of Francis, 51–52, 53
  and Sermon to the Birds, 63
Theocritus, 84

Thöde, H., 143
Thomas of Celano. *See* Celano, Thomas of
Thoreau, Henry David, 75–76
Tommasini, A., 23–24
Toynbee, Arnold, 5, 36
Tradition, and Francis, 39, 51, 54, 138–139
  and *Canticle*, 19, 117, 127, 130
  and demonic presence, 45
  and nature mysticism, 79, 91–92, 93
  and Sermon to the Birds, 66
Trasmene, Lake, 41, 42, 57
Trees
  and Francis' allegory, 43(tab.)
  Francis' concern for, 139
Troubadour poetry
  and *Canticle*, 106–8, 114, 131
  Francis' acquaintance with, 70–71
  and Francis' literalism, 140
  and Irish influence, 24

Ubertino da Casale, 119
Ugolino di Monte Santa Maria, 150(fig.), 153(fig.), 154
Unity, in *Canticle*, 135. *See also* Harmony
Utility
  in *Canticle*, 123, 131, 133, 134
  in *Description of Clairvaux*, 33, 36

Vasari, Giorgio, 143
Vegetarianism
  of Cathar elite, 77
  and Francis' views, 6
Vengeance, divine, 132
Vergil, 10, 23, 84
Vicinelli, A., 108–9, 114
Vision (*certificatio*), of Francis, 119, 120, 135
Vita Prima (Celano), 7, 51, 95, 116–17, 149, 150(fig.), 152, 153(fig.), 154, 155. *See also* Celano, Thomas of
Vita Secunda (Celano), 117, 119, 150(fig.), 151. *See also* Celano, Thomas of
Voyage of St. Brendan, 23–25, 64, 88
Vulgate Bible, and Francis' outlook, 7–8. *See also* Bible

Waldo, Peter, 24
Water
  in *Canticle*, 104, 105, 126, 127, 131, 136
  and Francis' allegory, 43(tab.)
  and Francis' thaumaturgy, 43(tab.), 47
Waterfowl
  Francis' freeing of, 36, 44(tab.), 95, 133
  and Martin, 156
Wesley, John, 81
White, Lynn, Jr., 5, 147–48
Wild flowers, and Francis' concern for animals, 44(tab.). *See also* Flowers
William of Conches, 13
Williams, G., 15
Wine
  and Francis' concern for animals, 44(tab.)
  and Francis' thaumaturgy, 43(tab.), 47
Wolf, and Severus on Egyptian asceticism, 20
Wolf of Gubbio, 133, 169–70n.47
Women
  and ascetic view, 15
  and Benedict of Nursia, 21
  Francis' relationship with, 148
Wordsworth, William, as quotable, 35
Workman, H. B., 15
Worms
  and Francis' allegory, 43(tab.)
  Francis' concern for, 44(tab.), 48
Writings of Leo et al., 150(fig.)

Zaehner, R., 80, 81